THE SOVIET
PROPAGANDA
NETWORK

THE SOVIET PROPAGANDA NETWORK

A DIRECTORY OF ORGANISATIONS SERVING SOVIET FOREIGN POLICY

CLIVE ROSE

Pinter Publishers, London
in association with John Spiers

St. Martin's Press, New York

First published in Great Britain by
Pinter Publishers Limited,
in association with John Spiers
25 Floral Street, London WC2E 9DS
and in the USA by
St. Martin's Press, Inc.
175 Fifth Avenue, New York, NY 10010

British Library Cataloguing in Publication Data
A CIP catalogue record for this book is available from the
British Library

ISBN 0-86187-000-X

Library of Congress Cataloging in Publication Data
Rose, Clive
The Soviet propaganda network: a directory of organizations
serving Soviet foreign policy/Clive Rose.
p. cm.
Bibliography: p.
Includes index.
ISBN 0-312-02811-3
1. Propaganda, Russian—Societies, etc—Directories. 2. Soviet
Union—Foreign relations—1975– —Societies, etc.—Directories.
3. International agencies—Directories. 4. International agencies—
Soviet Union—Directories. 5. Peace—Societies, etc.—Directories.
6. Disarmament—Societies, etc.—Directories. I. Title.
DJ270.R67 1988
327.1′4′02547—dc19   88-39384
                                                                      CIP

First published 1988

Index compiled by
BRIAN HUNTER

Printed and bound in Great Britain by
Biddles Limited, Guildford and King's Lynn

CONTENTS

v

NOTE Organisations which are the subject of individual profiles are marked in the text with *

ACKNOWLEDGEMENTS

The greater part of this book consists of profiles of the organisations which together make up the Soviet Propaganda Network.
Producing them has involved the collation of a mass of detail
drawn from a large number of published sources. I am indebted
to all those, officials and non-officials, who have contributed to
this task and have thus made it possible to present a comprehensive picture of the network. I should also like to thank the
Librarians of University College, London, the Royal Institute of
International Affairs and the Foreign and Commonwealth Office
for giving me access to material which is not readily obtainable
elsewhere. Malcolm Mackintosh kindly read and commented on
the Foreword and Section I. I am most grateful for his expert
advice which helped to sharpen my own perceptions. Finally I
must express my warm appreciation to John Spiers, not only for
encouraging me to write this book but also for his constant help
throughout. All this said however, I must make it clear that I
alone am responsible for the views expressed and the judgements
about what to include and what to omit.

Clive Rose
August 1988

GLOSSARY OF INITIALS

AALAPSO	Afro-Asian/Latin American Peoples' Solidarity Organisation
AAPSO	Afro-Asian Peoples' Solidarity Organisation
ABCP	Asian Buddhist Conference for Peace
ASL	Association of Soviet Lawyers
AASU	All-African Students' Union
AUCCTU	All-Union Central Council of Trade Unions of the USSR
BC	Berlin Conference of European Catholics
BITEJ	International Bureau of Tourism and Exchanges of Youth
BPA	British Peace Assembly
BSFS	British-Soviet Friendship Society
CIMEA	International Committee of Children's and Adolescents' Movements
CND	Campaign for Nuclear Disarmament (UK)
CPC	Christian Peace Conference
CPGB	Communist Party of Great Britian
CPSU	Communist Party of the Soviet Union
CPUSA	Communist Party of the United States of America
CYO	Committee of Youth Organisations of the USSR
END	European Nuclear Disarmament Movement
FELAP	Latin American Federation of Journalists
FIR	International Federation of Resistance Fighters
FISE	World Federation of Teachers' Unions
IADL	International Association of Democratic Lawyers
ICESC	International Committee for European Security and Cooperation
ICFTU	International Confederation of Free Trade Unions

ID	International Department of the Central Committee of the CPSU
IFJ	International Federation of Journalists
IID	International Information Department of the Central Committee
IIP	International Institute for Peace
ILF	International Liaison Forum of Peace Forces
IMEMO	Institute of the World Economy and International Relations (USSR)
IMO	International Mineworkers' Organisation
IOJ	International Organisation of Journalists
IPB	International Peace Bureau
IPPNW	International Physicians for the Prevention of Nuclear War
IUS	International Union of Students
KPD	German Communist Party
LRD	Labour Research Department (UK)
MEM	Esperantist World Peace Movement
NAW	National Assembly of Women (UK)
NGO	Non-Governmental Organisation (UN)
OIRT	International Radio and Television Organisation
SAASC	Soviet Afro-Asian Solidarity Committee
SCESC	Soviet Committee for European Security and Cooperation
SCSLAP	Soviet Committee for Solidarity with Latin American Peoples
SPC	Soviet Peace Committee (Soviet Committee for the Defence of Peace)
SPF	Soviet Peace Fund
SSOD	Union of Soviet Societies for Friendship and Cultural Relations with Foreign Countries
TUI	Trade Union International
WFDY	World Federation of Democratic Youth
WFSW	World Federation of Scientific Workers
WFTU	World Federation of Trade Unions
WIDF	Women's International Democratic Federation
WILPF	Women's International League for Peace and Freedom
WPC	World Peace Council

'THE GORBACHEV
REVOLUTION': AN OVERVIEW

This book was completed early in 1988. The Summit Conference in Washington, at which the US–Soviet Intermediate-range Nuclear Forces (INF) Agreement was signed, had taken place only a few weeks earlier; Mikhail Gorbachev's book 'Perestroika', which is discussed in Section 1, had recently been published in the West; and the Law on State Enterprise, the first major measure intended to give practical effect to economic restructuring in the Soviet Union, had come into force on 1 January. The 'Gorbachev revolution', effectively launched at the 27th Party Congress in February/March 1986, was on the point of bearing fruit. Or so it seemed.

The first seven months of 1988 have seen an astonishing quickening of the pace. The main focus has been on the development of 'glasnost' (openness), 'perestroika' (restructuring) and 'democratisation' of the political system within the Soviet Union. Interest concentrated on the discussions and preparations which led up to the 19th Conference of the Soviet Communist Party held in Moscow at the end of June, the first such conference since 1941. During this period, an unprecedented public debate was allowed to take place, in the press and on the radio, in public speeches and even, within strict limits, by way of demonstrations, on the merits and demerits of the changes proposed in the name of 'perestroika'. Criticism of past policies became more outspoken. Condemnation of Stalin's 'gross errors' and acknowledgement of his personal guilt for the crimes committed under his rule are not new, though Gorbachev has been careful also to recognize his positive contributions to the 'struggle for socialism'. Nevertheless the rehabilitation of Bukharin and others of Stalin's victims has necessitated the rewriting of Soviet history (with the awkward consequence that school history examinations have had to be suspended). But especially marked has been the widespread condemnation of Brezhnev's policies and their effect on the economy and the bureaucracy. Mikhail Gorbachev has made plain that his purpose is to reverse the stagnation and the deviation from Leninist principles for which Brezhnev is held responsible. His proposals are radical but he has been careful to stress the ideological basis for them. As he said: 'We are not retreating even one step from Socialism, from Marxism–Leninism.' But Gorbachev has not had it all his own way; there has been publicly expressed opposition, from those who consider he is trying to move too fast, from those who consider he wants to go too far, from those who see their personal positions and vested interests as being adversely affected and from those who are fearful of having to accept the new responsibilities which 'perestroika' will impose on them. Yegor Ligachev has long been seen as the leader of those within the Politburo who are demanding restraint on the pace and extent of reform. But whatever modifications Gorbachev may have been, and may still be, forced to accept to his own preferred measures in order to secure collective support, the principle that reform is needed is not in question. At the highest levels, the essence of the debate has centred on what should be done to revitalise the economic and political life of the country without weakening the effectiveness of control by the CPSU. 'Democratic centralism', Gorbachev told the Party Conference in June, 'lies at the basis of the structure of the activity of the CPSU', which must continue to fulfil its functions as the guiding force in government and society. So far at least Gorbachev – whether from conviction or necessity – is in agreement with his more conservative colleagues. Implementation of the resolutions approved by the Conference for democratisation and devolution of authority are not likely to violate this principle. The 'Gorbachev Revolution' is essentially a 'revolution from above': initiated from above, and intended to be controlled from above. But it cannot work unless it gains support from below.

The Party Conference was an undoubted success for 'glasnost'. If Gorbachev had hoped to be able to manipulate the election of the 5000 delegates so as to ensure that the vast majority would be supporters of his proposals rather than traditional local party nominees, he was largely disappointed. But the predominantly conservative composition did nothing to inhibit the outspoken views voiced by the 61 speakers who took the floor during the four days of the Conference. The critics of the new policies expressed themselves as freely as the supporters, and often evoked the warmest applause. As if to warn the 'liberals', who were demanding more 'glasnost', and perhaps to reassure the conservatives, who were demanding less, Gorbachev reminded the Conference of the limitations within which democratic freedom will be permitted: 'Recently we have seen attemps to use democratic rights for anti-democratic ends. Some people think it is possible to solve any issue by these means, from the redrawing of borders to the creation of opposition parties. The CPSU considers that such abuses of democratisation run fundamentally counter to the tasks of restructuring and are contrary to the interests of the people.'

Two events served to underline these remarks. A demonstration by the fledgling opposition 'party', Democratic Union, launched in May in a flush of enthusiasm for 'glasnost' by a handful of radicals, was violently dispersed by the KGB outside the hall in which the Conference was taking place. The concept of 'socialist pluralism' does not admit of such deviations. Similar manifestations of dissent which do not fall within the strict limits permitted to 'glasnost' are ruthlessly suppressed. The other, much more significant, threat to Gorbachev's reforms has been the upsurge of ethnic nationalism in the non-Russian Republics. The most serious manifestion of this has been the dispute between Azeris and Armenians over the future status of the small, predominantly Armenian, region of Nagorno-Karabakh in Azerbaijan. This dispute erupted in violent demonstrations and strikes, resulting in political and military intervention from Moscow, throughout the first six months of 1988. It was eventually referred for decision in July to the Praesidium of the Supreme Soviet, when Gorbachev rode roughshod over the aspirations of the Armenians to insist on the strict application of the boundaries fixed in the 1977 Constitution, which originated from decisions imposed by Stalin. Although the most violent, this has not been the only ethnic dispute which has erupted following the greater freedom of expression permitted by 'glasnost'. The nationalist aspirations of the Tatars and the peoples of the Baltic States have already presented problems for Moscow, where there is growing awareness of the potential for trouble from the diverse non-Russian nationalities which make up 48 per cent of the Soviet Union's population. A resolution of the Party Conference recognised the grave dangers and difficulties involved in the complex ethnic and nationality problems which are to be considered by a Special Central Committee Plenum. Its task will not be easy, and the subject is likely to prove a continuing stumbling block in the path of political reform.

Although the principal proposals sponsored by Gorbachev and endorsed by the Central Committee were approved, the Conference was not an unmitigated success for Gorbachev, some of whose ideas failed to secure inclusion in the final resolutions. Nevertheless the resolutions on 'glasnost' and legal reform, despite some major qualifications, at least open up the theoretical possibility for a less authoritarian society with safeguards for the citizen. In immediate practical terms the Conference paved the way for reorganisation of the Soviet Union's political structure. At the end of July the Central Committee agreed that elections throughout the country for a new Congress of People's Deputies should take place in March 1989. The Congress will then elect a Supreme Soviet, which in turn will choose a President: Gorbachev has made clear his view that the President should have wide executive authority and his expectation that the office would be doubled with that of General-Secretary of the CPSU. Besides ensuring, and demonstrating, the Party's continuing firm control over all aspects of Government, such an arrangement would also concentrate enormous power in the hands of one individual. Gorbachev no doubt had both these points in mind when proposing it. Although it seems likely that his expectation will be realised, there has been no indication so far that it has the support of the Central Committee. The way ahead for restructuring the economy is less certain. At the same Central Committee meeting Gorbachev also outlined far-reaching proposals for agricultural reform including the leasing of land to private individuals. But, speaking in early August, Ligachev made an outspoken attack on those advocating radical changes, including Gorbachev's agricultural proposals, when he declared that Western capitalist models for economic reform were totally unacceptable in a Socialist society.

'Perestroika' is indeed still very much on trial. Many speakers emphasized at the Conference that, for the population at large, the acid test would be whether it resulted in more food and consumer goods in the shops and less queues for ordinary citizens and less special privileges for the elite. So far it has not passed this test. And, in a final intervention at the Conference, Ligachev pointedly recalled that Gorbachev owed his election as General Secretary in March 1985 to support from the conservative members of the Politburo, including Gromyko and Chebrikov, the head of the KGB. The point was not lost on the largely conservative gathering.

Nor has it been lost on Western Governments in their reactions to the 'New Thinking' in foreign policy. NATO has adopted a guarded attitude, recognising the encouraging signs but requiring tangible evidence of real changes in policy and practice. In the international arena the two highlights of the period have been the Soviet agreement in April to withdraw Soviet forces from Afghanistan and the Reagan-Gorbachev Summit in Moscow at the end of May. The Afghanistan agreement was achieved with great difficulty and against the evident misgivings of Moscow's Afghan protégés. Although much can still happen in the nine-month period set for the withdrawal, the agreement removed an increasing source of domestic embarrassment for Gorbachev, which resulted from what was generally admitted as a major error on the part of Brezhnev. More than that, the continued Soviet occupation of Afghanistan remained a serious obstacle to Gorbachev's declared policy of closer cooperation with the United Nations and to any real hopes for an improvement in relations with the West. Indeed, failure to reach agreement would have soured the atmosphere for the May Summit meeting. The latter was significant not, as was the previous summit in Washington, for progress on arms control—there was relatively little—but for the outspoken way in which President Reagan publicly attacked the Soviet record on human rights. Perhaps even more important was the fact that Gorbachev refused to allow this subject, which at Reagan's insistence dominated the agenda, to deflect him from his purpose of avoiding a return to confrontation. Such public gestures as the subsequent visit of the American Defence Secretary to Moscow at the invitation of his Soviet opposite number have sustained this purpose.

They are in line with the 'New Thinking', supposedly the foreign policy equivalent of 'glasnost' and 'perestroika', as it was outlined by Gorbachev to the Party Conference. There was nothing new in his description of Soviet foreign policy since the Second World War as being the natural and proper reaction to the aggressive behaviour of the imperialist *bloc* and its military threat to the Soviet Union and its allies. His break with the past, already indicated in previous speeches, came with his disavowal of the errors which had resulted from applying the 'administrative command methods', which had proved so disastrous for the economy, to foreign policy. Having been 'drawn into the arms race', with an adverse effect on the country's economic development, the Soviet Union's 'traditional political and social activity in favour of peace and disarmament began to lose its power to convince'. The basis of the 'New Thinking' is therefore to move from 'confrontation to cooperation', so that 'guaranteeing the security of states will move more and more out of the sphere of the correlation of military potentials to that of political interaction and strict compliance with international obligations'. But Gorbachev emphasised that all this was in keeping with Marxist–Leninist principles. 'New Thinking' would involve a broader range of contacts with Governments and others in the non-communist world based on respect for national independence; and Shevardnadze, the Soviet Foreign Minister, has subsequently emphasised in an address to Soviet diplomats that, at this level, peaceful co-existence must not be identified with the class struggle. But Gorbachev was at pains to make clear to the Party Conference that 'New Thinking' did not in any way affect the 'Class nature of international relations' nor the role of the World Communist Movement, and moreover that the continuing threat to peace from imperalist militarism and aggression had not vanished. The ideological approach was emphasised by Ligachev in a speech in August when, in clear contradiction of Shevadnadze, he maintained that international relations must be considered from the point of view of class interests. This, he declared, is 'of fundamental importance'; any other presentation would only confuse the Soviet people and 'our friends abroad'. The debate about the role of ideology in the practical conduct of foreign policy is still continuing.

A substantial contribution to 'glasnost' over the past failures in Soviet foreign policy was contained in an article in the Literary Gazette of 18 May by Professor Dashichev, of the Institute of Economics of the World Socialist System, which may be assumed to reflect Gorbachev's views. After condemning the 'distortions' of Lenin's principles under Stalin, he asserts that the 'hegemonism' which Stalin's successors inherited led to the essential task of preventing the threat of war being subordinated to 'the interests of the expansion of social revolution' and to the propaganda argument that, since the West was resisting the social and territorial changes emanating from the Soviet Union, it was the aggressor. 'On the one hand we heightened the level of the danger of war by advancing on the West's positions, and on the other we mounted a broad campaign in defence of peace and spared no resources to organise a mass movement of champions of peace.' 'Over the years', he added (in an unusually frank admission coming from a Soviet source), the leadership had become 'effectively prisoners of their own propaganda'. These policies allowed the United States to use the 'Soviet military threat' as a means of advancing its own 'hegemonist interests' and to argue that the Soviet Union was actively exploiting detente as a cover for building up its own military forces. The resultant 'massive arms race' and the Soviet invasion of Afghanistan precipitated a crisis which was caused by 'the miscalculations and incompetent approach of the Brezhnev leadership towards the resolution of foreign policy tasks'. In reality the genuine interest of the Soviet Union 'lay in ensuring a favourable international situation for profound transformations in the Soviet Union's economy and socio-political system'. But 'no serious efforts were made to settle the fundamental political contradictions with the West'. This is now seen as the principal task, requiring mutual efforts to remove political and military tension between the Soviet Union and the West. But the aim is to create 'favourable international conditions for building socialism', which 'has become an invincible force', on a national basis throughout the world.

External, Gorbachev depends on three essential conditions if he is to succeed in his objectives of remodelling the political structure and revitalising the economy, in short, of making 'perestroika' work. They are: maintenance of a stable basis for East–West relations, especially for relations with the United States; creation of an international climate in which the Soviet Union can obtain the benefits of enhanced economic and commercial cooperation with the West; and progress in arms control which will permit a reduction in the high proportion of the Soviet GNP being spent on defence. Developments in the past seven months have underlined the importance of these conditions. The much publicised break with the past and the espousal of 'New Thinking' are the starting point for achieving them. Soviet public actions and initiatives in the field of foreign policy have all been consistent with them. In so far as they meet the desire in the West for a real improvement in the international climate and correspond to Western initiatives to this end, which mostly long pre-date the advent of Soviet 'New Thinking', they deserve a cautious welcome. Willingness to explore any new openings they present conforms with the West's own interests. Soviet withdrawal from Afghanistan, the INF Agreement, the prospect of Cuban withdrawal from Angola, all fall in this category, even if they are presented as Soviet concessions rather than the response to Western pressures. It is to be hoped that the new Soviet interpretation of peaceful co-existence in the era of 'perestroika' will lead to more such 'concessions'.

But the bottom line is not the tactical conditions for the success of 'perestroika'. It is the enduring objectives of Soviet foreign policy. These are discussed and spelled out in Section 1. 'New Thinking', however it may be presented to the Soviet people or to the West, does not in any way reduce their validity. They may be given less prominence, but nothing said by Gorbachev or by any other Soviet leader provides any ground for supposing that they have been modified. Indeed, the passages on 'New Thinking' quoted above serve to underline the essentially 'Socialist' basis for Soviet foreign policy. Moreover the evidence for any lasting change at the tactical level is still thin. Despite the much-publicised 'concessions' referred to above, there has so far been no reduction in the rate of the Soviet military build-up, the meaning of the new slogan of 'non-offensive defence' is far from clear, progress in the Vienna Review Conference on European Security and Co-operation has been delayed because of the equivocal Soviet attitude to human rights, there are still some hundreds of people in prison or otherwise detained in the Soviet Union on political and religious grounds, and many of the Soviet proposals on arms control and other so-called 'peace initiatives' are designed primarily to appeal to public opinion in the West and in the Third World, and often bear little relation to the stance adopted by the Soviet Union in actual negotiations. And the West is still waiting for publication of the true figures for the Soviet defence budget following Gorbachev's statement to the United Nations in August 1987 that 'we are for more "glasnost" and openness in respect of military activities and expenditure'. Since Western estimates of what the Russians actually spend on defence are vastly in excess of the official Soviet figures, Soviet proposals for a freeze or limitation on military spending must be seen for what they are: meaningless propaganda gestures. Moreover, the unsettling effect of the 'Gorbachev Revolution' on Russia's allies in Eastern Europe may even yet put to a practical test the assumption that the 'Brezhnev Doctrine', coined to justify the suppression of the Prague Spring in 1968, has really been abandoned.

General-Secretary Gorbachev is reported to have said, during the Washington Summit meeting in December, 1987, that he had given instructions that there were to be 'no more lies, no more disinformation'. This would indeed be a welcome contribution to the improvement of East–West relations. But if any such instruction was given, it has so far had little apparent effect on the activities of the KGB. Some of the principal recent disinformation campaigns are described in Section I. They have continued in 1988. Allegations that the AIDS virtus was created at a United States military establishment and deliberately spread in the Third World were still being repeated on Radio Moscow in February. Despite official Soviet disclaimers, following American protests, they have continued to appear in press reports throughout Africa, and a new variation alleging that a West German firm is associated with this American-financed research, surfaced on Moscow Radio in March. Charges, dismissed by American scientists as 'absolutely ridiculous', that the United States has developed in cooperation with South Africa (or in some versions with Israel) an 'ethnic weapon' which can discriminate between whites and non-whites, killing only the latter, were still being carried in 1988 by the official Soviet media and repeated in the African press. For many years it has been the practice of the KGB to accuse the United States of responsibility for the assassination or attempted assassination of any prominent non-American personality. During 1988 the Soviet official media have repeated such accusations in respect of the murders of Indira Gandhi, Olof Palme and Aldo Moro and the attempted murder of Pope John Paul II. As recently as April they promoted in the Arab press the allegation that the Americans actively conspired with the Israelis to kill Abu Jihad, Deputy Commander-in-Chief of the Palestine Liberation Organisation, in Tunis. These examples are typical of the disinformation themes, aimed primarily at discrediting the United States in Third World countries—in Africa, the Middle East, Latin America and Asia—which are still being actively promoted in 1988 by those responsible for Soviet 'active measures'.

Meanwhile the activities of the Soviet propaganda network continue undiminished. The emphasis which Gorbachev has placed on the interconnection between domestic and external policies has given a new impetus, and a new direction, to its role. The new General Secretary of the World Peace Council, Johannes Pakaslahti of Finland, has embarked on the task of improving the credibility of the Council. Attendance at the annual meeting of the Presidential Committee, held in Prague in March, was extended beyond the normal complement of some 250 office-holders and elected members to include representatives from 120 peace organisations and other movements not affiliated to the WPC. The President, Romesh Chandra, announced that this should be regarded as a first major step towards a new joint strategy by the peace movement throughout the world; the next triennial session of the Council in 1989 would discuss 'global security'. Pakaslahti claimed that the 1989 session, in the Council's 40th anniversary year, would be of crucial importance as providing the occasion to discuss the positive contribution which the WPC could make to the work of national peace movements. It is clear that the WPC's aim will be to broaden the base of it support and extend the scope of its influence by softening the hard edges of its blatantly anti-Western propaganda and emphasising the principal themes enunciated by Gorbachev: interdependence, 'the survival of mankind', disarmament, the 'demilitarisation of international relations', cooperation in the conservation of natural resources, and 'the Common European Home'. Where the WPC leads, the other Soviet front organisations usually follow, but there may be resistance from some, such as the Prague-based International Organisation of Journalists, which are not yet wholly reconciled to the implications of 'glasnost'. One organisation which is playing an increasing part in spreading Soviet propaganda is the Christian Peace Conference, which may be expected to capitalise on the ecumenical relations established during the June celebrations in Moscow staged by the Russian Orthodox Church to mark the millennium of Christianity in the Soviet Union. The limited concessions made to the Church indicate the Soviet authorities' intention that these relations should be exploited for propaganda purposes. In the West, the trend is increasingly to rely on the newer Soviet-influenced organisations, single-issue and professionally-based bodies which have sprung into prominence in recent years and of which examples are still emerging. Not only is Soviet involvement less obvious in these organisations, but the principles of 'glasnost' and 'perestroika' are calculated to have an immediate appeal to their members and potential members, irrespective of their political sympathies. There are also signs of renewed Soviet attempts to use Communist parties in non-communist countries, both as vehicles themselves for Soviet propaganda, and also as bases for cooperation with other left-wing parties in promoting Soviet views on 'peace', disarmament, etc., possibly an attempt to revive the old 'popular front' technique which was not conspicuously successful in the past. This was a theme of Gorbachev's and other speeches at the meeting in Moscow of representatives of Communist and socialist parties at the time of the 70th Anniversary of the October Revolution, and its importance was emphasised again by Gorbachev at the Party Conference in June.

Though it has already changed much, the 'Gorbachev revolution' still has a long way to go. Its outcome is not predictable. It is difficult to believe that, short of a return to outright repression, the gains achieved for 'glasnost', whatever its limits, could now be wholly reversed. More uncertainty surrounds the future development of 'perestroika', which has to face hard physical problems as well as entrenched attitudes. Proposals for democratisation remain incomplete; their detailed elaboration is likely to prove contentious. Two years of 'New Thinking' have proved little except that, for the time being, the atmosphere may be conducive to a more realistic and pragmatic approach to the settlement of some issues. What is however certain is that the expanding worldwide propaganda network will continue to be available to purvey Moscow's message in whatever form best serves the interests of Soviet foreign policy. Openness about the network's methods and activities is as important for an understanding of the nature of the Soviet Union as is openness about what is taking place inside the country itself. In short, experience of the past seven months has served only to reinforce the conclusions reached in the introduction to Section 1.

August 1988

SECTION I

Soviet Propaganda and Foreign Policy

INTRODUCTION

This book is a directory of organisations which comprise the Soviet propaganda network. Their structure, functions and activities as they exist today are described in the profiles contained in Sections II to V. While every effort has been made to ensure that these profiles are comprehensive and factually up-to-date, the directory cannot claim to be exhaustive or to take account of changes occurring subsequent to its compilation. The role they play in the total projection of Soviet policy can only properly be understood in the context of their origins and subsequent development. This section contains an account of the historical ideological and organisational background against which these organisations, which are witting or unwitting instruments of Soviet propaganda, have evolved and currently operate.

Just as important is the current political background to these operations. The wind of change has been blowing through the Soviet Union since Mikhail Gorbachev assumed the appointment of General-Secretary of the CPSU in March 1985. That change was urgently needed, if the steady deterioration of the Soviet economy was to be arrested, can hardly be disputed. Whether or not the policies initiated by General-Secretary Gorbachev, under the principles of 'perestroika' and 'glasnost', restructuring and openness, will succeed in doing this, or be allowed to succeed, is still very much an open question. (A strict translation of the Russian word 'glasnost' would be 'permission to speak', which more accurately reflects the limits imposed on 'openness' in practice.)[a] Much has been said and written about these policies. Authoritative accounts are to be found in the Central Committee's report, presented by the General-Secretary to the Twenty-

---

[a] This interpretation is provided by Malcolm Mackintosh

3

seventh CPSU Congress in February 1986, in the General-Secretary's report to the CPSU Central Committee Plenum on twenty-fifth June 1987 and other similar official sources. But in the context of Soviet propaganda, more significant than these set-piece statements is the description given by Gorbachev himself in his book published in 1987 with the title *Perestroika: New Thinking for our Country and the World*. 'In writing this book,' he says, 'it has been my desire to address directly the peoples of the USSR, the United States, indeed every country.' He goes on to discuss the origins, purpose and progress of the new policies. Although the book is repetitive, contains many platitudes and oversimplifications and glosses over some awkward facts, it is of major importance for understanding not only what Gorbachev intends for the Soviet Union but also how he wishes it to be presented to public opinion throughout the world. It must be assumed that what is said in this book will be adopted as a source of policy guidelines for the campaigns to be conducted by the propaganda network. This is consistent with the new style intro-duced by Gorbachev, whose ability to communicate, to handle public relations, has been in marked contrast to the stilted formality of his predecessors. For the first time since Lenin—if the erratic performance of Khrushchev is discounted—a Soviet leader has emerged who is capable, in effect, of being his own chief of propaganda. It is therefore worth examining briefly what he says.

Gorbachev defines 'perestroika' as 'a revolutionary process', involving 'radical changes on the way to a qualitatively new state', and sees it as a 'direct sequel to the great accomplishments' of the party of Lenin. Thus he declares that 'in politics and ideology we are seeking to revive the living spirit of Leninism' in order to sweep away the corruption and stagnation of a bureau-cracy-ridden society. If it is to work, perestroika must involve 'more Socialism and more democracy'. Democracy means glas-nost: openness about what is happening in the country and in the Government, truthful (and 'responsible') reporting by the media, and the development of criticism and self-criticism.

All this represents an ideal which must seem to many a remote prospect. It is accompanied by the professed aim of constituting a Socialist society in which all citizens participate in decision taking, from the Politburo downwards and from the shopfloor upwards; in which the principle of 'from each according to his ability, to each according to his work' is restored; and in which social welfare and social justice for all are guaranteed. But the ideological framework remains intact, as a firm restraint on the process: there is to be no deviation from the principle of 'democratic centralism'; criticism must be directed to promoting 'observance of socialist law and order' and 'the social principles and ethical standards of the Soviet way of life'; the system of privileges for people who have performed 'socially useful work' (though not the 'abuse' of the system) is upheld; and, above all, the supremacy of the Party and its direction by the leadership are sacrosanct.

In short, there are limits, in terms of doctrine and practice, to the scope to be allowed both for openness in society and for 'democracy' in the restructuring of the economy. Precisely where these limits lie is not clearly defined and is evidently still subject to trial and error. Many things have already begun to change in the Soviet Union, in the direction outlined by Gorbachev, and there are promises of further progress towards the implementation of his programme of reforms during 1988. Whatever the future of this programme and of its principal instigator, it is probable that no successor would find it easy to reverse the process entirely. Nevertheless current realities fall far short of Gorbachev's ideals. Public criticism and debate have been allowed to an extent not previously tolerated, but they have been confined to subjects which the leadership wishes to see criticised and debated. Some demonstrations have been permitted and some political prisoners released and allowed to emigrate. But the process has been carefully controlled, and it is still not clear whether it represents the start of a genuine loosening up and, if so, how far the régime can afford to let it run without encountering serious risks. The summary dismissal of Boris Yeltsin, one of Gorbachev's foremost supporters in the Politburo, in November 1987, showed the strength of those who wish to narrow the limits. Jews, human rights activists and others who have interpreted the new policies as permitting peaceful rallies and meetings have found to their cost and dismay that the KGB adopt a much less flexible interpretation. It is small wonder that the attitude of the general public towards the reforms is still one of caution. Gorbachev confines himself to the assurance that bills are being drafted which 'should guarantee glasnost' and that 'everything which is not prohibited by law is permitted'. Moreover the measures for restructuring the economy which came into force on 1 January 1988 can hardly be expected to have a smooth passage. The limited shift of responsibility for decision-making from the Moscow bureaucracy to the factory management for which they provide is likely to be resisted by the former and may not be altogether welcome to the latter. But probably the greatest threat to Gorbachev's policies comes from the non-Russian republics, where different nationalist groups have been emboldened by the limited freedom of expression permitted by glasnost to give vent to grievances and demands which have formerly been ruthlessly suppressed.

Half the book is devoted to foreign policy. Here the key phrase is 'New Thinking'. In fact much of it turns out to be the familiar comparison of constructive Soviet initiatives with negative Western, especially American, responses. Emphasis is, however, placed on the 'realities' of the world scene—the existence of different states with different political systems and different interests, the emergence of 'global issues' and, above all, nuclear weapons. These dictate the policy of 'interdependence', which, despite the preference of 'the West' for cooperation in small groups of like-minded countries, can best be realised through the United Nations. The suggestion that there is—or has ever been—a Soviet policy 'of imposing communism throughout the world' or of 'exporting revolution' is dismissed as 'crude falsification or at best ignorance'. 'Every nation is entitled to choose its own way of development'—this is said with particular reference to the Third World—and 'differences in political systems are the result of the choice made by the people'. So the West is warned to 'set aside the psychology and notions of colonial times'. In Eastern Europe, however, the commitment to Socialism is assumed. The way in which it was forced on the satellite countries in the years immediately following the Second World War is ignored; and the subsequent brutal application of the Brezhnev Doctrine (not mentioned) in order to maintain Soviet dominance over Hungary, Czechoslovakia and Poland as they 'went through serious crises in their development' is glossed over by the bland assertions that 'Each of these crises had its own specific features. They were dealt with differently.' The result, not surprisingly to those who remember how they were dealt with, was that 'a return to the old order did not occur in any of the socialist nations'. This leaves, finally, the question of relations with the capitalist West. Gorbachev leaves no doubt of his view that, as a result of the inevitable 'economic, political and ideological competition between capitalist and socialist countries', the latter's system will prevail. But it will prevail without war. This at least has been official policy since 1956, when the Twentieth CPSU Congress declared that 'war is by no means an indispensable prerequisite for social revolutions'. Now that nuclear war would result in universal destruction, rather than (as in pre-nuclear days) 'social upheavals which would finish off the capitalist system' and would 'spell global peace', the possibility of a new world war has been removed from the 1986 edition of the CPSU Programme 'as not corresponding to the realities of the nuclear era'. So General-Secretary Gorbachev can in sincerity agree with President Reagan that 'a nuclear war cannot be won and must not be fought'.

Much is made of the need for Pan-European unity; the concept of a 'Common European home' in which the interests which unite East and West Europeans are more important than those which divide them. But Gorbachev finds it 'regrettable' that NATO governments yield to pressure to support extreme American policies 'thereby assuming responsibility for the escalation in the arms race and international tension'. Continuing this blatant wedge-driving he warns of the threat to European culture which 'emanates from an onslaught of "mass culture" from across the Atlantic'. In a long section on US–Soviet relations, Gorbachev breaks no new ground. The emphasis is on the need for the two super-powers to avoid confrontation and the hope, as yet largely unfulfilled, that the United States will respond positively to Soviet initiatives designed to halt the arms race and lead to the elimination of nuclear weapons. This last point—the aim of a world free of nuclear weapons—is the underlying theme of the 'New Thinking'. This theme is already, and will undoubtedly remain, a key element in Soviet propaganda campaigns. Little is said about the problems of achieving it, still less about those of verification, and the question whether it would really lead to greater peace and stability is not addressed. Nor is its relationship to the balance of conventional armaments considered. A crucial question left unanswered is the effect that the removal of the restraints imposed by the 'nuclear era', which is presumably the intended result of the total elimination of nuclear weapons, would have on the means for conducting the 'struggle against imperialism' in order to achieve the Marxist–Leninist objective of the world-wide victory of Communism.

It may be debated how far 'New Thinking' represents any more than an up-dated version of the familiar Soviet 'peace offensives' and how the concept of interdependence differs from 'peaceful co-existence'. But if it reflects the genuine need by the Soviet Union for a period of stability in East–West relations during the disturbance which is bound to result from perestroika, however much the latter may have to be modified to take account of Soviet political realities, it may be given a cautious welcome. In so far as it corresponds to Western interests, it is likely to meet with a positive response. There is however no evidence to show that it denotes any change in the strategic aims of Soviet foreign policy, which indeed General-Secretary Gorbachev's book generally confirms.

It is the purpose of the present book to identify and describe the extensive network of organisations existing throughout the world whose role is to disseminate propaganda in support of Soviet policies. The tactical requirements of Soviet foreign policy may fluctuate. But the network remains in being, responsive to directives laid down by Moscow. In this respect, at least, the practices of Mikhail Gorbachev's Russia in no way differ from those of his predecessors. The approach may have become more subtle and more differentiated. This only serves to underline the need for those who are its targets to be alive to the methods and vehicles used to convey Moscow's message. Addressing the Twenty-seventh Congress of the Communist Party of the Soviet Union on 25th February 1986, Gorbachev said: 'The psychological war is a struggle for people's minds, their world outlook and their orientation in life, society and culture.' He himself makes a notable contribution to this struggle, which is however defined in terms little different from those used by Andropov and others before him.

EVOLUTION OF THE NETWORK

"A struggle is going on for the hearts and minds of billions of people in the world. The future of mankind depends, in no small measure, on the outcome of this ideological struggle." YURI ANDROPOV, General Secretary of the CPSU, addressing the Central Committee, 15 June 1983.

This emphasis on struggle, as a dynamic factor in the building of Communism, has been a constant theme in statements by all Soviet leaders from Lenin down to, and including, Gorbachev. The struggle for peace, for democracy, for Socialism, for national liberation; the struggle against Capitalism, against Imperialism, against bourgeois values. Such terms have become so familiar that it is easy to dismiss them as ritual clichés which have long since ceased to have any reality. This would be a serious error. Not only is the concept of struggle deeply embedded in the political thinking of the Soviet leaders but, in its numerous and varying forms, it represents the basis of the massive propaganda campaign which has been conducted in defence and in further-ance of the world-wide expansionist ambitions of Soviet Commu-nism for the past 70 years. Communists, Lenin wrote 'must be capable of any sacrifice, of overcoming the greatest obstacles, in order to carry on agitation and propaganda, systematically, perserveringly, persistently and patiently';[1] they must be ready 'to resort to all sorts of tricks, slyness, illegal methods and concealment of truth . . . to carry on communist work at all costs.'[2] Propaganda has always been one of the principal weapons for conducting the struggle; its practitioners today have no hesi-tation over employing all the methods advocated by Lenin.

As defined in the Shorter Oxford English Dictionary, propa-ganda is 'any association, systematic scheme or concerted move-ment for the propagation of a particular doctrine.' Such a bland

9

definition may appropriately be applied to the efforts made by political parties in the Western democracies to promote the policies in their election manifestoes. But it would be a mistake to make any comparison between these efforts and those made by Soviet propagandists. The OED definition conveys none of the aggressiveness and hostility, of the alternations between subtlety and crudity and between threats and seduction, of Soviet propaganda directed at non-Communist audiences. The Great Soviet Encyclopaedia (1975), in the course of a lengthy article, spells out clearly, albeit in rather turgid language, the purpose of political propaganda in Communist terms: 'the dissemination of views, ideas and theories with the aim of forming among the masses a specific outlook and concepts reflecting the interests of the subject of the propaganda, and stimulating in them corresponding practical action. A specific class ideology forms the kernel of political propaganda. In the contemporary world, two opposing types of propaganda are noted; the bourgeois and the communist.' In short, the purpose of propaganda is the pursuit of the class struggle.

This is not just a question of influencing but of positively manipulating the attitudes, opinions, and actions of the target to which propaganda is addressed. It is intended to serve both Soviet long-term strategic goals and short-term tactical requirements. It may be designed to prevent something happening which is considered hostile to Soviet aims (for example, deployment of nuclear weapons by NATO) or to promote something which will further those aims (for example, support for Soviet disarmament proposals or specific campaigns to undermine western, especially American, credibility and influence in the Third World). Soviet propaganda may be overt or covert; it may be deliberately false of subtly misleading: it is always 'one-sided' and never 'objective'. Above all, it is systematic, comprehensive and monolithic. In these respects, apart from its content, it differs fundamentally from the fragmented and uncoordinated public relations and information activities of Western Governments which make no pretence to having any of these characteristics, not only because they are alien to the nature of the democratic system but also because the system itself makes them impossible to achieve. Democracy, for all its faults, is incapable of the Big Lie which is the hallmark of totalitarianism.

The principal vehicles for overt propaganda are the orthodox ones of statements by Soviet leaders and officials and the legitimate activities of Soviet diplomatic missions, official delegations and other bodies responsible for conducting relations between the Soviet Union and foreign states. Whether or not the purpose of the message emanating from these sources is always recognised by the recipient, the identity of the messenger is openly acknowledged. The message may be threatening, like Khrushchev's warning at the time of Suez in 1956 or Brezhnev's attack on NATO's INF proposals in October 1979, or seductive, like the various 'peace offensives' launched by Brezhnev and Gorbachev; it may be crude, like the running campaign against alleged American use of biological and chemical weapons in Korea (1950), Vietnam (1960s) and Afghanistan (1980s), or subtle, like the campaign against the so-called 'neutron bomb' in 1977. But at least it is recognisable for what it is, part of a continuing process of trying to persuade, browbeat, divide and weaken those who stand in the way of Soviet aims.

These official sources are, in a sense, the tip of the propaganda iceberg. Under the surface—at least notionally—is a vast machine whose task is to organise the dissemination of Soviet propaganda without formal attribution to Soviet sources. In practice the existence of this machine and of its role has long been generally recognised. But the fiction of non-attribution is sedulously maintained. The machine controls a world-wide network of organisations, the functions and associations of many of which have already been exposed. But so wide are the ramifications of this network that the nature of many of the organisations within it is not understood and they are still able to operate with their credibility largely unaffected. All the organisations within this network are used as vehicles for Soviet propaganda, both in the West and in the non-aligned and Third World countries. They find a ready market in the latter for their portrayal of the various manifestations of the 'struggle' referred to above, and they derive advantage from the ingrained anti-western, and especially anti-American, prejudices, which are never far from the surface in many of these countries and which they take every opportunity of fuelling and exploiting. In the West, the task of the network is facilitated by the asymmetry between the open societies in NATO and other countries in Western Europe and the managed societies of the Communist East. Individuals and organisations engaged in Soviet propaganda are able to operate freely in the West and so have the advantage of being able to initiate, support and infiltrate indigenous campaigns in opposition to Western policies. Moreover they are able to do this in confidence that the controls exercised in the Soviet Union and other Communist countries will effectively insure against embarrassing repercussions in those countries. The Western 'peace movements' provide ideal instruments for their purpose and have been fully exploited. They can safely encourage these movements' attacks on NATO's nuclear policies without any risk that parallel criticism of Soviet policies, which even if it is admitted is heavily muted, will find any echo in the Soviet Union.

So propaganda plays, and always has played, a key role in the projection of Soviet policies. It is closely associated with—and some would describe it as part of—the whole range of techniques which the Russians refer to as 'active measures'. This term is defined by one leading authority as 'clandestine operations designed to extend Soviet influence and power around the world'.[3] Such operations include disinformation, forgeries, the use of 'agents of influence' and the infiltration of political parties and special issue groups. Another category of active measures is such para-military activities as support for 'freedom fighters' and guerilla movements. Many active measures in the former category overlap with particular propaganda campaigns. Principal among them, and most aptly descriptive of the purpose of the others, is 'disinformation'. This distinctively Russian word is not to be confused with the English word 'misinformation', which normally carries no implication of ill-intent. 'Disinformation'— again to take the definition in the Great Soviet Encyclopaedia— is 'the dissemination, in the press, radio etc., of false information with the intention to deceive public opinion'. This definition perhaps requires two glosses; the information may not in itself be false, but what may be basically true information is presented in a tendentious and misleading way which is deliberately designed to convey a false impression in the minds of its recipients; and 'public opinion' should be interpreted in the widest sense to include Governments or specific groups which may be the targets of a particular disinformation campaign. The same authority mentioned above distinguishes between the object of propaganda as being to improve the Soviet Union's public image by promoting positive support for its policies, and that of 'active measures' as being to discredit and disrupt the policies and influence of governments regarded as hostile to the Soviet Union. No doubt this is a valid conceptual distinction. Certainly, most of the content of the programmes and campaigns of the propaganda network are geared to the former object. But the latter object is never far from their intentions, and the extent of high-level orchestration of themes and activities is always evident.

Often a disinformation operation is initiated or supported by the use of forged letters or documents designed to 'substantiate' the information disseminated; sometimes also the information may be given formal public endorsement in statements by Soviet officials or in the controlled Soviet press; and the initial disinformation operation may be followed up as a theme for use by the propaganda network. All these operations combined are used to reinforce the hands of those whose function it is to conduct the regular diplomatic relations of the Soviet Union with other states. Stalin once said: 'With a good diplomat, words must diverge from acts—what kind of a diplomat would he otherwise be? Words are one thing and acts something different. Good words are masks for bad deeds. A sincere diplomat would equal dry water, wooden iron'.[4] An illustration of the practical application of this principle was given by the duplicity of Soviet diplomatic dealings with the British and French Governments in the period immediately preceding the Second World War leading up to the 1939 Nazi–Soviet Pact, a classic example of the mutually reinforcing capabilities of diplomacy, disinformation and propaganda.

It is not necessary to assume that all Soviet diplomacy today is conducted in accordance with Stalin's crude principle. Worldly experience and enlightened self-interest have combined to demonstrate that subterfuge may often prove risky and counterproductive and that traditional methods may be more expedient, at least in relation to short-term objectives. Nevertheless outstanding examples such as the categorical denials given to the United States Government in 1962 by the Soviet Foreign Minister and Ambassador in Washington of the installation of Soviet missiles in Cuba in face of photographic evidence to the contrary and the palpably false explanations given in 1979—which did not fit the known facts—that the Soviet troops had entered Afghanistan at the invitation of the Afghan Government show that Stalin's maxim has not been repudiated. These are but two instances of the use of diplomatic channels to convey information which is demonstrably incorrect. Experience shows that not only are Soviet diplomats briefed to take advantage of successes achieved by Soviet propaganda campaigns and active measure operations, but they are regularly and actively associated with their promotion whenever, and to the extent that, this can safely be done without prejudicing their diplomatic status.

Of the countless Soviet propaganda and other 'active measures' operations all over the world, two very different cases will serve as examples. Both have had high propaganda exposure. This first is the running campaign against NATO's plans for maintaining the effectiveness of the nuclear element in its defences. This acquired a new focus with the attack on the American proposal in 1977 to deploy the so-called 'neutron bomb', the Enhanced Radiation Warhead. This is an anti-tank weapon intended to enhance NATO's defensive capability against the vastly superior numbers of Soviet tanks on the Central Front which because of its reduced blast effects and high degree of accuracy would minimise collateral damage, for example on West German territory, in the event of Soviet aggression. Its introduction would thus have made a significant contribution to enhancing the credibility of the NATO deterrent. For this reason the Russians launched a major attack on plans to deploy the weapon, although its range and explosive power bear no comparison with that of many Soviet nuclear weapons already based in the European theatre, on the grounds that it was a capitalist weapon designed to kill 'people' (ie the tank crews) while preserving property. It was described as a 'horrific' new means of mass destruction and a major threat to peace.

The campaign was given maximum coverage on Moscow Radio and in the Soviet press and strenuous efforts were made to mobilise opposition to the 'neutron bomb' in the Third World. The principal international organisations of the Soviet propaganda network were actively engaged in organising conferences and media coverage world-wide. Articles were placed in the press with the help of sympathetic journalists. Forged letters purporting to emanate from NATO Headquarters were also employed. And Brezhnev wrote to heads of NATO Governments warning them that the deployment of the device would greatly endanger detente. The issue became so divisive within the Alliance that in April 1978 President Carter suspended his proposal. The Russians regarded this as a major success, as indeed it was, for the combined efforts of propaganda and diplomacy in support of an important policy objective. They thus moved with confidence into the campaign against NATO's plans to modernise its intermediate-range nuclear forces (INF) in 1979. This campaign was conducted over a period of five years, and contained every ingredient used in the 'neutron bomb' campaign. There were threats of dire consequences which would result from deployment of NATO's Pershing II and cruise missiles and of Soviet retaliatory measures, notably in Brezhnev's speech in East Berlin in October 1979 (two months before NATO's decision)

and in frequent statements subsequently by senior Soviet officials
and generals. Totally false allegations were made about the capabilities of the NATO missiles. There was a regularly published
supply of misleading statistics designed to prove that NATO's
plans would seriously disturb the existing stability based on
'parity' of INF systems between East and West.[5] Leaving aside
the different characteristics of systems on each side (there was
no Western theatre system in any way comparable in range and
power to the Soviet SS20), these statistics were based on a selective use of data which included in the NATO total systems whose
counterparts were conveniently omitted from the Soviet figures.
So the propaganda campaign was based on deliberate distortion
of the figures to 'prove' that a balance already existed at the time
of NATO's 1979 decision. Although the first NATO missiles
were not deployed for another four years during which the build-
up of SS20s continued steadily, the Soviet claims that a balance
existed were maintained throughout. Given the complexity of
the statistical analysis and the instinctive dislike of Western public
opinion for what was presented by its opponents as a new level
of escalation in the nuclear arms race, the Russians were confi-
dent that their campaign would succeed. They were assisted by
the whole propaganda network, for which the campaign was
during the period the principal theme in the programme, and by
the CND and other indigenous 'peace movements' in Western
Europe, which needed little encouragement to mount sustained
attacks on the NATO plans unmatched by any parallel demands
for Soviet restraints and which readily reproduced the inaccurate
information made freely available from Soviet sources. Forged
NATO documents were again employed to 'prove' American
intentions to bring pressure on NATO Governments which were
hesitant to accept deployment of the new missiles. Nevertheless
the campaign failed, despite the unprecedented and sustained
effort co-ordinated by Moscow.[6] The Russians on this occasion
over-played their hand and vastly over-estimated the influence
which national protest movements were able to bring to bear on
NATO Governments. The Alliance on the other hand had
learned from the 'neutron bomb' affair the importance of facing
the Russians down. A tougher US administration and more
robust Governments in the key NATO countries ensured that
the combined pressures, domestic and external, were resisted.
This was not, and is not, the end of the story. Because it is a
subject in which, so far as public opinion is concerned, emotional
reactions often prevail over rational thinking, NATO's nuclear

policies will remain highly vulnerable to Soviet propaganda and subversion.[7]

Soviet disinformation campaigns against NATO have, as the above examples show, aimed at preventing the Alliance from taking measures to strengthen its military capability and at dividing the United States from its European Allies. Campaigns in Third World countries have been designed to discredit the West, in particular the United States, by imputing to Western governments activities and policies which involve gross inter-ference in the affairs of those countries. Most of these campaigns are directed against the United States, and are often crudely executed. Many of them are too disreputable to risk the compro-mise to diplomatic relations which would be involved by giving them overt official support. A common feature is to attribute to the CIA responsibility for efforts to subvert or destabilise the political situation, for example in Fiji in 1987. A particularly outrageous report revived in 1987 was the accusation that the United States was developing 'ethnic weapons' which could distinguish between different racial targets; it was suggested that the Americans were working with the Israelis to make a weapon which would be effective only against Arabs and with the South Africans to produce a bomb which would kill blacks and spare whites.[8] A technique commonly used is to get the story published in the local press or radio, and then to use these 'sources' as a basis for wider and increasingly 'authoritative' dissemination by the Soviet media.

This technique was used extensively in the campaign to pin responsibility on the United States for the spread of AIDS. This originated in a letter to the Indian pro-Soviet newspaper *Patriot*, alleging that 'the AIDS virus escaped in the late 1970s from an Army biological warfare factory' at Fort Detrick, Maryland, where it was said to have been produced by US military research. This allegation was exploited—and embellished—since 1985 by Soviet propagandists in order to direct blame onto the United States for causing the AIDS epidemic in African countries and to stimulate fears in countries which are hosts to American bases that they run a high risk of exposure to the AIDS virus owing the presence of American servicemen. So-called evidence was adduced from purported, but bogus, scientific experts to the effect that the AIDS virus was a man-made creation of the Americans. Despite categorical denials by United States virolo-gists, the 'evidence' was used to fuel the campaign. According to one account, in two years from the start in October 1985 'more than 200 newspaper articles, radio reports and forged documents surfaced in 74 countries attributing the AIDS epidemic to American military research gone awry.'[9] The initial story and its elaborations were a blatant effort to discredit the United States by harping on a theme in which emotions and fears run high. Moscow Radio and the controlled Soviet newspapers and press agencies carried the allegations, often quoting reports in Third World media (where they had been placed originally by Soviet agents) as the source, thus giving them maximum currency without having to acknowledge their Soviet origin. They were also disseminated widely through the publications of the World Peace Council*. The Soviet press refused to publish official American denials and the Soviet Ambassador in Washington is said to have rejected suggestions that the campaign was being orchestrated by the Soviet Union or that his Government had any responsibility for reports in the Soviet press. But by November 1987 the Soviet authorities were compelled officially to dissociate themselves from this campaign. Leading members of the Soviet Academy of Sciences, at a press conference to celebrate the 70th Anniversary of the Revolution, denied that there was any substance in the allegations against the Americans. The Soviet official press reported that the Soviet Government supported these views. Nevertheless this repudiation came too late to undo the harm already done to American interests in countries where the about-turn in Moscow went unreported. Though built on an implausible tissue of lies, this was a particularly effective campaign. It is typical of countless others similar in method and purpose which form the continuing output of the Soviet disinformation industry.

Those responsible for directing the Soviet propaganda network draw freely on the whole range of propaganda and disinformation techniques, and other 'Active Measures', described above when determining the priorities and methods to be adopted by organisations comprising the network. The purpose of this book is to identify these organisations, to describe their structure and functions, and to show how they fit into a world-wide network which is controlled or manipulated from Moscow. Their role, as seen from Moscow, is to act as vehicles, whether conscious or not, for the dissemination of Soviet propaganda. Whether they are described as 'transmission belts'—Lenin's term—or, in the more recent formula, 'closely cooperating non-governmental organisations', this role is unchanged. Whatever the content of the message, the messenger's task is to deliver it. It is therefore important to set their role in the context of the nature and objectives of the Soviet régime.

The whole network is geared to operate in support of Soviet foreign policy and so to promote the aims and interests of the Soviet Union. Formally, Soviet foreign policy is conducted, on a state-to-state and day-by-day basis, by the Soviet Government, through the Foreign Ministry and Soviet Missions and Delegations abroad. It is not however the Soviet Government but the Soviet Communist Party, the CPSU, which determines and controls foreign policy, both in theory and in practice. The Party is the guardian and interpreter of the ideological basis against which Soviet aims and interests, and the foreign policy conducted in pursuit of them, have to be defined. The Soviet Constitution of 1977 says: 'The Communist Party of the Soviet Union is the leading and guiding force of Soviet society and the nucleus of its political system, of all state and public organisations. The CPSU exists for the people and serves the people. Armed with the Marxist–Leninist teaching, the Communist Party shall determine the general perspective of Society's development and guideline of the internal and external policy of the USSR.' In practice CPSU control of policy is absolute, and much more detailed and specific than the constitution implies. Only a few of the senior figures in the Soviet Government are also leading members of the CPSU, as members or candidate members of the Politburo, which is in theory the executive body of the CPSU's Central Committee but in practice the centre of all political power in the Soviet Union. Their power derives from their position in the Party rather than in the Government; General-Secretary Gorbachev for example, is Chairman of the Politburo, and of the Defence Council (in effect the Politburo in Defence session)[10] but occupies no Government appointment.

So the objectives of the Soviet régime must be defined in Marxist–Leninist terms. They are determined by three basic factors. The first is the historical inevitability of the ultimate world-wide victory of Communism and the defeat of bourgeois capitalism. The second is that it is the duty of Communists everywhere to do all they can to promote that victory. The third is that fulfilment of this duty is the sole criterion of Communist moral and ethical conduct. According to Lenin 'morality is entirely subordinate to the interests of the class war'. It is sometimes fashionable to dismiss these factors as being the products of out-of-date thinking and no longer having the same significance in relation to Soviet policy-making as they had in the early years following the Revolution. No convincing evidence has been adduced to support this view which seems to rely more on the credulity and wishful-thinking of those who assert it than on any objective arguments. Such evidence as exists all demonstrates the essential continuity of these factors throughout the past 70 years. That the new revised edition of the CPSU programme adopted, with Gorbachev's endorsement, by the 27th Party Congress in March 1986, contained the statement that 'the movement of mankind towards Socialism and Communism is inexorable' may not in itself be remarkable. It might be compared with the stock clichés of any 'party' manifesto the world over. But the same statement appeared in the programme adopted by the 20th Party Congress in 1956 under Khrushchev, and it has a pedigree going back to Lenin. The timescale has changed; the latest version prudently sets no deadlines. But the continuity of expectation is there and has been reaffirmed time and again in speeches by Soviet leaders from Stalin onwards. It is not just that the ultimate victory is held up as the goal, but that, in speech after speech, successive Soviet leaders emphasise the 'correctness' of Marxism–Leninism as the standard by which all policies are to be judged and invoke Lenin's name in support of particular policies they are advocating. The similarity between Gorbachev's speech to the 27th Party Congress and Khrushchev's to the 20th Party Congress in this respect is striking. Both quote Lenin in support of the need for pragmatism in developing the revolutionary doctrine to apply to evolving circumstances. This has served to legitimise the tactical flexibility which, within prescribed limits, each has needed for dealing—in his different way—with the situation he had to face on assuming power; Khrushchev, in taking over a system distorted by the crimes and repressions perpetuated by Stalin, and Gorbachev, in inheriting the stagnation and corruption of the Brezhnev years.

To ask whether the Soviet leaders believe in Marxism–Leninism is largely meaningless or at least irrelevant. The commitment to Communist victory is the rock on which the CPSU's authority stands. The legitimacy of the party's claim to be the sole repository of Marxist–Leninist orthodoxy depends on its ability to demonstrate that progress is being made towards this goal. As one scholar has expressed it; 'If there were no such goal and no authoritative knowledge of the way to it, the party could not present itself to the people as their "conscious vanguard" in the long march to what its propaganda has called the "glittering heights" of Communism.'[11] But this is the basis for the legitimacy also of the leadership within the party. Each successive Soviet leader needs to have his ideological roots firmly planted in the soil of Marxism–Leninism as the only basis on which his legitimacy can be justified; if he deviates from this fundamental orthodoxy, he risks making his position vulnerable. Since Stalin's death however, this is unlikely to present such a difficult intellectual problem as might be supposed. Successive generations of Soviet leaders have been conditioned by their education or their careers or both to accept that Marxist–Leninist objectives are historically determined. This underlines the extent to which ideology is built into their thought process, so that the debate is more likely to be about the limits of permitted flexibility than about ideological deviation. This is the balancing act which Gorbachev is having to perform.

The background then is the objective of the ultimate world-wide victory of Communism. In Lenin's perspective victory was imminent; Brezhnev in 1972 set his sights on 1985; and now, in the 1986 version of the Party programme, no date is set. But it is against this background that the strategic and tactical decisions on Soviet foreign policy are taken. At the strategic level there is consistency on four broad lines of policy. First, permanent conflict with Western democracy. Whether it is described as imperialism, capitalism or 'bourgeois ideology', this is the enemy whose defeat is necessary for the realisation of Communist victory. This line has remained unchanged since the Revolution. Second, the 'correctness' of Soviet policies and actions. This has been discussed above. When Gorbachev speaks of 'the open, honest, Leninist nature of the CPSU's foreign policy strategy' he relates this to 'the truly scientific theory of social development' contained in Marxism–Leninism according to which 'the course of history is irreversible'.[12] In fact his speech to the 27th Party Congress contained a classic exposition of the thesis that every Soviet move is designed to promote peace and social progress and every Western, and especially American, response is designed to frustrate these desirable Marxist–Leninist goals. Third, the opportunist encouragement of 'socialist' (sc. Communist) and anti-imperialist (sc. democratic) tendencies in the developing countries. This flows directly from the duty to promote Communist victory wherever possible. Fourth, the exploitation of the inherent weaknesses of imperialism and capitalism in order to undermine their resistance to Communism. These are Lenin's famous 'contraditions' of imperialism, whose reasoned exposition by Gorbachev is very different in style from their crude exposition by Stalin. But allowing for changes to take account of international developments since the 1920s and differences in the political climate of East–West relations between 1924 and 1986, the substance of the message remain essentially the same.[13]

Within this strategic framework there is considerable tactical flexibility. Short-term aims, and the methods of achieving them, are varied to suit the opportunities and realities of the current international scene. On a day-to-day basis these provide the issues with which the conduct of diplomatic relations between non-Communist countries and the Soviet Union is primarily concerned. But in conducting both its public and its private diplomacy, the Soviet Union has, almost from its birth, seized and held one great asset. This is the way in which it has hijacked the word 'peace' as a platform from which to launch its foreign policy initiatives, even those which are as obviously 'unpeacelike' as, for example, the 1979 invasion of Afghanistan. The pursuit of 'peace'—whether it is presented as 'the preservation of peace' (as in the North Atlantic Treaty) or as 'the struggle for peace' (in Communist parlance)—appeals irresistably to the peoples and governments of all countries. By equating 'peace' with the building of 'socialism' and victory over 'capitalism', Communists can present anything done in the name of 'socialism' as contributing to 'peace'. 'Peace', in short, is not an end in itself but a condition for the triumph of Communism. This is very different from the Western concept that peace must be associated with freedom. The 'struggle for peace' is the struggle against the enemies of peace, the capitalists and imperialists. 'Peaceful coexistence', the basis for the Soviet Union's relations with non-Communist states, constantly reaffirmed by Khrushchev, Brezhnev and Gorbachev, has never meant, to the Communists, either non-interference in the affairs of non-communist states or acceptance of the right of capitalism to continue to exist; on the contrary, it has always been a prescription for intensification of the struggle against capitalism and imperialism in pursuit of the triumph of Socialism. But it was under Khrushchev's leadership that the first public renunciation of war as a means to this end was made. In terms of the formulation enshrined in the Declaration of the 81 Communist Parties of December 1960, 'ideological and political disputes must not be settled through war'. This same struggle is the basis for the policy of support for 'national liberation movements' in Asia, Africa and Latin America who serve the cause of peace because they are engaged in the struggle against the enemies of peace, often, in this context, described as 'racialists'. The Soviet military build-up is justified by the assertion that 'strength in imperialism's hands is a source of danger of war . . . strength in socialism's hands becomes a source of ensuring peace';[14] thus, Soviet military superiority is a necessary condition for successfully waging the struggle for peace. This principle applies equally to Soviet policy on disarmament. The aim is to disarm those who resist the spread of Soviet influence and who are, by definition, opponents of peace; the method is publicly to announce proposals designed to embarrass Western governments by appealing over their heads to Western public opinion and to produce an outcome favourable to the Soviet Union. This dual purpose is apparent from an analysis of the periodic Soviet 'peace offensives', as for example Gorbachev's beguiling proposals for the total elimination of all nuclear weapons within 10 years (or by the year 2000) and for a 'freeze' on defence expenditures. In so far as agreements are reached, this has been because Western—particularly American—policies have successfully denied to the Soviet Government the realisation of its aims. This applied for example to the INF case where the failure of the Soviet propaganda campaign (summarised above) as a result of NATO resistance led eventually to an agreement acceptable to both sides.

It may be argued that the 'peace equation' is an element of Soviet propaganda rather than a platform for Soviet foreign policy. This is true only in the sense that the word 'peace' is used in order to manipulate the opinions and influence the actions of those to whom it is addressed, whether in the West, in the United Nations or in the Third World. But this is because the word 'peace' conveys to these people what they want to hear, not what the Russians intend it to mean. It is the other half of the equation, the build-up of 'socialism', which reveals unmistakably the association with Soviet foreign policy. In practical terms, there is no distinction between the aims of Soviet propaganda and those of Soviet foreign policy, the former being not only a direct reflection but also a powerful instrument of the latter.

Of course propaganda, being for the most part addressed to mass audiences, whatever their level of sophistication, tends to be shrill. That is to say, the message is hammered home by repetition and by employing all the methods already described. The purpose of diplomacy, the formal means of conducting foreign policy, is to apply Soviet aims to specific issues and circumstances. What actually takes place in arms control negotiations in Geneva, for example, may bear little apparent resemblance to the public presentation of what is going on by Soviet spokesmen. Moreover, while the conduct of diplomacy can be quickly adapted to suit the shifts of day-to-day requirements, propaganda campaigns, once launched, are not susceptible to such fine tuning. Nevertheless the main lines of foreign policy within which Soviet diplomacy operates also form the basis for Soviet propaganda campaigns. What are these 'main lines'? It is only possible to speculate on the basis of observation and practical experience of Soviet diplomacy and propaganda in action. But on this basis, it is reasonable to suggest that the 'main lines' have changed little during the past three or four decades and that the principal aims which determine Soviet foreign policy decisions have been and continue to be, the following:

(1) to present the Soviet Union as the driving force in the 'struggle for peace' by interpreting all its policies and actions in terms of the 'struggle';

(2) to present the United States as the principal enemy of peace whose policies and actions are designed to obstruct the 'struggle', thereby undermining American international influence and standing;

(3) to weaken NATO by exploiting divisions between the United States and its European allies (and Canada), and, as opportunities arise, between the European Allies;

(4) to use all the above means in order to promote among public opinion in the West dissatisfaction with and criticism of the United States and NATO;

(5) to support internationally and in the United Nations the aspirations of the non-aligned and developing countries where these are consistent with the above aims;

(6) to support, in the name of 'peace', movements in these countries which are committed to the struggle against 'imperialism', capitalism and 'racialism';

(7) to negotiate and conclude with the West practical agreements on arms control, confidence-building measures and other aspects of security provided these can be achieved on the basis of 'equal security', that is to say, a reduction in NATO's defence capabilities without any significant restraints on Soviet freedom to maintain the forces needed for the defence of socialism;

(8) to seek practical accommodations with the West in areas where these bring economic and technological benefits for the Soviet Union or relieve potentially dangerous tensions,

provided they do not restrict Soviet ability to pursue the ideological struggle; and

(9) to ensure that the 'gains of socialism', in Eastern Europe and elsewhere in the world, are defended and not eroded.

Together these add up to the single all-embracing aim of shifting the 'correlation of forces'—that elusive formula which, in communist terminology, represents the sum total of a country's political, economic, social and military potential—irreversibly in favour of the Soviet Union.[15] From these aims the recurrent Soviet propaganda themes are derived.

Just as foreign policy is directed by the CPSU, so is propaganda and the whole range of 'active measures'. At the apex, decisions are taken by the Politburo, and formally endorsed by the Central Committee. The principal bodies involved in the execution of decisions in these areas are the Secretariat of the Central Committee, the KGB and the Foreign Ministry. The latter is responsible for the conduct of orthodox diplomatic relations. So far as possible it, and its staff in Moscow and abroad, try to distance themselves from those who are engaged in less orthodox activities. This is essential for the successful pursuit of Soviet foreign policy through all normal means of international diplomacy; as already noted it does sometimes present some problems, but by and large the separation is maintained. The operations of the Foreign Ministry need not be further considered here.

Since the 27th Party Congress in 1986, two organs of the Secretariat and one of the KGB have been responsible for propaganda and 'active measures'. Service A of the First Chief Directorate of the KGB is responsible for all the KGB's disinformation activities, including forgeries and the operation of 'agents of influence'. These activities are distinct from intelligence and internal security, which are the responsibility of other Directorates. This service is heir to the original Department D established by Shelepin in 1959 as part of Khrushchev's drive to restore the international image of the Soviet Union and the influence of Communism, which had been tarnished and damaged by Stalin's excesses and distortions. The purpose was—and is—to give the KGB a major role in the dissemination of disinformation in support of the propaganda operations directed by the Central Committee organs, with which Service A's activities are co-ordinated.

The two organs of the Central Committee are the Propaganda Department (PD) and the International Department. The former took over the functions of the International Information Department (IID) in 1986, just as the IID had in 1978 succeeded to some of the functions of the Department of Agitation and Propaganda (Agitprop), whose head in the early post-war years was Mikhail Suslov, later to become the CPSU's principal hard-line ideologist and senior member of the Politburo until his death in 1982. The PD is responsible for the direction of overt Soviet propaganda. Its functions include control of the foreign operations of the Soviet news agencies *Novosti* and *Tass*, the external broadcasts of *Radio Moscow*, the presentation of foreign news in the Soviet press and the production of foreign language publications such as *New Times* and *Moscow News*, as well as the information activities of Soviet Embassies abroad. Its new head, appointed in 1986, is Yuri Sklyarov, formerly Chief Editor of the International Communist journal *World Marxist Review* in Prague; the new First Deputy Head, Albert I. Vlasov has emerged as an influential figure in the new style Soviet information apparatus; and the importance placed on the external propaganda effort is underlined by the promotion of the former head of the PD (and a former Soviet Ambassador to Canada), Aleksandr Yakovlev, to become a Party Secretary and full member of the Politburo, retaining responsibility for supervision of all propaganda activities.

The International Department (ID) is the successor to the Foreign Affairs Department (FAD), established in 1943 following the dissolution of the Comintern (the Third or Communist International). The Comintern was closed down by Stalin partly because it had, by 1943, become an ineffective instrument for its original purpose, the control of foreign Communist parties, and partly because its activities were seen as obstructing the development of good relations with the Soviet Union's wartime allies. Its dissolution proved beneficial in terms of inter-allied relations, and its functions were transferred to the Foreign Affairs Department. In practice this ensured that more effective direct control could be exercised by the CPSU over foreign Communist parties and also that its exercise could be carried on with much less public exposure. This arrangement was continued throughout the immediate post-war period when it suited the CPSU to maintain a low profile for its foreign links so long as prospects of cooperation between the Soviet Union and its wartime allies remained. But with the outbreak of the Cold War, Soviet requirements changed. The need then was to reassert firm ideological control and to ensure that all propaganda against the

West was effectively co-ordinated. With the announcement of
the 'Truman Doctrine' in March 1947[16] and subsequent Soviet
refusal even to discuss the Marshall Plan for economic aid to
Europe which was put forward by the US Secretary of State,
General Marshall, in June, the die was cast. The Communist
Information Bureau (the Cominform) was established in October
1947 to direct political activities in the struggle against imperialism, of which these two developments were seen as the latest
manifestations. The idea came from Georgi Malenkov, the Politburo's principal ideologist, who declared at the inaugural meeting
that: 'Experience has shown that the absence of contact between
the Communist parties is a hindrance in co-ordinating the action
of Communists in various countries . . . in our opinion it is
necessary to put into effect definite measures designed to eliminate the present abnormal situation in this respect.' But it was
not only in Europe that the struggle against imperialism was to
be co-ordinated. The colonial territories of the European powers
provided fertile soil for both overt and covert Soviet propaganda.
Following the creation of the Cominform, a Conference was held
in Calcutta in 1948 at which the Communist parties in Asian
countries were ordered to go on the offensive. This they did,
and they consequently played a major part in the unrest and
violence which erupted in these countries during their 'struggle
for independence'. The first head of the Cominform was Andrei
Zhdanov, Stalin's right-hand man until he died in mysterious
circumstances in 1948. He was succeeded by Suslov. Its original
members were the Communist parties of the Soviet Union,
Poland, Czechoslovakia, Bulgaria, Hungary, Romania, France,
Italy and Yugoslavia. Its first headquarters were in Belgrade, but
they were moved to Bucharest after the expulsion of Yugoslavia
in June 1948. The Cominform presided over the establishment
of all the principal Soviet-controlled International Front Organisations which are described below.

The Cominform lasted until 1956, when it was disbanded as
being no longer appropriate in the new climate of East–West
relations which Khrushchev was seeking to establish by his
emphasis on 'peaceful co-existence'. Its functions reverted to
the Central Committee, which had in fact always effectively
controlled them. The Foreign Affairs Department was split into
three parts. Two of them took on, respectively, the tasks of
handling relations with the Communist parties of the Soviet *bloc*
and of supervising party discipline. The most important functions, those of directing political activities and covert propaganda

towards non-communist countries, were given to the new International Department (ID), set up in 1957. The ID's first head was Boris Ponomarev, a veteran of the Comintern Executive Committee, who became a candidate member of the Politburo in 1972 and exercised a major influence over the whole field of international affairs. He was replaced in 1985 by Anatoliy Dobrynin,[@] formerly Soviet Ambassador in Washington for many years, and now a Central Committee Secretary. Dobrynin has two powerful First Deputies, Vadim Zagladin, who has held the appointment for the past ten years, and Georgi Korniyenko, formerly First Deputy Minister of Foreign Affairs, who was appointed in 1987. Both are full members of the Central Committee. The ID appears to be playing an increasingly important role in co-ordinating advice on foreign policy to the Politburo and in implementing the latter's decisions. Its principal responsibilities also include handling the CPSU's relations with Communist parties in countries outside the Soviet *bloc*; directing the activities of the Soviet-controlled international front organisations and their national affiliates; and ensuring that the activities of the Soviet-influenced organisations faithfully conform to the requirements of Soviet policy. It is with these last two categories that this book is primarily concerned.

It has already been observed that these organisations have an important function today in the projection and promotion of Soviet foreign policy. An account of their origins and history will show how their role has evolved from the principles laid down by Lenin in the years immediately following the October Revolution, and the way in which this role has been manipulated from Moscow to suit the requirements of the frequent, and often bewildering, changes in the tactics of the CPSU, especially during the long period of Stalin's leadership.

Disillusioned by the failure of the Second (Socialist) International, which had proved incapable of maintaining its policy of solid opposition to participation in the 'imperialist' war and whose increasingly social-democratic membership he regarded as lacking sufficient enthusiasm for the revolution, Lenin issued invitations in 1919 to an inaugural congress for a Third (Communist) International (the Comintern). This took place in Moscow in March, and was attended by only 40 representatives from Britain, France, Ireland and the United States. What it lacked in numbers however it made up for in propaganda appeal. Its

[@] Dobrynin was replaced by the chief of Novosti, Valentin Falin, in October 1988, when other major changes were also made in the Politburo and Secretariat.

immediate purposes were to demonstrate support for the Bolshevik Revolution in Russia and keep alive the hope for imminent revolution elsewhere. Its aim was clearly set out in its statutes as being 'the overthrow of the international bourgeoisie and the establishment of an international Soviet Republic as a transition to the complete abolition of the Capitalist State'.[17] Any idea that those joining the Comintern were to be left to pursue their individual methods for achieving this aim were quickly dispelled. In his *Left Wing Communism, An Infantile Disorder*, published in April 1920, Lenin set out his instructions to which non-Soviet Communist Parties were expected to conform. Lenin condemned the exclusive approach of those who, by refusing to compromise the purity of their revolutionary doctrine, failed to exploit the opportunities presented by democratic institutions. He emphasised the necessity 'for the Communist Party, the vanguard of the proletariat, its class-conscious section, to resort to changes of tack, to conciliation and compromises with the various groups of proletarians, with the various parties of the workers.' 'It is,' argued Lenin, 'entirely a matter of knowing how to apply these tactics in order to raise—not lower—the general level of proletarian self-consciousness, revolutionary spirit, and ability to fight and win.' British Communists were enjoined to establish themselves within such democratic institutions as the Trade Unions and to support the Labour Party 'as the rope supports a hanged man'. Similar injunctions were given to other foreign Communists.

Any remaining idea that those joining the Comintern were to be allowed to follow their own independent path to the revolution was dispelled by the Second Comintern Congress in July 1920 when its President, Grigory Zinoviev, made clear the intention to transform the organisation into a single world Communist movement responsive to the direction of the CPSU. The prestige and authority of the CPSU, as the only party which had achieved power, helped to secure this. The Congress adopted, with little opposition, '21 Conditions' for membership which were designed to model all national parties on the Russian pattern and to ensure their acceptance of the policy laid down by Moscow. Lenin's tactics were endorsed. It was resolved to bring about 'a close alliance of all national and colonial liberation movements with Soviet Russia' and to support 'national revolutionary movements' (the 'national liberation movements' of modern Communist jargon) in the struggle against 'imperialism'. By the time of the Third Congress, in 1921, the prospects for further imminent revolutions, after failed attempts in Poland, Hungary and Germany, had receded and the New Economic Policy (NEP) had

been introduced, which underlined the urgent need for establishing commercial relations with the capitalist countries and,
if possible, obtaining from them financial assistance. So Lenin
sounded a tactical retreat from the aim of world revolution. At
the same time, although the Social Democrats were denounced
as 'social patriots' (a term of severe abuse), the Comintern reaffirmed the policy of infiltrating democratic political parties and
trades unions, which became known as the 'united front from
below'. This was complemented, at the Fourth Comintern
Congress in November 1922, in one of those reversals of tactics
which proved so disconcerting to the CPSU's fellow members,
by the adoption of the policy of the 'united front from above',
which envisaged direct cooperation between Communists and
leaders of the social democratic parties and trades unions in their
democratic (and parliamentary) opposition to capitalist governments. Although imposed on the compliant membership of the
Comintern, which by then numbered 34 Communist Parties,[18]
many, including the British Party (CPGB), did not find it
comfortable to implement or easy to achieve.[19]

Lenin's ideas however went beyond the advocacy of Communist infiltration of or cooperation with non-Communist political
parties. He understood that such tactics might meet with resistance from those who, suspicious of their Comintern origin,
perceived the threat to democracy that they represented. This
indeed proved to be the case in Britain where the CPGB's
attempts to form a 'united front' with the Labour Party were
roundly defeated. Entry by the front door having been barred
the Communists fell back on the tactic of the 'united front from
below', individual infiltration of local Labour Party branches.
Once again they were rebuffed, and, after a series of measures
designed to frustrate the tactic, the British Labour Party decided
by an overwhelming majority in 1924 that 'no member of the
Communist party should be eligible for individual membership
of the Labour Party'.[20] To overcome difficulties of this kind,
Lenin saw a need for the establishment of ostensibly non-communist mass organisations over which however the Coninterm would
exercise effective control or, better still, the capture of existing
organisations by strategic penetration of Communists or Communist sympathisers into key positions. Such organisations would
serve as 'transmission belts' for promoting the Soviet cause in
the West. They would exist side by side with overtly Communist
organisations such as the Red International of Trade Unions (the
Profintern) formed in 1921, which, although successful as a co-

ordinating body for Communist trade unions, made no attempt to conceal its Comintern connections. A particularly effective Communist international organisation was the Communist Youth International (which from its formation in 1914 until 1919 had been known as the Association of Social Youth Organisations) under the leadership of the German Communist, Willi Muenzenburg. Muenzenberg, a tireless campaigner, imaginative propagandist and brilliant improviser, spent his whole adult life working for the cause. Recognising the dangers, he strove hard to maintain the Youth International's independence of the Comintern, but lost the battle in July 1921 when a proposal by the Russian Youth Organisation, the dominant group in the International, to move the headquarters from Zurich to Moscow was adopted. The leader of the Russian organisation took over from Muenzenburg and the International became fully subordinated to the Comintern.

A month later, in a move which was to have significant consequences for the whole future of Soviet propaganda operations in the West, Lenin invited Muenzenburg to form an organisation whose purpose was to raise funds in aid of the starving population of Russia. Muenzenburg was convinced by Lenin's view that, if it was to be successful, the organisation must seek to avoid the appearance of being Communist-controlled. He also realised that people would be more likely to contribute if they felt the cause— help for starving Russian workers engaged in constructing a great working-class enterprise—was worthwhile supporting. Applying these two principles Muenzenburg concluded that the organisation should combine propaganda with fund-raising and must secure from the start the public support of prominent international personalities. Thus the first international 'front' organisation was created known as International Workers Aid (IWA). Its headquarters were in Berlin, under the direction of Muenzenburg. Among those in whose names its first appeal was launched, and who gave it 'respectability' were George Bernard Shaw, Albert Einstein and Anatole France. Many non-communist politicians and intellectuals in the West gave their support. In the United States an American Relief Association was set up, with Herbert Hoover at its head, which contributed a large proportion of the total aid. IWA—which became known as Red Aid— proved an enormous success in propaganda as well as in financial terms. The extent of this is shown by two examples: in 1923, IWA was specifically exempted from the ban imposed by the Weimar Government on the Communist Party and other

Communist organisations because of its valuable relief work; and in 1924 the British Labour Party and the Trades Union Congress adopted resolutions confirming the view that IWA pursued its relief activities without indulging in political propaganda. Muenzenburg soon used IWA as a base for expanding his activities in other fields; he acquired a publishing business and launched a series of successful newspapers in Germany, including *Sichel und Hammer* (a pictorial about life in the Soviet Union) and *Welt am Abend*.[21]

Following the success of the IWA (Red Aid), a crop of new national societies grew up based on sympathetic support for the plight of workers in Russia and, by extension, on friendship for the Soviet Union. Initially known as 'Friends of New Russia' (later 'Friends of the Soviet Union', the forerunners of the modern Soviet Friendship Societies), they counted a high proportion of non-communists among their members. Muenzenburg described them disparagingly as 'Innocents Clubs'. In 1923, in an address to Red Aid officials he said:

> We exist basically to make large-scale propaganda for Soviet Russia . . . the IWA can take steps which the political parties cannot take . . . we must avoid being a communist organisation. Now especially we must bring in other names, other groups, to make persecution more difficult. The question of the New Russia Clubs is particularly important in this context . . . Let us have no illusions about the importance of these clubs. But it is a question of penetrating the broadest sections of the population, of gaining the support of artists and professors, of using the theatre and the cinema and stressing everywhere that Russia abandons everything, that Russia humbles herself, that Russia is doing everything to preserve world peace. We ourselves must join these Clubs.[22]

By the time of the Fifth Comintern Congress in 1924 after Lenin's death the emphasis on 'united front from above' had declined; the social-democratic parties were once again denounced as 'bourgeois'. Moreover Stalin's advocacy of the idea of first perfecting 'socialism in one country' before attempting to export it, though in direct conflict with the views of Trotsky and Zinoviev, was in line with the reality that, after a series of failures, the Comintern saw little prospect of the early achievement of its revolutionary aims. But the policy of seeking mass support of non-communists using the methods devised by Muenzenburg was strongly endorsed. An official Directive by the Executive Committee of the Communist International (ECCI) declared:

> For certain specific purposes mass organisations which are uncommitted but

potentially pro-communist represent an important means of organising communist influence on the masses. They can be autonomous or independent organisations. Their organisational form must be as elastic as possible.[23]

Otto Kuusinen, the Finnish Communist leader who was Secretary of the Comintern Presidium, summed up the policy:

We must create a whole solar system of organisations and smaller committees around the Communist Party, of smaller organisations working actually under the influence of our Party but not under mechanical leadership.[24]

In other words, it was acceptable that they should be self-governing with a non-communist Chairman or other leading official provided effective control was able to be maintained through the presence of Communists within the organisation. The official Comintern description for these bodies, adopted in 1926, was 'sympathising mass organisations for definite special purposes'.[25]

The 1920s saw the creation of further such organisations, at both national and international levels. Directly or indirectly Muenzenburg was the driving force behind these developments, with the backing, if sometimes grudging, of the Comintern secretariat. In Britain, the Society for Cultural Relations with the USSR was established in 1924, the Minority Movement (the British affiliate of Profintern) also in 1924, and the Friends of the Soviet Union in 1927. Similar bodies were set up in other Western countries. All attracted support from non-communist well-wishers but remained firmly under Communist control exercised from Moscow through the Soviet co-ordinating organisation known today as the 'Union of Soviet Societies of Friendship and Cultural Relations with Foreign Countries' (SSOD)*.

Red Aid struck out in a new direction. Following the Fifth Comintern Congress (see above) it offered financial support for workers striking at the instigation of Communists and in opposition to official trade union policy, and to their families. A parallel organisation was established, International Class War Prisoners' Aid, with Muenzenburg as Secretary, to provide help for 'political victims' of the Class War. The former organisation offered assistance to workers taking part in the British General Strike of 1926 and the latter organised support for Sacco and Vanzetti, two left-wing extremists condemned to death for murder in the USA in 1927. By the mid-1920s, Comintern involvement in these organisations was openly admitted—Zinoviev, the Comintern President said 'The Executive Committee of the Comintern regards international Red Aid as one of its branches'. But its membership continued to be composed largely of what one of its Soviet officials described as 'the great non-Party masses', many of them no doubt remaining oblivious of the extent to which they were being used for the purpose of Soviet propaganda.

In 1926 Muenzenburg founded the international League for the Struggle against Imperialism, taking over the name from an earlier body formed by Chinese Communists in Moscow. With help from national Communist parties branches were formed in many Western countries and were invited to send delegates to a 'Congress against Colonial Oppression and Imperialism' in Brussels in 1927. This was a typical example of Muenzenburg's propaganda methods, which set a pattern which conferences of Communist front organisations have tried, with only limited success, to follow down to the present day. The Congress was Communist-organised and financed by the Comintern. But Muenzenburg was careful to keep the League, of whose links with the Comintern few people can have been unaware, firmly in the background, and he contrived to conceal the extent of direct Communist involvement. With such a politically emotive title, he had no difficulty in securing sponsorship by such eminent international personalities as Pandit Nehru, Upton Sinclair, Albert Einstein, Romain Rolland, Madade Sun Yat-Sun and George Lansbury MP. The last, subsequently leader of the British Labour Party, was Chairman of the Congress's Executive Committee. The Congress achieved a great propaganda success by demonstrating (as was to be expected) widespread non-communist support for a major plank of Communist policy. One hundred and thirty-four organisations from 37 countries were represented. By the time of the Second Congress, in Frankfurt in 1929, Soviet policy had changed. The Comintern insisted that the League should play a leading and more overtly Communist role. As a result the Second Congress, which was completely stage-managed, had none of the spontaneity of the First and lost the support of many of its prestigious sponsors. Stalin's unwillingness to tolerate anything but total submission to the line dictated by Moscow spelled the end of the League as an effective propaganda body in the West.

This change of policy was decreed at the 6th Comintern Congress, which met in Moscow from July to September 1928. It came at a time of disarray in the Soviet leadership. Stalin, having ousted Trotsky and his 'left-wing' allies, was shortly to

turn on Bukharin and others on the 'right-wing' of the CPSU in
order to eliminate resistance to his aim of replacing the NEP by
a policy based on rapid industrialisation and the accelerated and
enforced collectivisation of agriculture involving the wholesale
liquidation of the Kulak class. Meanwhile Stalin obtained Comintern endorsement for a complete reversal of the existing tactic
of the 'united front' with Social Democrats, who were branded
as 'the most dangerous enemies of Communism and of the
dictatorship of the proletariat.'[26] The main political and propaganda effort was in future to be directed against them and against
those in foreign Communist parties—the so-called 'right-wing'—
who had supported the policy of alliance with the Social Democrats. What is remarkable is that Stalin's new policy of 'Class
against Class', a foretaste of things to come in the Soviet Union,
was imposed on the Comintern by a Soviet delegation in which
Stalin and Bukharin managed virtually for the last time to present
a semblance of unity.

This sudden about-turn by the Comintern caused bitter
upheavals in the Western Communist parties, all of which were
compelled to fall into line behind Moscow's new policy. Disre-
garding the compliant obedience of his own German Communist
Party (the KPD) which, on Comintern orders, actually supported
the Nazis in their campaign to destroy the SPD, Muenzenburg
continued to pursue his Communist propaganda activities with
his customary energy and flexibility. At a time when the Western
democracies were hardly conscious of the dangers of fascism, he
recognised it as a target against which Communists and non-
communists could make common cause. So he launched the
International League against War and Fascism (also known as
the Amsterdam-Pleydel Movement), which gained immediate
support from Edo Fimmen, Secretary of the International Transport Union, and Ellen Wilkinson, MP, a leading left-wing
member of the British Labour Party. A group of internationally-
known intellectuals, many of them non-communists—Shaw,
Heinrich Mann, Theodore Dreiser and others—joined the
Organising Committee for a Conference held under the League's
auspices in Amsterdam in August 1932. Two thousand one
hundred and ninety-five delegates attended from 29 countries
(none from the Soviet Union). But the Comintern was giving
secret instructions to Muenzenburg, and the Amsterdam Manifesto was as much an anti-imperialist as an anti-fascist document.[27] Other organisations followed, such as the World
Committee for the Struggle against War, supported by Bertrand

Russell and Havelock Ellis. Then, in January 1933 came the Reichstag fire, responsibility for which the Nazis tried to pin on the Communists. To escape arrest Muenzenburg fled to Paris, from where he launched the World Committee for the Relief of Victims of Fascism, ostensibly a philanthropic organisation, with branches in many countries headed by non-Communist celebrities who, according to Arthur Koestler, 'thought that the Comintern was a bogey invented by Goebbels'.[28] These organisations also attracted the support of an impressive list of 'fellow travellers', among them Malraux, Hemingway, Auden, Spender and Silone.

In Paris Muenzenburg organised the publication, anonymously but with attribution to the World Committee for Relief, of the two famous 'Brown Books'; *The Reichstag Fire and Hitler Terror* and *Dimitrov contra Goering: Revelations about a Red Fire-Raiser*. The publishers, *Editions du Carrefour*, were owned by the Comintern, which supplied the material for the Brown Books. As the first comprehensive report on Nazi atrocities, the books made a major impact and, according to Koestler, were translated into 17 languages.

With Hitler's rise to power, which the Communists had done little to prevent and much to promote, the Comintern abandoned the policy of 'class against class' and set about trying to re-establish links with the Social Democrats, especially in Germany. The Soviet Union now openly proclaimed itself the foremost opponent of Nazi Germany. In 1934, Communist parties were instructed to demand the creation of a 'Popular Front against Fascism'. This took most of them by surprise. The French Party, after some initial hesitation, took up the demand, which led, in 1936, to the formation of a Popular Front Government. In Britain overtures from the CPGB were firmly resisted by the Labour Party, which had denounced and proscribed identified Communist front organisations since the early 1930s; the list of those proscribed by the National Executive Committee in 1933–34 is given in Appendix B. In July 1935, at its 7th (and last) World Congress, the Comintern, now headed by Georgi Dimitrov, formally promulgated the policy of the 'united front with social democratic workers', a revival of the 'united front from above' tactic which had been in force from 1922 to 1928, and called for a 'broad peoples front with the labouring masses who are still far from Communism but who nevertheless can join us in the struggle against fascism', in other words, the 'united front from below'. Muenzenburg's headquarters in Paris was the focal point for the expanding 'solar system' of international and national front organisations and for effective propaganda through newspapers acquired by the 'Muenzenburg Trust'—*Le Soir* in Paris and *PM* in New York. More prominent personalities were roped in to lend their distinguished names—Aldous Huxley and E. M. Forster among them—to the first 'International Congress of Writers for the Defence of Culture' held in Paris in June 1935.[29] By the time of the Second Congress in 1937 many left-wing intellectuals and others were already engaged, from genuine idealism, in supporting the Communist cause in the Spanish Civil War, the first active struggle against fascism. Then in August 1939 came the shattering volte-face, Stalin's conclusion of a Non-Aggression Treaty with Nazi Germany, shortly to be followed by a Treaty of Peace and Friendship. This threw the Western Communist parties into total confusion and, more than any of Stalin's previous switches of policy, demonstrated their complete subservience to Moscow.[30] Utterly discredited, the CPGB failed to derive any lasting benefit even from the subsequent *renversement des alliances* following Hitler's invasion of the Soviet Union in 1941.

Confused and embarrassed as the leaders of the Communist Parties in the West may have been by successive changes in Moscow's tactics, they had no alternative but to conform. Their total dependence on the Comintern had been established from the early 1920s and the latter's task was to ensure that the non-Soviet parties correctly reflected the CPSU's requirements of the moment. When Harry Pollitt, the British leader, showed initial hesitation over the Nazi-Soviet Pact in 1939 he was smartly summoned to Moscow and instructed to toe the line, just as Maurice Thorez, the French leader, had been in 1934 when he doubted the wisdom of the 'Popular Front' policy. National Communist Parties were useful tools, but their own interests and opinions were irrelevant to the tactics adopted by the CPSU within the broad framework of Soviet strategic aims. This relationship survived into the post-war period. Although Moscow's control over the West European Parties was sorely tried by such Soviet actions as the invasion of Hungary in 1956 and of Czechoslovakia in 1968 and began to falter with the advent of 'Eurocommunism' in the mid-1970s, the continued failure of these parties to achieve any real political breakthrough did not—and does not—give them a strong hand in their dealings with Moscow. The dismal record of the Communist Party in Britain is an object lesson. From about 10,000 in 1932, its membership rose to a peak of around 60,000 in 1942. But this had nothing to do with the efforts of the CPGB; it was the result of a sudden accession of fellow feeling with Russia, which had joined the Western Alliance following Hitler's invasion of the Soviet Union. Since then the CPGB has been in continuous decline, its membership in November 1987 being very little more than it was in 1932, and the Young Communist League, the bright hope for the Party's future, is able to muster no more than 40 members.

But as experience in the 1920s and 1930s had shown, the success of Soviet propaganda did not depend on the overt political activities of the national parties. Three factors were important: first, a cause with which ordinary people could identify, whether or not they had any sympathy with Communism; second, the public support of distinguished and well-known individuals, preferably non-communists, so as to give the cause respectability; and, third, a hard core of Communist activists working behind the scenes and under control from Moscow in the organisation set up to promote the cause. This was the formula which Muenzenburg had devised. It had worked initially over aid for the starving workers of Russia, then for the campaign against imperialist exploitation, and pre-eminently for resistance to fascism and support for its victims. All these causes had captured popular imagination and in each case the organisation set up to promote them had been so manipulated as to ensure that the policies it advocated served the Comintern's interests. But the pre-war organisations had been brilliant improvisations, largely the creation of one man. In the immediate aftermath of the Second World War, the Soviet leaders saw the opportunity to take advantage of the genuine admiration in the West for the major contribution of the Soviet Union to the defeat of Nazism and sympathy for the vast losses the Soviet people had suffered. It was evident however that to match the more sophisticated techniques of mass communication which had been developed since the 1930s, especially by the Nazis themselves, a more deliberately co-ordinated structure was needed. Thus, although Muenzenburg's formula remains in essence unchanged, the rudimentary 'solar system' of the 1930s has evolved into the vast and differentiated propaganda network of the present day.

All the major Communist international front organisations were set up in the years immediately following the end of the Second World War. Although not the first, the World Peace Council, established in 1949, has from the start played a leading and co-ordinating role in the activities of these organisations.

Ten of the organisations whose profiles are included in Part A of Section II were set up in the late 1940s and, by 1950, had managed to get rid of virtually all non-communists from key positions. Moreover such non-communist bodies as initially participated had by then withdrawn. Besides the favourable attitudes towards the Soviet Union already mentioned, the widespread hope that the Russians would not only cooperate in preserving peace but would also support the aspirations of the colonial peoples for independence provided fertile ground for Communist propaganda. The latter was especially important because, whereas the pre-war 'solar system' had concentrated mainly on Europe and the United States, the new organisations were intended to operate world-wide and paid particular attention to the countries of the Third World. In the early years, the 'front organisations' were to some extent able to disguise the degree of their control by Moscow, if not from the non-communist bodies which withdrew in disgust at the blatant Communist manipulation behind the scenes, at least from the mass of ordinary people who were seduced by the emotive appeal of the causes they promoted or supported. Moreover the technique of seeking support of well-known personalities was continued, although they tended to be more obvious fellow travellers than before the war. The Stockholm Peace Appeal which called for the prohibition of nuclear weapons is an example of a typical operation. Launched in 1950 by the WPC, at a time of clear Soviet nuclear inferiority but overwhelming superiority in conventional forces, the theme of the Appeal exactly parallelled the official line on disarmament being taken by the Soviet Union in the United Nations. The organisers claimed 500 million signatures for the Appeal, which was however abruptly suspended in 1953 as the Soviet Union began to develop a more sophisticated nuclear capability following its first thermonuclear test. The public record of the WPC—and its sister organisations—shows remarkable consistency: they support unquestioningly Soviet policies and actions as being conducive to peace, and oppose automatically all United States and NATO policies and actions as being hostile to peace. The only exception is when it suits Soviet tactics to drive wedges between the United States and her European Allies. Any dissentient voices among participants at congresses are quickly and effectively stifled.

For many years after the Second World War the British Labour Party continued the practice of publishing annual 'proscribed lists' of Communist front organisations. The last was in 1972 (see

Annex C). By this time the true nature of the organisations was widely known, and while it is not possible to establish how many members of the Labour Party have joined them, only a relatively small number of Labour Members of Parliament have done so. Eight years later the term 'disguised instrument of Soviet foreign policy' was first used in a British Ministerial statement with reference to the WPC, which Labour Prime Minister Clement Attlee had in 1950 baldly declared to be 'an instrument of the Politburo'. Since then the same term has been used frequently by British Ministers to describe the group of international front organisations. But the disguise has worn pretty thin over the years to the point where most of the organisations are recognised for what they are, and most of those who join them do so deliberately and with their eyes open. Most but not all: some organisations apparently still manage to conceal their association at least from some of those who participate in their activities. The Christian Peace Conference (CPC)*, for example, and the Women's International Democratic Federation (WIDF)* to this day succeed in attracting sincere followers who are evidently naive and unsuspecting enough to accept their claim to objectivity. Moreover, the indiscriminate and ambiguous use of 'peace' as the brandname for all their policies has enabled these organisations to acquire a certain respectability in United Nations circles, where its combination with anti-imperialism and anti-racialism has attracted support from the developing countries of the Third World. As a result, as will be seen from the profiles in Section II, many of the organisations have gained NGO consultative status in the appropriate organs of the United Nations. Their progress has not been unchecked, as the failure of the WPC's application in 1981 for higher status in ECOSOC showed. But at least they have achieved general recognition of their right to proffer advice in the appropriate UN fora, even though there is little doubt as to the true source of the advice.

The Western 'peace movements' were tailor-made for exploitation as vehicles of Soviet propaganda. These movements were at their height, especially in Western Europe, in the early 1980s following NATO's INF decision. Much earlier, the WPC was actively involved from 1966 in the anti-Vietnam War movement in the United States; and by 1975 had succeeded in harnessing the various 'peace' groups which emerged from this movement in support of the New Stockholm Appeal, launched by the WPC, on 'a great new world-wide offensive against the arms race'. By the early 1980s, when the 'nuclear freeze' campaign was gaining momentum, with widespread support throughout the country and the backing of leading Congressmen and other prominent Americans to whom Communist sympathies could not reasonably be imputed, leading members of the WPC and other international front organisations enthusiastically encouraged the concept of a freeze which they saw as a means of blocking NATO's plans for modernising its theatre nuclear forces. In Western Europe, apart from the Campaign for Nuclear Disarmament (CND), which was founded in 1958 to campaign for the unilateral renunciation of nuclear weapons by the United Kingdom, the 'peace movements' did not emerge until the late 1970s in opposition, first, to the so-called 'neutron bomb' (the Enhanced Radiation Warhead) and subsequently to NATO's INF deployment plans. The bulk of the members of these movements were no doubt inspired—as many still are—by genuine concern at the failure of efforts to reduce the growing number of nuclear weapons on both sides and fear of what they saw as the likely effects of this failure on the prospects for preserving peace. But the movements were wide open to Communist infiltration, which indeed was often welcomed by the non-communist leaders, who were naive enough to believe that anyone who professed support for 'peace' was an ally. CND is not, and has never been, a Communist front organisation, but it came near to being taken over during the 1970s when key positions were continuously held by members of the CPGB. In the Netherlands the two principal 'peace' organis-ations, the Inter-Church Peace Council (IKV) and the Commun-ist-based Joint Committee, which had strong support from both the WPC and the Soviet Peace committee, worked together between 1977 and 1983, when the IKV severed its association with the Communists which it found increasingly embarrassing. In West Germany the West German Communist Party (now the DKP) was involved in the 'peace movement' from 1980 onwards, either directly or through infiltration or control of the numerous peace groups which emerged (estimates vary from about 500 to 2000 at the height of the movement in 1983). The DKP co-operated closely with the Green Party in organising the 'Krefeld Appeal' in November 1980, which called for rejection of NATO's INF deployment plans. The Social Democrats' (SPD) attempt to remain independent of the Communists by launching a separate appeal was unsuccessful, and within three years the Krefeld organisers claimed 5 million signatures, including many from SPD members.

The Soviet Peace Committee (SPC) claims to be the counterpart of the non-Communist peace movements in the West; it seeks to sustain this claim by holding meetings in Moscow, followed by joint statements, with visiting representative groups from the CND and others. Such credibility as the SPC had with Western peace movements was however largely dissipated in 1982 by the affair of the Zhukov letter. The events that led up to this are worth recording. In 1980 a number of Western peace organisations launched the campaign for European Nuclear Disarmament (END), which issued the 'European Appeal'. This Appeal called on the United States and the Soviet Union to withdraw all nuclear weapons from Europe, avoided apportioning blame for the East–West confrontation and proposed that each side should 'act as if a united, and pacific Europe already exists'. END's hopes that the unofficial (effec-tively, dissident) peace movements in Eastern Europe would be allowed to attend its conventions, that its Appeal would be published in the Soviet Union and that its activities would not be subjected to Soviet interference were all disappointed. In response to END's firm rejection of the Soviet Peace Commit-tee's demand to co-sponsor the second END Convention due to be held in West Berlin in May 1983, G. A. Zhukov, then Presi-dent of the Soviet Committee, wrote a lengthy letter in December 1982 to some 1,500 leaders of the peace movements in Western Europe. In this he claimed that 'the real mass peace movements of the Socialist countries' had been excluded from the first convention and those invited were active 'not in the struggle for detente and disarmament but in undermining the Socialist system'. He alleged that the attempt to apportion 'equal responsi-bility' to East and West was aimed at the 'disorientation, demob-ilisation and undermining of the anti-war movement' and threat-ened that the Soviet Peace Committee would 'not be a party to this wrecking undertaking'. END's co-ordinating committee and other recipients of Zhukov's letter reacted angrily to this blatant Soviet attempt to dictate to the campaign, and no representatives of the Soviet or East European Peace Committees attended the second convention. They returned in 1984, but stayed away again in 1985. (This particular quarrel appeared to have been patched up by 1987 when Soviet delegates attended the END Convention in Coventry.) Summing up the situation in October 1985, the Secretary-General of the Dutch IKV wrote that: 'The Western peace movement is at a crossroads.' This was—and is still—true. Much of the steam has gone out of the Western peace movements since serious bilateral negotiations between the United States and the Soviet Union began, following the Geneva Summit in December 1985. Nevertheless, leaving aside END's quixotic but abortive initiative, the strident attacks on NATO and American policies which still emanate from the CND and the German Green Party in particular, unbalanced by any but ritual criticisms of the Soviet Union, show that Moscow has little need for concern at Western disenchantment with the WPC and the Soviet Peace Committee. The emotional response which the Western peace movements are able to arouse in Western public opinion on any issue relating to nuclear weapons means that, however sincere their motives and purpose, they remain a potential and readily exploitable vehicle for propaganda in support of Soviet policies.[31]

The developments described above, relating to the traditional international front organisations and the 'peace movements', have given added importance to the organisations described in Section III. These are professional, or pseudo-professional, bodies, founded ostensibly on the initiative of non-communists. They generally have some laudable aim such as the promotion of mutual confidence and reciprocal exchanges with their professional counterparts, often on matters which go beyond their strictly professional concerns. This is indicated by the frequent use of the word 'peace' in their titles. For this reason they are the more insidious because it is easier to conceal the true purpose and sympathies of their leading officials from the general membership. Soviet control over them is not only less obvious but less total than over the traditional organisations. Many of their members, and even some of their leaders, are no doubt motivated by the desire to support what they may believe to be constructive Soviet initiatives. Others are blatantly sympathetic to Soviet aims and methods. Whatever the motives or intentions, the skilled Soviet propagandists have no hesitation—and little difficulty—in exploiting them to the full. It is these organisations which are the true successors to Muenzenburg's 'Innocents' Clubs'.

The international and national organisations described in this book constitute an impressive network for disseminating Soviet propaganda. Geographically, they are present in, and concerned with the problems of, all parts of the world. Functionally, they are comprehensive in the range of interests they cover. They are therefore well-placed to provide fora in which and channels through which Soviet policies can be extensively promoted without direct attribution to Soviet sources. Between them, they are able to mount a co-ordinated and virtually continuous programme of activities—conferences, seminars, 'solidarity weeks' and other events. Their principal target being public opinion in the West, efforts are made, wherever possible, to organise conferences in NATO and other Western countries. This is much easier for the newer Soviet-influenced organisations, whose true nature is largely unrecognised and which are able to sustain their public claim to impartiality, than it is for the international front organisations. Among the former, for example, the IPPNW* held its 1986 annual conference in Bonn and the IMO* held a major conference in Australia in November 1987. The traditional national front organisations are less successful since their true purpose is widely known and Western governments generally are unwilling to tolerate too many major manifestations which can be attributed to them. For example, United Kingdom policy, publicly announced by the then Home Secretary in February 1953, was to refuse visas to people seeking to organise or attend events connected with the international front organisations. Indeed, the first full conference staged by the WPC in a NATO country, and the first for over 20 years in a non-communist country, was held in Copenhagen in 1986, and that was only saved from undisguisable failure as a result of a last minute rescue operation by the Soviet Peace Committee, which, together with the WPC itself, had hoped to evade local objections by keeping in the background. More successful have been the events staged in Third World countries, where the governments and professional classes are usually the main targets. Often these are regional meetings of the international organisations, or subsidiaries with local appeal, or special conferences on a topic of importance to the region: for example, the WPC alone envisaged in its Programme for 1987 holding at least a dozen such conferences in Third World countries. Besides these major events, the international front organisations are actively engaged in lobbying international bodies, sending delegates to conferences, promoting 'solidarity' with diverse causes and organising exchange visits of all kinds. The WPC Programme for 1987 contained plans for one 'Solidarity Month' (with the 'People of Korea') five 'Solidarity Weeks' (including the 'Chilean people' and 'Turkish Peace Activists') and fourteen 'Solidarity Days' (among them, for the 'struggle of the Namibian People', the 'struggle of the Cypriot people' and the 'struggle of the People of Bahrain'); and there were at least 27 proposals in the 1987

Programme for WPC Delegations to visit individual countries, attend international meetings or lobby United Nations bodies.

In practice, the major international conferences sponsored by the international front organisations frequently take place in Moscow or in the Communist countries of Eastern Europe. Although this means that Communist sponsorship cannot be concealed, it does avoid political problems and simplifies organisation. When the venue is Moscow, the deliberate purpose is to demonstrate the leading role of the Soviet Union in the 'struggle for peace'. In February 1987, for example, a major international forum was held in Moscow on the theme 'For a Nuclear-Free World, for the Survival of Humanity'. Some 1,000 people from 80 countries are said to have participated, among them many internationally renowned personalities from the worlds of the arts, literature, the theatre and science. The proceedings of the forum were given wide publicity in the media not only in the West but also in non-aligned and Third World countries. Speeches by leading Western participants, all eminent in their own fields but not all known either for their Communist sympathies or for any special expertise in the complexities of international relations, extolled the virtues of the 'new' policies of the Soviet Union under General Secretary Gorbachev's leadership, which were, generally, contrasted with the outdated or reactionary policies of Western governments and especially of the United States administration. This was also the thrust of a major speech to the conference by General-Secretary Gorbachev himself. Primary responsibility for organising this forum lay with the Soviet Peace Committee, but a major role was played in this conference by both the IPPNW and the Generals for Peace and Disarmament. Many, though not all, of the Western participants were no doubt oblivious to, or chose to ignore, the fact that they were being used for the purpose of Soviet propaganda just as their predecessors had been used in the 1920s and 1930s. The sequel, nearly a year later, has been the establishment of the International Fund for the Survival and Development of Mankind, launched in Moscow on 15 January 1988, with Academician Yevgency Velikhov (USSR) as Chairman, Jerome Wiesner (US) as Deputy Chairman and a Board of Directors which includes Armand Hammer, the American businessman, Robert McNamara, former US Secretary of Defence, Federico Mayor, Director-General of UNESCO, David McTaggart, Chairman of Greenpeace and Metropolitan Pitirim of the Russian Orthodox Church as members. The purpose of the Fund, which was given a warm send-off by General-Secretary Gorbachev, is to operate 'independent of governments or any financial or political groups' in support of projects concerned with the 'end of the arms race', environmental protection, 'presentation of cultural values' and 'the problem of information'. How genuinely independent the Fund will be and how far it succeeds in eschewing propaganda remain to be seen. It is to be financed by 'private contributions', of which the largest so far has come from Armand Hammer.

The Moscow forum is but one example, albeit an especially prominent one, of the conference organised by bodies whose claims to independence and objectivity are transparently not credible. Later in 1987, the 9th World Congress of Women was held in Moscow under the title 'Towards 2000, without Nuclear Weapons for Peace, Equality and Development'. Innocent seeming invitations were sent to prominent women in the West by the Soviet Women's Committee; many who attended were no doubt genuinely, if naively, unaware that this body is the Soviet arm of the Women's International Democratic Federation (WIDF), a long-standing and well-known Soviet international front organisation, whose British affiliate is the National Assembly of Women*. Both the latter body and WIDF itself were for 20 years proscribed by the Labour Party, until the Party abolished its annually published Proscribed List in 1973. No one should have been surprised that this conference too, which was also addressed by General-Secretary Gorbachev, was intended and used as yet another forum for Soviet propaganda.

These examples could easily be multiplied. It might be assumed that those who accept invitations to attend mass conferences in Moscow are aware that they will be participating in propaganda occasions. Unfortunately this assumption is not always realised, and the hospitality offered by the organisers often provides a powerful incentive to attend. This is even more true of conferences and activities organised in order to promote sympathy for Soviet aims and policies in countries outside the Soviet *bloc* by bodies whose credentials may be less obviously compromised by direct association with Moscow.

The themes adopted for these Communist-sponsored conferences, wherever they are held, and the declarations which invariably issue from them are published in the journals which each of the front organisations produces regularly. Irrespective of the nature of the organisation there is a consistency—and a dreary monotony—about the content. Take, for example, CIMEA (the Children's and Adolescents' Committee)* in its

Information No. 4 of 1986: 'The Presidium is of the opinion that the preservation of life on Earth, the safeguarding of peace and prevention of nuclear war have primary importance for mankind.' The CPC takes up the theme, in a declaration from its West German Committee (published in *Information No. 377* of 10 February 1987): 'Our Yes to God's creation and to Peace is our No to the Militarisation of the Earth and Heavens.' So, says the CPC in the same issue: 'The new political thinking in the USSR creates a new quality in the international dialogue and strengthens the growing movement for the preservation of life on earth.' The International Trade Union Committee for Peace and Disarmament (the 'Dublin Committee')* poses the stark alternative: 'Either the people of the world will unite and wipe out all nuclear weapons, or nuclear weapons will wipe out all life from the face of the planet' (from WFTU *Flashes*, issue of 22 May 1987).

It may be argued that these rather meaningless generalisations are of little significance. But the object of constant repetition is to create among the undiscerning, the impressionable and sometimes even among those who are less so, a climate in which the Soviet Union is constantly represented as the power in favour of peace, against nuclear weapons, against racialism and in favour of 'equality'; and the author of all positive initiatives in favour of all these objectives. The themes and declarations are used as pegs on which to hang more detailed propaganda in support of Soviet positions on specific issues. Such propaganda is, as has already been shown, backed up by carefully elaborated disinformation campaigns. The process is not by any means universally successful. Nuclear weapons in the hands of the United States and NATO—though never those of the Soviet Union—have been the constant target. Less has been said about conventional weapons, in which the Soviet Union has and intends to retain superiority, except when NATO shows signs of improving its conventional capabilities. The campaign against NATO's deployment of INF (1979–83) failed,, as have, so far, the long-running campaigns for nuclear-free zones in Central Europe, in the Nordic countries and in the Mediterranean. The AIDS disinformation campaign has had some success in sowing mistrust of the United States in Third World countries, and no doubt helped to fuel criticism of American military bases. The campaign against the 'neutron bomb' (1977–78) was successful; that against the SDI (1983 onwards) had not, by the end of 1987, made much progress.[32] The campaign against Western 'imperialism' was somewhat weakened after 1979 by the Soviet invasion and continued occupation of Afghanistan, which has resulted in annual defeats for the Soviet Union by large majorities in the United Nations. Nevertheless, after eight years, the fall-out effect of Afghanistan has largely worn off, and, combined with 'racism', the charge of 'imperialism' remains a powerful weapon against the West. It is used effectively in such diverse issues as South Africa, Chile, Nicaragua, Palestine and Puerto Rico. (It is however an interesting comment on the flexibility of Soviet propaganda that, in their publicity for the 1989 Youth Festival in North Korea, the International Union of Students refer to it as being held in 'the 50th Year since the outbreak of the Second World War'. The IUS evidently hope that their supporters will conveniently forget that 1989 is, in terms of Communist history, the 50th anniversary of the Stalin–Hitler Pact and that they will have to wait until 1991 before celebrating the 50th anniversary of the start of the 'Great Patriotic War' against Nazi Germany.)

Whether the aim is to promote a Soviet initiative, to oppose action by NATO or by the United States, or to foment anti-western attitudes in the Third World, the techniques used in every case have one important thing in common. They are based on a well-tried device: the manipulation, fabrication and suppression of facts and arguments in order to support only the Soviet objectives. The organisations in the propaganda network described in this book are the 'transmission belts' through which the results of this process are conveyed throughout the world, the messengers through which the message is broadcast. The message is, as it always has been, inherently hostile to Western values and Western concepts of peace and democracy. Such a conclusion in no way invalidates the principle of realistic negotiations between East and West: on the contrary, it reinforces the need to seek solutions which can reconcile the perceived and conflicting interests of both sides. But it does underline the difficulties which such negotiations will always face so long as the fundamental objectives of the two sides remain irreconcilable.

Notes

1. *Left-Wing Communism, an Infantile Disorder*, p. 38.
2. Lenin, *Collected Works*, vol. 31, p. 37, quoted by Ian Greig in *They mean what they say*.
3. Ladislav Bittman, *The KGB and Soviet Disinformation*, p. 43.
4. Quoted by Stanley Kober in 'The Arms Control Arena: Target on Policy

Initiatives' included in *Contemporary Soviet Propaganda and Disinformation*, p. 197.

5. The International Institute for Strategic Studies in *The Military Balance 1982–83* estimated that the balance of Theatre Nuclear Forces was 3.6 to 1 in favour of the Warsaw Pact. An estimate, in *The Economist* of 17 October 1981 put the figures at 2441 for the Warsaw Pact against 864 for NATO.

6. A comprehensive review of the Soviet campaign is contained in *Soviet Propaganda against NATO* published by the US Arms Control and Disarmament Agency (October 1983).

7. For a more detailed account of these campaigns see the author's *Campaigns against Western Defence: NATO's Adversaries and Critics*.

8. *Soviet Influence Activities: Active Measures and Propaganda 1986–87* published by the US State Department contains an account of this and other campaigns in the Third World.

9. Reported in the *International Herald Tribune* of 1 September 1987.

10. See Malcolm Mackintosh, 'Changes in the Soviet High Command Under Gobachev' in *The RUSI Journal*, Spring 1988.

11. Robert Tucker, *Political Culture and Leadership in Soviet Russia*, p. 132.

12. Quotation from Gorbachev's speech to the 27th Party Congress, 25 February 1986.

13. Compare the relevant passages in Stalin's *The Foundations of Leninism* (1924), in *Problems of Leninism*, with those in Gorbachev's speech to the 27th Party Congress.

14. *Pravda*, 21 April 1974. The same concept appears in other official statements.

15. A useful short definition of the 'correlation of forces' is given in Shultz and Godson, *Dezinformatsia*, pp. 10–13 and 194.

16. This was enunciated by President Truman in his address to a joint session of Congress in the following terms: 'I believe that it must be the policy of the United States to support free peoples who are resisting attempted aggression by armed minorities or by outside pressures'.

17. Quoted in *The Communist Solar System* published by the British Labour Party, September 1933.

18. Figure taken from Golitsyn's *New Lies for Old*, p. 17.

19. The main line of this account of the early development of the Comintern is drawn from Professor Leonard Schapiro's *The Communist Party in the Soviet Union*.

20. Quoted in *The British Road to Stalinism*, an IRIS Survey (1958), p. 9.

21. Much of the detail about Muenzenburg's activities is derived from *Willi Muenzenburg* by his widow Babette Gross (1974).

22. Ibid. p. 133, quoted from an ADGB pamphlet of 1924.

23. INPRECORR, vol. 6, no. 68, quoted on p. 181 of *Willi Muenzenburg*.

24. Quoted in *The Communist Solar System*, published by the British Labour Party, September 1933.

25. INPRECORR, 13 May 1926 quoted in 'The Communist Solar System', an IRIS survey (1957).

26. Quoted by Schapiro, op. cit., p. 371.

27. Babette Gross, op. cit., and the British Labour Party's *The Communist Solar System*.

28. Arthur Koestler's *The Invisible Writing* (1954), p. 198.

29. In the following year Muenzenburg was ordered to return to Moscow to work at the Comintern Headquarters. Fearing arrest after interrogation, he refused the appointment and fled the country. Having broken with the Comintern he was expelled from the KPD in 1937. He escaped from internment in France in 1940 and, soon after, was found hanged in a wood near Grenoble. Who killed him has never been established.
30. See *Campaigns against Western Defence*, pp. 48–51.
31. This is not this place for a detailed analysis of the Western Peace Movements. For a further account of their origins and activities see *Campaigns against Western Defence*, *passim* and Paul Mercer, *Peace of the Dead*.
32. This concerns only the effectiveness of the Soviet propaganda campaign. It is not the purpose of this book to consider the desirability or feasability of the SDI programme.

SECTION II

Soviet-controlled Organisations

INTRODUCTION

The organisations described in this Section are those which are commonly referred to in the West as international front organisations. This is not a term which is used by the CPSU or by Communists in the West. It is however descriptive of the purpose of the organisations. They purport to be democratic and non-governmental but are, in fact, as British ministers have often stated, disguised instruments of Soviet foreign policy.

In recent years Soviet official publications have also begun to use a new term for these organisations: 'closely cooperating non-governmental organisations'. This still falls short of an open admission of the extent of Soviet control and the new term in practice applies to a rather wider range of organisations than those covered by this Section. The title 'Soviet-controlled organisations' is used here because it accurately describes the group of organisations, most of which were established during the five years following the end of the Second World War. These organisations were the successors to the pre-war network of 'mass organisations' which were used as 'transmissions belts'—the description originally given to them by Lenin—for the spread of Soviet propaganda in the 1920s and 1930s. This pre-war 'solar system' was under the firm control of the Third International, the Comintern.

As did their pre-war counterparts, these organisations exist today for the exclusive purpose of promoting Soviet policies and influence worldwide. All the leading positions in them are held either by key officials from the Soviet matrix organisations described in Section V or by trusted representatives from other countries, of whom Romesh Chandra, the Indian Communist President of the World Peace Council (WPC)*, is a prominent example. But, of course, some of the individual members are

53

not Communists and many of those who take part in their congresses and other events do so without realising that they are supporting an organisation which is directed from the Politburo and whose whole purpose is the dissemination of Soviet propaganda. This is indeed the object of the 'front' organisations. The organisations are largely financed by Soviet subsidies, usually channelled through the Soviet Peace Fund. (A table of estimated subsidies in 1979 is given at Appendix D.) Responsibility for the direction of these organisations rests with the International Department of the Central Committee of the CPSU (see Section I), the lineal heir to the pre-war functions of the Comintern. The policy and propaganda lines to be pursued are laid down in an annual programme issued by the WPC, which serves as guidance also for the other organisations. Only occasionally have the international front organisations had to contend with internal dissension arising from Soviet actions. Khrushchev's disclosures of Stalin's crimes at the Twentieth Congress of the CPSU in 1956, the Soviet invasion of Hungary in the same year, and of Afghanistan in 1979 each resulted in defections and some loss of support. The expulsion of Yugoslav representatives from the organisations in 1949, and Chinese withdrawal in the 1960s following the Sino/Soviet dispute were, at the time, major setbacks because of their effect on the Soviet claim to sole authority in the Communist World. Some strains have emerged more recently as a result of criticism, especially from West European members, of the Soviet record on human rights. But, with the possible exception of this last issue, which is likely to prove a continuing problem, any apparent weakening of Soviet control has proved only temporary. The methods and objectives pursued have remained firmly under the direction of the Central Committee, acting through the International Department. Any idea that the organisations are likely to be democratised is dispelled by the procedures adopted at the regular Congresses run or sponsored by those organisations. The proceedings are carefully stage-managed, the main speeches are censored in advance, potential trouble makers are not given the floor, and resolutions are passed 'by acclamation' rather than by majority vote.

Descriptions of the origins, structure, policies and principal activities of these organisations, together with the names of leading officials associated with each, are given below in Part A. In this part mention is made of numerous subsidiaries. Many of these have been established to meet some temporary requirement or to fulfil a specific but limited purpose. Some however have a more permanent status and perform a wider function; these are listed and described in Part B.

For nearly three decades after the end of the Second World War, the network of international organisations controlled by the Soviet Union which are described in this section maintained the fiction that they were a loose group of independent 'democratic mass organisations' of spontaneous origin and with distinct identities. In 1978, however, the first of a regular series of group liaison meetings between representatives of the 'closely cooperating international non-governmental organisations' took place. Since then such liaison meetings have been repeated, usually at six monthly intervals (although only one took place in 1987). These are strictly business meetings, held for the purpose of co-ordinating Soviet propaganda activities through the participating organisations.

The turnout fluctuates. The usual attendance is about 12 representatives, eight being the lowest and seventeen being the highest recorded to date. The constant factor is the presence at all these meetings of the WPC. Each meeting takes place in a different capital and is hosted by a different 'front'. In addition to the WPC and the other principal Soviet 'fronts', representatives are sometimes present from Soviet-influenced organisations (see Section III), such as the Berlin Conference of Catholic Christians* or AALAPSO* and at least three meetings have also been attended by representatives of the Soviet-edited *World Marxist Review* in Prague, the world Communist movements' nearest surviving equivalent of the Comintern or Cominform publications of the 1930s and 1950s. At the latest such meeting, held in Prague in September 1987, the host was the WFTU.

PART A

PRINCIPAL INTERNATIONAL FRONT ORGANISATIONS

1. World Peace Council

The World Peace Council is also known under its French, German and Spanish titles which are, respectively, *Conseil mondial de la paix*, *Weltfriedensrat* and *Consejo Mundial de la Paz*. Its headquarters is at Lönnrotinkatu 25A, Helsinki 18, Finland.

Origins
The WPC was not the first of the International Front Organisations to be established after the Second World War. But it has from its inception been regarded as the most important and plays a coordinating role within the group. It grew out of the deliberations of the Soviet-backed World Congress of Intellectuals for Peace, held at Wroclaw (Breslau), Poland, in August 1948, the first of a series of regular pro-Soviet and anti-Western 'peace' Congresses held in the last 40 years. This Congress established an International Liaison Committee of Intellectuals which in turn convened the World Congress of Partisans of Peace organised in Paris in April 1949. The latter's sponsors were in the main French Communists, and the Congress conveniently (for the sponsored participants) took place immediately after the signature of the North Atlantic Treaty earlier in the same month. The latter event provided a spurious justification for the establishment by the Congress of the Permanent World Committee of Partisans of Peace. This Committee was renamed the World Peace Council (WPC) after the Second World Peace Congress held in Warsaw in November 1950, attended by 1750 delegates from 80 countries.

The WPC's first headquarters was in Paris, but it was expelled by the French Government in 1951 for what were described as 'fifth column activities'. After a short stay in Prague, the headquarters was moved in 1954 to Vienna, thus maintaining the image of an organisation based in the non-Communist world even though at the time the Austrian Minister of the Interior protested strongly because his Government's permission had neither been sought nor given. By 1957, however—two years after the conclusion of the Austrian State Treaty which provided for the withdrawal of the Soviet, and other, occupying powers— the Austrian Government, which had become concerned about the subversive character of the WPC, was emboldened to ban it for 'activities directed against the interests of the Austrian State'. (*The Observer*, London, 3 February 1957). As a result, the WPC ceased, temporarily, to operate under its own name, but the ban was not totally effective. A new cover organisation, the International Institute for Peace (IIP)*, was set up which carried on virtually the same activities from the WPC's former address in Vienna. Finally, in 1968, the WPC was re-established under its own name on moving to Finland, to its present headquarters in Helsinki.

Declared Aims

According to the *Yearbook of International Organisations*[a] (1986/ 87) the aims of the WPC are:

> Prohibition of all weapons of mass destruction and ending of the arms drive; abolition of foreign military bases; general simultaneous and controlled disarmament; elimination of all forms of colonialism and racial discrimination; respect for the right of peoples to sovereignty and independence, essential for the territorial integrity of states; non-interference in the internal affairs of nations; establishment of mutually beneficial trade and cultural relations based on friendship and mutual respect; peaceful co-existence between States with different political systems.

These aims sound irreproachable and, expressed in these very general terms, many of them are. Similar aims are to be found in declarations by the Warsaw Pact, Soviet statements in the United Nations and elsewhere. In fact they are standard Soviet propaganda jargon. Designed to attract the support of uninformed and unsophisticated public opinion and to rally the faithful sympathisers, they take little account of the practical

---

[a] The Yearbook of International Organisations is edited annually by the Union of International Associations (Brussels), based on an agreement with the United Nations, and published by KG Saur Verlag (Munich). It was first produced by the Union of International Associations in 1908.

problems and of the obstacles the Soviet authorities place in the way of their resolution. Their purpose is to provide a platform for the Soviet Union to use in its campaign against the United States and NATO.

Organisation and Membership
The WPC is the most important element in the Communist 'World Peace Movement'. The other International Front Organisations look to it for policy guidance, and leading members of the other principal organisations are members of its 'Presidential Committee' (see below).

Besides the other International Front Organisations, membership of the Council comprises affiliated national 'peace committees', which the WPC claims exist in 144 countries, and some other Soviet-influenced or sympathising bodies. Individuals may join as honorary members or observers, and organisations may apply for Associate Membership. Total membership is currently estimated (1987) at about 1600, although detailed figures are not published. The Council meets every three years, the last occasion being in April 1986 in Sofia.

Between meetings of the Council responsibility for running the organisation rests with the Presidential Committee, which is elected triennially by the Council. This Committee consists of the President of the WPC, the General Secretary, 52 Vice-Presidents and over 200 other members. It meets annually but may also hold *ad hoc* emergency sessions. The Committee appoints a Bureau which is charged with overseeing the implementation of decisions and planning new activities. The Bureau comprises the President and Vice-Presidents plus some representatives of the affiliated national 'peace committees'. It meets three or four times a year.

The Presidential Committee may invite a limited number of distinguished people to serve as 'Presidents of Honour', with the right to participate in WPC meetings. Currently there are six Presidents of Honour (1987).

The Secretariat is the permanent executive arm of the Presidential Committee and is appointed by it. It gives effect to decisions of the Council, Presidential Committee and Bureau, initiates further activities and administers the organisation and membership. It comprises a General Secretary and about 20 full-time secretaries, and is under the direction of the President.

Office-holders
Professor Frédéric Joliot-Curie, the distinguished French nuclear scientist, was the first President until his death in 1958. Thereafter, the British scientist, Professor J.D. Bernal, although not holding the office of President, discharged its functions until his resignation in 1965 when he was succeeded by the Belgian Mme. Isabelle Blume (until 1967). Meanwhile the post of General Secretary had been reactivated in 1966, after a gap of seven years, and was held by Romesh Chandra as, in effect, the head of the WPC until 1977, when he in turn became the first full President since Joliot-Curie's death. Chandra, a member of the Central Committee of the Indian Communist Party, won the Lenin Peace Prize in 1979.

Currently the Vice-Presidents (as listed in *New Perspectives*, No. 4, of 1988) are: Richard ANDRIAMANJATO (Madagascar); PHAN Anh (Vietnam); Eduardo AREVALO Burgos (Colombia); Mohammed Jaber BAJBOUJ (Syria); Vital BALLA (Congo); Genrikh BOROVIK (USSR); Freda BROWN (WIDF); Martha BUSCHMANN (FRG); Vasco CABRAL (Guinea-Bissau); Kerfala CAMARA (Guinea); Francisco da Costa GOMES (Portugal); Sonja DAVIES (New Zealand); Jacques DENIS (France); Karl DERKSEN (Netherlands); Andre DE SMET (Belgium); Georgi DIMITROV-GOSHKIN (Bulgaria); Günther DREFAHL (GDR); Luis ECHEVERRIA (Mexico); Orlando FUNDORA Lopez (Cuba); George GEORGES (Australia); Feleke Gedle GHORGIS (Ethiopia); HWANG Jang-yop (DPR of Korea); Abdullah EL HOURANI ('Palestine' (PLO)); Jorge KREYNESS (Argentina); Marcelino JAEN (Panama); Mitsuhiro KANEKO (Japan); Hieronim KUBIAK (Poland); James LAMOND (United Kingdom); Daniel LISULO (Zambia); Pascal LUVUALU (Angola); Sarwar MANGAL (Afghanistan); Rodolfo MECHINI (Italy); Hugo MEJIAS Briceno (Nicaragua); Ali Ameir MOHAMMED (Tanzania); Khaled MOHIELDIN (Egypt); John Hanley MORGAN (Canada); Gus Eugene NEWPORT (USA); Alfred NZO (South Africa (ANC)); Abdel-Ati OBEIDI (Libya); Camilo O. PEREZ (Panama); Matti RUOKOLA (Finland); Nadim Abdul SAMAD (Lebanon); Ilona SEBESTYEN (Hungary); Boubakar SECK (Senegal); Liber SEREGNI (Uruguay); Aziz SHERIF (Iraq); Nageshwar P. SINGH (Nepal); Filifing SISSOKO (Mali); T.B. SUBASINGHE (Sri Lanka); Mikis THEODORAKIS (Greece); Emma TORRES (Bolivia); Tomas TRAVNICEK (Czechoslovakia); Ibrahim ZAKARIA (WFTU).

The following are Presidents of Honour: Hortensia ALLENDE (Chile); Hans BLUMENFELD (Canada)[a]; Josef CYRANKIEWICZ (Poland); Dolores IBARRURI (Spain); Sergio MENDEZ Arceo (Mexico); and Yannis RITSOS (Greece).

The post of General Secretary, which lapsed when Chandra became President but was re-established in 1986, is held by Johannes PAKASLAHTI (Finland), (see below).

The Secretaries appointed since 1983 include: Dzanghir ATAMALI (USSR); Nathaniel HILL Arboleda (Panama); Pierre HUGUENIN (France); Kosta IVANOV (Bulgaria); Oleg KHARKHARDIN (USSR); Karoly LAUKO (Hungary); Rolf LUTZKENDORF (GDR); Max MOABI (South Africa, ANC); Bahig NASSAR (Egypt); Marilyn OLSSON (Sweden), Kvetoslav ONDRACEK (Czechoslovakia); Robert PRINCE (USA); Jesus REYES Arencibia (Cuba); Mamadou SAKO (Mali); Sana Abu SHAKRA (Lebanon); Philip SPILLMAN (Switzerland); Tobias THOMAS (FRG); Ryszard TYRLUK (Poland); Bhagat VATS (India); Mark WALLER (UK).

The office holders are, virtually without exception, members of the Communist Party in their own countries, or are closely associated with national organisations under Communist control or influence. The Soviet Union itself is strongly represented in key positions from which its influence can be effectively exercised. Genrikh Borovik, Chairman of the Soviet Peace Committee*, is a Vice-President; G.A. Zhukov, former chairman of the Soviet Peace Committee, is a member of the Presidential Committee as also is Vitaly Shaposhnikov, Deputy Head of the CPSU's International Department; Oleg Kharkhardin, formerly First Deputy Chairman of the Soviet Peace Committee, is a WPC Secretary (and Executive Secretary of the International Liaison Forum*). The other Soviet official, Dzanghir Atamali, is also a member of the Secretariat.

The General Secretary
Johannes Pakaslahti, a pro-Soviet Communist and formerly a leading member of the Finnish Peace Committee, is regarded as an expert on West European peace movements. He sees his task as being to restore the credibility of the WPC, which has been undermined by its continuous one-sided criticism of the United States, and to find a basis for uniting the peace movements, of both East and West, under the general umbrella of the WPC. His appointment seems intended to signal a departure from the

---

[a] Died 29 January 1988.

hard-line position which has been for years associated with Romesh Chandra and the adoption of a more moderate line in keeping with the policies of General Secretary Gorbachev and better calculated to attract the support of peace activists in the West. Such a move was urgently needed, given the outcome of the Copenhagen Congress (see below p.74).

Publications and Information
The Council has two main publications: *New Perspectives*, published every two months in English, French, Spanish, and German and *Peace Courier*, published monthly in English, French, Spanish and German. A quarterly publication in English, *International Mobilisation*, is published in Helsinki in cooperation with the United Nations Centre against Apartheid, and *Development and Peace* is published twice a year in English in Budapest in cooperation with the Hungarian National Peace Council. *Sintesis Informativa* is published for Latin America and the Caribbean in Havana. Publications are distributed by the Information Centre in Helsinki to direct subscribers and through the WPC's national affiliates throughout the world (the WPC has, for instance, been known to circularise its national committees requesting lists of names and addresses of 'organisations, groups or people' who should receive *Peace Courier*).

The WPC also issues such regional bulletins as *Solidarity with Cyprus, Palestine Solidarity Newsletter, Latin America Today* and *Solidarity with Chile* at irregular intervals. A new bulletin called *Spotlight on South Africa* appeared in August 1985. Apart from these regular and irregular publications, the wide range of the WPC's propaganda activities may be seen from the titles of numerous booklets it produces which have included since 1983: *The US Space Offensive—Road to Nuclear Annihilation; Euro-missiles and the Balance of Forces—Propaganda and Reality; Europe, A Time for Responsible Decisions; American Genocide; The Persecution of Leonard Peltier and the Violation of the Human Rights of the American Indians of the United States; Negotiations Not Confrontations—Security and Cooperation in Europe; Peace and Security in Asia and the Pacific; Against Imperialist Aggressions and Intervention in Central America and the Caribbean; Nicaragua* (in Spanish only); *A Life devoted to the Liberation of his People—Sandino Lives* (in Spanish only).

There are WPC Information Centres in Helsinki, Havana and Addis Ababa, and there is a Puerto Rico Information Centre in New York.

Finance

The WPC claims to be funded by contributions from national peace committees affiliated to it, donations to its World Peace Fund and special collections. In practice, the bulk of its expenses is met by the Soviet Union. This was admitted by Frank Swift, the former Executive Secretary, in an article in the British (CPGB) newspaper the *Morning Star* on 24 June 1985.

James Lamond (UK), Vice-President, said in an interview with the BBC *Today* programme on 24 April 1985, that some of the WPC's money came from the Soviet Peace Committee. According to the Soviet English-language weekly *Moscow News*, No. 19, 1981, the Soviet Peace Fund* helps to finance some of the WPC's and other such organisations' 'large public initiatives'. It has provided funds for such events as the World Parliament of Peoples for Peace in 1980 and the World Assembly for Peace and Life in 1983, and congresses of the Women's International Democratic Federation and the International Physicians for the Prevention of Nuclear War in 1987. The Fund, which purports to be supported spontaneously by over 80 million Soviet citizens, also helps to finance the activities of the Soviet Peace Committee—the WPC's senior affiliate and, in effect, controlling body. According to Stanislav Levchenko, a former KGB major and consultant to the Soviet Peace Committee, who defected in 1979 'the Peace Fund . . . comes under the guidance of the International Department, which ensures that the Soviet Peace Fund spends its money for the right causes' (Hearings of the Permanent Select Committee on Intelligence, US House of Representatives, 13/14 July 1982, p. 60).

In a letter published in the British *New Statesman*, 17 October 1980, Ruth Tosek, a 'former senior interpreter at several of the Moscow-controlled organisations', stated that 'all the funds of these organisations, in local and in hard currency, were provided above all by the Soviet Union but also by other East European satellite countries on the basis of set contribution rates, paid by the governments of these countries through various channels.'

At a session of the Committee on Non-Governmental Organisations (NGOs) held in New York from 9/19 February 1981, the WPC was forced to withdraw its application for reclassification to Category I consultative status with the UN Economic and Social Council (ECOSOC). Western delegations recorded their opposition to the application, pointing out that Paragraph 8 of ECOSOC's Resolution 1296 (XLVIV) required organisations to make a full and accurate declaration of their financial situation.

The British delegation noted the statement by the WPC representative that his organisation's accounts were not submitted to independent audit, and his admission under questioning that the financial statement submitted to the Committee covered only a fraction of the WPC's actual income and expenditures. The British delegation concluded that 'in other words, the World Peace Council has presented to the Committee a false statement of its accounts.' It was also clear that despite its claim to the contrary, the WPC 'has received large-scale financial support from government sources, and has gone to great lengths to conceal that fact from the Committee' (*ECOSOC Report*, 16 March 1981).

The Russians keep a relatively tight rein on their financial contributions. Frank Swift said in an interview reported in the London *Daily Telegraph* on 4 December 1982, that the Council had a staff of 52 and there had been no salary increases for two years; the Russians simply did not 'shovel out roubles'. The newspaper commented that, according to American sources, the WPC received some £25 million a year from the Soviet Union. This reflects the conclusion of the Sub-Committee on Oversight of the US House of Representatives on 6 February 1980 that the WPC received a Soviet official subsidy in 1979 estimated at US$49,380,000.

Relations with other bodies
(1) United Nations The WPC has always set great store by its efforts to increase its links with the United Nations and its specialised bodies. It maintains permanent representatives at the UN in both New York and Geneva and also at UNESCO in Paris. It has Category A consultative status with UNESCO (for explanation of Consultative Status in the United Nations see Appendix F) and consultative status with ECOSOC, UNCTAD and UNIDO. The UN generally sends representatives to the principal WPC meetings, including the regular Congresses.

It received a setback in February 1981 over its attempt to obtain reclassification to Category I consultative status with ECOSOC (see above under Finance). Prior to the withdrawal of its application, it was strongly criticised for pursuing policies opposed to those of the United Nations. WPC's consistent support for the Soviet invasion of Afghanistan, which has been overwhelmingly condemned by large majorities in the UN General Assembly annually from 1980 onwards, is one example. Its refusal to accept UN policy on Kampuchea is another. The complete one-sideness of its practice of attacking the defence policies of the United States and its Allies while making no reference to the steady build-up of armaments by the Soviet Union was referred to in 1981 by the United Kingdom representative to the UN who repeated the description of the WPC as 'a disguised instrument of one country's foreign policy'.

Despite its 1981 rebuff, the WPC continually tries to exploit its UN associations with a view to increasing its respectability, particularly among the developing nations. It is noticeable however that it only supports those UN activities which do not conflict with Soviet policies. Until 1985 it played an increasing role in the NGOs Committee on Disarmament in Geneva, of which Romesh Chandra had for more than 10 years been a Vice-President. He had also been President of the Sub-Committee on Racism, Racial Discrimination, Apartheid and Decolonisation of the Special NGO Committee on Human Rights. It was therefore a major blow to the WPC's standing in UN circles when, in September 1985, a majority of the NGOs who have consultative status with ECOSOC (and who together form the unofficial Conference of Non-Governmental Organisations, known as CONGO) decided not to re-elect the WPC to their Board of Management. Since the WPC had previously exercised a strong influence over the CONGO this was an especially bitter decision for the WPC, coming as it did at the start of the International Year of Peace (IYP), proclaimed by the UN for 1986.

The WPC attempted to use the IYP in order to camouflage the true origin of (and its own association with) the 'World Congress Devoted to the International Year of Peace' which was held in Copenhagen in October 1986 (see below under Congresses). On the other hand, the WPC made no secret of its full support for the World Congress of Intellectuals for Peace, which was held in Warsaw in January 1986 as Poland's contribution to the IYP.

(2) Other International Front Organisations The WPC's dominant role in relation to the Soviet-controlled International Front Organisations has already been mentioned. The leading officials from the seven principal organisations—AAPSO(1)*, CPC*, IOJ*, IUS*, WFDY(2)*, WIDF(2)* and WFTU(2)*—are members of the WPC's Presidential Committee. This ensures that the WPC is able effectively to coordinate the policies and activities of the Communist 'World Peace Movement'. As already noted (see Introduction) liaison meetings take place regularly

between the International Front Organisations normally at six-monthly intervals.

(3) Non-Communist Organisations Collaboration with non-Communist international bodies has usually failed because the WPC cannot sustain its claim to non-aligned status. For example, at the World Congress of Peace Forces in Moscow in 1973, members of the non-Communist War Resisters' International (WRI) tactlessly raised the question of the treatment of dissidents in the Soviet Union and Czechoslovakia. As a result, Romesh Chandra warned that 'certain peace organisations should be watched; because they had taken an anti-Soviet stance they ceased to be genuine peace organisations'.

After 1973, however, Chandra succeeded in persuading leading members of three non-aligned organisations to cooperate with him. The Vice-Chairman of the Continuing Liaison Council of the World Congress of Peace Forces (renamed International Liaison Forum of Peace Forces in January 1977), of which Chandra is Chairman, have included representatives of the International Peace Bureau (IPB), the World Association of World Federalists (WAWF) and the Women's International League for Peace and Freedom (WILPF)*. The WILPF's General Secretary, Edith Ballantyne, a Canadian of Czech origin, chaired the Coordinating Group of the International Preparatory Committee for the World Assembly for Peace and Life, in Prague in June 1983. Hermod Lannung presided over the World Congress Devoted to the UN Year of Peace in Copenhagen in October 1986.

As well as Soviet-controlled International Front Organisations, the following bodies are represented on the WPC Presidential Committee: All-Africa Students' Union, All-Africa Women's Organisation (AAWO), Arab Peoples' Congress, Asian Buddhist Conference for Peace (ABCP)*, Berlin Conference of European Catholics*, Esperantist Movement for World Peace (MEM)*, Federation of Latin American Journalists (FELAP), International Confederation of Arab Trade Unions (ICATU), Latin American Confederation of Associations of University Professionals, Organisation of African Trade Union Unity (OATUU), Afro-Asian/Latin American Peoples' Solidarity Organisation (AALAPSO)*, Permanent Congress of Trade Union Unity of Latin American Workers (CPUSTAL), the Anti-Imperialist Tribunal of Latin America (TANA), and the Continental Organisation of Latin American Students (OCLAE).

The WPC claims to cooperate with the Non-Aligned Movement (NAM), the Organisation of African Unity (OAU) and the League of Arab States. It also has links with the Vienna-based International Progress Organisation (IPO).

National Affiliates

As noted above, the WPC claims to have affiliated to it national 'peace committees' in 144 countries. Apart from the Soviet Peace Committee, which exercises a controlling influence, all the other national committees are in a subordinate position. That is to say, they receive, and follow, directions from the WPC on the line they should take. The regular vehicle for such directions is the annual *Programme of Action* (see below) approved by the WPC at the end of each year and issued early in the next. According to the Secretariat's letter forwarding the 1985 *Programme*, it 'outlines positions of the WPC on major issues and calls for action around these issues'. In addition 'specific events and actions are called for on the international, regional and national levels'. While it is recognised that national committees will need to place different emphases on the various points in the programme, they are asked to keep the WPC informed of their plans and activities. To ensure that the affiliates adhere to the party line, the WPC holds periodic meetings of national officials on a regional or continental basis. Besides the national 'peace committees' there is a large number of pro-Soviet friendship societies in different countries—such as the British/Soviet Friendship Society—which are wholly Communist-controlled.

Subsidiaries

The WPC has set up numerous subsidiary bodies to direct specific campaigns. Some of these have been ephemeral and have been disbanded once they are no longer required. Those currently or recently active include the International Campaign Committee for a Just Peace in the Middle East; the International Commission of Enquiry into the Crimes of the Military Junta in Chile; the International Commission of Enquiry into Israeli Crimes against the Lebanese and Palestinian Peoples; the International Committee for Solidarity with Cyprus; the International Committee for Solidarity with the Palestinian People; the Vienna Dialogue on Disarmament and Detente.

WPC's Policies

In pursuit of its declared aims quoted above, the WPC makes little attempt to disguise the one-sided nature of its policies. It has always been unashamedly pro-Soviet and anti-American, pro-communist and anti-Western. The policies of the Soviet Union and its allies are extolled, those of the United States and NATO vilified. Despite the protestations of objectivity and even-handedness which are routinely made, there is, in practice, no real evidence of balance or impartiality. The vast network of fraternal organisations, affiliates and subsidiaries which take their cue from the WPC exists for one purpose only: to rally support for the policies of the Soviet Union throughout the world.

Romesh Chandra, in statements before and since he became President, has been quite explicit about the alignment of the WPC with the Soviet Union. Speaking in Moscow in 1975 he said: 'The Soviet Union invariably supports the peace movement. The World Peace Council in its turn positively reacts to the Soviet initiatives in international affairs.' (*New Times*, Moscow, July 1975). In an article in the *World Marxist Review* (No. 1, of January 1981), Chandra said:

> The foreign policy goals of the USSR . . . are to establish lasting peace and peaceful co-existence between States of different social systems . . . The Soviet Union's military policy fully corresponds to these goals. It is of a purely defensive character . . . In the hands of Socialism force has for the first time in human history become an instrument for safeguarding peace and social progress. So much for the 'Soviet threat'. If it does exist, it is, figuratively speaking, not a threat to peace but a threat of peace in the name of peace.

The record speaks for itself: the WPC did not waver in its support of the Soviet Union's suppression of the Hungarian uprising (1956), the Soviet attempt to instal ballistic missiles in Cuba (1962), the invasion of Czechoslovakia by Warsaw Pact forces (1968) and the Soviet invasion of Afghanistan in 1979. All these Soviet actions were condemned by the United Nations. Resolutions severely critical of the continued Soviet occupation of Afghanistan have been adopted by overwhelming majorities in the General Assely each year since 1980.

Annual Programmes
At its triennial meeting the WPC issues a statement which provides general policy guidance until its next meeting. The lengthy statement issued by the Council in 1986 was, to all intents and purposes, a summary of current Soviet propaganda themes and foreign policy objectives. At the beginning of each year the Bureau approves a draft *Programme of Action* prepared by the

Secretariat. The programme follows the general guidance in the Council's statement. Although intended primarily as a directive for the WPC's own affiliates, it also serves as guidance for the other international front organisations. The style, emphasis and precise content of these programmes are carried from year to year to suit Moscow's current requirements. In substance, however, there is a common thread running through them which reflects the continuity of Soviet policies. For the purpose of comparison extracts from the *Programme* for 1985, the last one approved before General Secretary Gorbachev was appointed, and for 1988, the latest available, are given in Appendix E.

The introduction to the 1985 *Programme* is aggressively anti-American:

> The year that has ended saw tens of millions of women and men . . . expressing . . . their refusal to participate in the war preparations of the United States Administration . . . The overwhelming majority of governments have once again voted at the United Nations General Assembly in support of the most vital demands of the peace movement for the ending of the global arms build-up.

In fact, in 1984 the bankruptcy of Soviet arms control policies had been demonstrated. Soviet efforts to prevent the deployment of NATO INF missiles had failed, and the Soviet Union had withdrawn abruptly in November 1983 from the bilateral negotiations with the United States on INF arms control. It suffered a massive defeat in the UN General Assembly when it opposed, with the support only of its Communist allies, a resolution calling for the immediate resumption without preconditions of negotiations with the United States. During 1984 Soviet policies were evidently in disarray, and by the end of the year even the Western peace movements, on which the Soviet Union had relied to apply pressure on NATO governments, were showing signs of running out of steam. So the introduction to the 1985 *Programme*, with its recital of the familiar agenda of the Soviet 'peace offensive' and its anti-American incantations, while fully reflecting Soviet propaganda, had little to do with the realities of the international situation.

Gorbachev's influence is clearly shown in the change of style apparent in the introduction to the 1988 *Programme*. There are none of the customary anti-Western polemics, either in the introduction or in the subsequent sections. The United States Strategic Defense Initiative, which was bitterly attacked in 1985 and subsequent years, is not mentioned. In fact, apart from a reference to the Soviet-American INF Agreement, as a manifestation of the growing 'possibilities for enhancing the process of peace and real disarmament' and to the need 'to ensure the long-term adherence to [the US/Soviet Anti-Ballistic Missile Treaty] by the US and the USSR', neither the United States nor NATO are named anywhere in the programme. The emphasis in the introduction is on the importance of mobilising public opinion in support of peace, of developing the peace activities of national organisations and of strengthening cooperation between the WPC and professional and special interest groups of all kinds. All this action is to be aimed at 'overcoming the enemy images of the "Cold War" ' and the 'promoting of people to people diplomacy'. The whole document is consistent with the subtler and more realistic public relations style of the Gorbachev régime. It will appeal to a much wider audience than any programme of recent years has done.

The principal section in each of the two programmes concerns Arms Control and Disarmament. Here a similar contrast is apparent. In 1985, the instructions for action were detailed, combative and comprehensive. Every one of them was designed to promote Soviet interests at the expense of American and western interests. The whole thrust was to counter western policies and resist western activities everywhere in the world. In effect, the instructions were tantamount to a declaration of 'Cold War'. The 1988 *Programme* is quite different. The 'instructions' are less specific, much shorter and less peremptory. The tone is no longer aggressively polemical. There is no overt suggestion of anti-American or anti-NATO bias. The main purpose of the action proposed is to support, by way of conferences and studies, arms control negotiations, bilateral and multilateral, which are currently taking place and especially proposals favoured by the Soviet Union. The contrast is even more marked in the section on human rights. Here the blatant posturing of previous years has been abandoned. The serious tone of the few practical and positive themes is clearly intended to support the Soviet Union's efforts to convince its CSCE partners—and others—of the suitability of Moscow as the venue for a human rights conference.

The difference is less obvious in the remaining sections in the two programmes, although the 1988 version is more concise, with the emphasis on practical dialogue, and contains much less rhetoric than 1985. They include the Middle East, Mediterranean, Africa, Latin America and the Caribbean, Asia and the Pacific, the Environment, the United Nations, Trade Unions and so on. The annual programmes cover a remarkably wide range of activities, omitting no aspect of international relations. They provide an invaluable vehicle for the world-wide dissemination, through the organisations of the propaganda network, of the thrust of Soviet public attitudes on all aspects of foreign policy, which can be fine-tuned annually at Moscow's direction. The fine-tuning in 1988 shows a far greater sensitivity than previously to what is likely to impress and what to antagonise Western public opinion.

Congresses

The main events staged by the WPC, either directly or indirectly, are the World Peace Congresses. These are large propagandist gatherings, designed to attract non-communist individuals and organisations as well as the party faithful. The large number of resolutions approved at these Congresses are 'passed by acclamation'; voting is avoided. Frequently the participants who are not members of the small controlling group do not see the texts which they have adopted until they are published. In recent years they have attracted relatively little publicity in the Western media, but they are published in *Peace Courier* and in booklet form. Since the Wroclaw Congress of Intellectuals for Peace in August, 1948, there have been 14 'Peace Congresses' held under the auspices of or at the instigation of the World Peace Council (or its precursor, the Permanent Committee of Partisans of Peace). These are:

April 1949:	main Congress in Paris but, owing to the French Government's refusal of visas for some Communist delegates, continued in Prague: First World Congress of Partisans of Peace.
November 1950:	opened in Sheffield but, owing to the British Government's refusal to admit the Soviet and other Communist delegates, switched immediately to Warsaw: Second World Peace Congress.
December 1952:	Vienna: Congress of the Peoples for Peace.
June 1955:	Helsinki: World Peace Assembly.
July 1958:	Stockholm: Congress for Disarmament and International Cooperation.
July 1962:	Moscow: World Congress for Disarmament and Peace.

July 1965:   Helsinki: World Congress for Peace, National Independence and General Disarmament.
June 1969:   East Berlin: World Assembly for Peace.
May 1971:   Budapest: World Peace Assembly.
October 1973:   Moscow: World Congress of Peace Forces.
May 1977:   Warsaw: World Assembly of Builders of Peace.
September 1980:   Sofia: World Parliament of Peoples for Peace.
June 1983:   Prague: World Assembly for Peace and Life, against Nuclear War.
October 1986:   Copenhagen: World Congress devoted to the International Year of Peace.

The *Prague Assembly* in June 1983 was initiated by the WPC and organised by the Czech Peace Committee. Like its prede-cessors it was intended to attract non-communists, and, following the precedent of previous congresses, its title was designed with that purpose in mind: 3,625 delegates attended from 132 coun-tries and 119 international organisations; of the delegates, 20 per cent came from 'socialist' countries, 40 per cent from 'developing' countries and 40 per cent from 'advanced capitalist' countries (figures from the Czech News Agency *CTK* on 4 June 1983). The Assembly was announced in advance as the most important of the Congresses so far initiated by the WPC. But, despite the large attendance, in terms of its international impact it must have been something of a disappointment to its organisers. Of the well-known foreigners invited to attend as guests of honour, only Yasser Arafat accepted and the proceedings did not attract as much publicity in the world media as had been hoped. The Czechoslovak President and Prime Minister and the UN Deputy Secretary-General, Vyacheslav Ustinov (USSR), were present at the opening ceremony and Romesh Chandra attended throughout the five days. Only two plenary sessions were held, at the beginning and end, at which the speeches were couched in familiar and predictable terms. At the final session, Chandra adopted an up-beat note: 'To those who try to divide use, we say: Your efforts will only make us more united . . . We can say: Yes, I was in Prague, and I know we shall win.' The work of the Assembly had taken place in the 'dialogue groups' with titles such as 'The dangers of nuclear war, the threat to life and how to prevent it', 'The arms race and how to stop and reverse it', and 'The role of the Non-Aligned Movement for peace and life'. The Assembly adopted an appeal which, after a warning that all talks on limiting and reducing arms were virtually blocked and new types of weapons of mass destruction were being developed, noted that a particularly acute danger 'is posed by plans to deploy new first-strike nuclear missiles in Western Europe' which it was 'utterly essential' to stop. The Appeal concluded by declaring that: 'We are deeply convinced that, whatever differences there may be between us over some problems, nothing shall divide us in the face of our common goal to save peace and life and prevent a nuclear war.' Given the importance of securing support from the many non-Communist delegates present from Western countries, the Appeal was careful not to put the blame on any single country for the stalemate in the arms control negotiations at Geneva (on INF and START) or for aggression in any part of the world, although individual speakers had not been so restrained and there was no doubt about the unanimous opposition to the NATO plans to deploy INF missiles. Closing the Assembly, the British Labour MP, James Lamond, President of the British Peace Assembly and a WPC Vice-President, said (according to *CTK* on 26 June 1983) that it had been an extremely valuable opportunity for an exchange of views and the Appeal, which had been formulated on a broad basis upon which all sections of progressive opinion could unite, should become the starting point for the future work of the international peace movement. The Assistant Secretary of the British Peace Assembly, Florence Croasdell, was quoted (by the *Daily Telegraph* on 27 June 1983) as saying the Soviet Union is working for peace '24 hours a day'. She went on: 'The only social order that is going to bring any progress for our children is Socialism, and real Socialism is in the Soviet Union. Nevertheless the Soviet Union does not impose its system on anybody, but America is out to dominate the world.' She was warmly applauded.

Outside the official proceedings, things did not run so smoothly. Three leaders of the Czech human rights group, Charter 77, were refused permission to attend the Assembly, despite the organisers' pledge that it would be 'open to all movements'. The two observers from CND, Roger Spillar and Jon Bloomfield, made it clear that they intended to meet all individuals and groups working for peace, including Charter 77. Together with representatives of the West German Green Party and of the Dutch Pax Christi Organisation, they arranged a meeting with Charter 77 which was, however, broken up by Czech police. This incident, and the arbitrary exclusion of Charter 77 and other human rights groups, were the subject of representations to the Czech organisers, demonstrations and publicly-voiced complaints by several of the delegates from West European countries. The Green Party representatives summed up their reaction by saying that police action over the Charter 77 meeting 'stands in crass contradiction to the propagated principles of this world peace conference'.

The *Copenhagen Congress*, from 15/19 October 1986, was the first (excepting the 1949 Paris Congress) to be held in a NATO country and the first for over 20 years in a non-Communist country. As usual it was initiated by the WPC which was however anxious to play down its role and went so far as to claim publicly in 1985 that the initiative had come from a 'group of Danish personalities'. To maintain this fiction the preparatory committee set up in autumn 1985 was headed by a non-Communist coordinator with long-standing WPC connections, 90-year old Hermod Lannung, Chairman of the Danish/Soviet Friendship Association and a Vice-President of the International Liaison Forum of Peace Forces (ILF). Practical arrangements and finance were placed in the hands of a Danish secretariat. But it proved impossible to escape the WPC and communist association. Both the original sponsoring group and the international preparatory committee were dominated by WPC members. The secretariat was provided by the WPC's Danish affiliate, the Cooperation Committee for Peace and Security (SAK), and the work of preparation and organisation of the Congress was effectively taken over by the small Danish Communist Party (the DKP, which in the 1984 Danish election obtained only 0.7 of the votes). In the event, however, the Danish Secretariat proved unequal to the task and, with only four months to go, the WPC and Soviet Peace Committee stepped in in June 1986 and put Dzhangir Atamali, a Soviet WPC secretary from Helsinki, in charge of a new International Secretariat. This strong Communist role alienated non-communist Danish organisations; the Social Democratic Party and the Socialist Youth Movement, among others, refused to take part.

The slogan adopted for the Congress was: 'Safeguard Peace and the Future of Mankind'. This enabled Lannung to maintain that its main emphasis would be on 'peace' rather than human rights and thus to justify the exclusion of any of the independent groups from Eastern Europe, such as Charter 77, the Moscow Trust Group and Polish Freedom and Peace Group. Members of these groups—and of other dissident bodies—were however included in the non-communist Danish delegation. Attendance, according to the organisers, was by 2,468 delegates from 136 countries and 60 international organisations. This figure, much lower than that achieved three years earlier in Prague, was half the original target and only achieved by flying in hundreds of additional delegates by way of Moscow. Unlike Prague, there was on this occasion no official representative of the UN, despite the personal efforts of Lannung to secure one. In fact links with the UN and the International Year of Peace were minimal, being confined to a recorded message from the UN Secretary-General for use at the opening session. More serious was the fact that the Congress was boycotted by most non-communist Western 'peace' movements. Neither the CND from the UK nor the European Nuclear Disarmament Movement (END) were officially represented. Most Danish non-communist bodies had withdrawn during the preparatory stage. Only the Socialist People's Party (Marxist) and the Radical Party participated, but they were highly critical of the WPC's involvement.

At Prague the principal target for attack had been NATO's planned deployment of Pershing II and Cruise Missiles in Europe. At Copenhagen, the target switched to the US Strategic Defense Initiative (SDI). Opening the proceedings, Lannung set the tone by denouncing the SDI and calling upon delegates to mobilise an ever wider circle of people in the campaign against 'nuclear insanity', which he ascribed entirely to the Reagan Administration. By chance the Congress opened three days after the Summit meeting between President Reagan and General-Secretary Gorbachev in Reykjavik had ended. Inevitably, virtually all the speakers placed responsibility exclusively on Washington for wasting what the Soviet *New Times* described as a 'unique historic chance to drastically change the dangerous course of events'. The reason was President Reagan's insistence on going ahead with the SDI. Zhukov, then Chairman of the Soviet Peace Committee who was head of the Soviet delegation to the Congress, told *Tass* correspondents at the end of the meeting that Gorbachev's policy statement at Reykjavik had received 'unanimous support' in Copenhagen and that 'everyone' wanted an immediate end to nuclear weapon tests, a ban on the militarisation of space and the elimination of nuclear weapons by the year 2000 as proposed by Gorbachev. Zhukov did however admit that there had been some disagreement over 'organisational matters'.

Virtually all the other topics on the agenda—the dissolution of military blocs, the creation of nuclear free zones, the removal of foreign military bases—were said to have produced a consensus in favour of speedy moves towards disarmament (on Soviet terms), though no formal resolutions were passed. Several appeals to world public opinion were launched, notably the 'Copenhagen Appeal', initiated by the six countries which had met in Delhi earlier in the year ('the Delhi Six')—India, Argentina, Mexico, Greece, Sweden and Tanzania—for an immediate nuclear test ban and a 'resolute no' to the SDI. Signatures are to be collected worldwide, the hope being that the ideas embodied in the Appeal will become the principal aim of 'anti-war' activities. Discussion of problems in specific geographical areas, notably Central America, produced predictably anti-American sentiments. As the independent Danish newspaper *Berlingske Tidende* commented on 17 October, the organisers' control of the debates and lists of speakers was so effective that panic ensued if any 'outsider' succeeded in voicing a controversial or critical opinion.

The Copenhagen Congress was in gestation for nearly two and a half years. Since the proposal was first made known by the WPC in July 1984, it had been discussed at numerous meetings of representatives of the international communist 'peace movement' and there were high hopes that this Congress in a Western capital during the UN's International Year of Peace would attract massive support in the non-communist world. Such hopes were undoubtedly disappointed; not only did non-communist organisations show little interest in the proceedings but the Western media virtually ignored the event. The coincidence with the Rejkavik Summit meeting, coverage of which, and of its aftermath, dominated the Western media at the time, cannot have helped, even though it provided a useful topical anti-American theme for speakers. At any rate, the outcome of this venture must have raised doubts in the WPC about the success of its present policies in the West and the propaganda value of holding mass meetings in a NATO country. It showed how opportune was the appointment of Pakaslahti as General-Secretary (see above).

Other campaigns and activities
These, for the most part, have developed from the directives contained in the annual *Programme of Action*. From the start, the principal campaigns have been concerned with opposition to nuclear weapons (meaning, of course, American nuclear weapons). The earliest campaign—and possibly even now the best known—was the 'Stockholm Appeal' launched in March

1950, which called for 'unconditional prohibition of the atomic weapon as a weapon of aggression and mass annihilation of people, and that strict international control for the implementation of this decision be established'. This demand was calculated to attract mass support, and the organisers claimed to have secured 500 million signatures worldwide. But although it reflected the official Soviet line in the United Nations at the time, Soviet veto of the American 'Baruch Plan', with similar objectives, two years earlier cast serious doubts on the sincerity of its authors. The Appeal was launched six months after the first Soviet atomic test, at a time of clear Soviet nuclear inferiority; it was suspended three years later after the Soviet thermonuclear test in 1953 gave the Soviet Union the basis for developing its own sophisticated nuclear capability. In June 1975 the WPC launched a second Stockholm Appeal under the slogan: 'To make detente irreversible, stop the arms race'. The text made its real purpose clearer, stating that 'the arms race, the stockpiles of weapons in the hands of imperialists, incite and encourage the forces of aggression, militarism and fascism, colonialism and racism.' Since then the WPC has orchestrated major campaigns against specific United States initiatives on nuclear weapons: against the Enhanced Radiation Warhead (ERW—the 'neutron bomb') in 1977 and 1978; against the modernisation of INF—the production and deployment of Pershing II and cruise missiles—from 1979 onwards; and, more recently, against the US Strategic Defence Initiative announced by President Reagan in March 1983. These campaigns have been directed primarily at public opinion in West European NATO countries, but they have also been designed to promote opposition worldwide to the American proposals. Thus, for example, more than a hundred WPC affiliated organisations which were represented at a WPC Presidential Bureau meeting held in Madagascar in January 1981 supported the declaration that 'through NATO's nuclear weapons the countries of the Mediterranean, the Middle East, the Gulf and the entire world' were at risk. This was just one of the frequent meetings which the WPC has organised in various countries to campaign for objectives similar to those in the 1975 Stockholm Appeal.

Other topics on which the WPC has organised special meetings include: economic development—discussed at a seminar on Problems of Socio-economic Transformation in Developing Countries in Aden in January 1978, a seminar on Peace and Development in Kathmandu in April 1984, and on 'International Conferences on Developing Countries' in Budapest in January 1985; human rights—although naturally the subject of human rights in communist countries is never mentioned, the 'suppression of human rights' in such countries as Chile, South Africa, Namibia and Northern Ireland are frequently condemned and a seminar on the 'Human Right to Peace' was held in Geneva in June 1984 and an International Conference for Peace, Democracy and Human Rights in Quito in July 1984; and disarmament—an International Forum on Disarmament was held in Helsinki in September 1976 (transferred from York (England) because of the refusal of visas to some Soviet and East European delegates in March) and a 'Conference against the Arms Race and for Confidence and Security in Europe' was organised in Stockholm in June 1981.

The WPC is also active on national and regional issues; this is reflected in the list of its subsidiaries quoted above, many of which hold regular meetings. The most active among them are the International Commission of Enquiry into the Crimes of the Military Junta in Chile; the International Committee for Solidarity with Cyprus, which was set up at a conference in Nicosia in 1975 to support the Greek Cypriot position and criticise NATO for the island's troubles and which has met in Athens (1975), Nicosia (1976), Nicosia (1979), Paris (1980), Helsinki (1982), Lisbon (1983), Nicosia (1984) and Sofia (1987); and the various committees set up to deal with ostensibly different but largely overlapping aspects of the Arab–Israel conflict, all of which meet regularly and whose main connecting theme is denunciation of Israel for being an 'aggressor' and a 'tool of US imperialism'. In Latin America, the WPC gave full vent to its anti-imperialist, anti-NATO bias by backing the Argentine junta in the war with the United Kingdom over the Falkland Islands in 1982; in April 1983 the Council organised a Conference for Peace and Sovereignty in Central America and the Caribbean in Managua to demonstrate its support for the Sandinista Government of Nicaragua, and a follow-up conference was called in Mexico City in November of the same year to discuss—and denounce—US intervention in Grenada. Other regional meetings have been held in Panama City in September 1981, Guayaquil in July 1984 and Havana in January 1985. Though its affiliates in Africa are not very strong, the WPC has worked closely with African 'liberation movements' and has been actively involved in campaigning against Apartheid. Details of bodies established in support of this campaign are given in the profile on the Afro–Asian Peoples' Solidarity Organisation (AAPSO)*.

Finally, the WPC has not ignored the scope for propaganda in Asia and the Pacific. For many years the war in Vietnam was the main focus and provided ample opportunity for denunciation of United States 'aggression' and 'imperialism'. Among other organisations the WPC set up a Stockholm Conference on Vietnam, and claimed to have made a significant contribution towards the American withdrawal, which was hailed as a 'glorious victory' against the 'aggressors'. More recently, the Council has campaigned for the closure of US military bases in Asia and the Pacific (as well as in the Indian Ocean, where it supports the Soviet proposal for establishment of a 'zone of peace'). It held a Forum on Peace in South-East Asia in Phnom Penh in February 1983, a Conference for Peace and Security in Asia and the Pacific in Ulan Bator in April 1983 and further conferences on similar themes in Manila in December 1984 and Sydney in October 1985.

It has not been possible to include here details of all the conferences organised or sponsored by the WPC round the world. Enough has been said however to illustrate the constant and comprehensive activity directed from the headquarters in Helsinki, which is the hub of the whole system of communist front organisations operating under the control of the CPSU's International Committee.

2. Afro–Asian Peoples' Solidarity Organisation

The Afro–Asian Peoples' Solidarity Organisation (AAPSO) is also known under its French and German titles which are, respectively, *Organisation de la solidarité des peuples afro–asiatiques* and *Organisation für Afro–Asiatische Völkersolidarität*. Its headquarters is at 89 Adbul Aziz Al Saoud Street, Manial, Cairo, Egypt.

Origins
The WPC* has spawned a number of organisations which, in the course of time, have emerged as autonomous international front organisations in their own right. AAPSO is a prime example. It was founded by the Soviet Union as a means of reasserting Soviet influence in Africa and Asia following the Soviet Union's exclusion, despite its vast Asian empire, from the inter-governmental Afro–Asian Conference held in Bandung, Indonesia in 1955, the founding conference (as it later proved) of the Non-Aligned Movement. In practice AAPSO, although formally run

from Cairo under the terms of a constitution drafted when Egypt, under Nasser, was in many ways a Soviet client State, is still controlled directly by the Russians acting through its main constituent, the Soviet Afro–Asian Solidarity Committee in Moscow.

AAPSO had its origins in the WPC's Meeting for Lessening International Tension, held in Stockholm in June 1954, and its successor, the Asian Nations' Conference for the Relaxation of International Tension held in New Delhi in April 1955. Its sponsors claimed that the New Delhi Conference was associated with the forthcoming Bandung Conference, and secured the attendance of Prime Minister Nehru. But it was organised (by Mrs. Rameshwari Nehru, a distant relation by marriage of the Indian Prime Minister) with WPC support and led directly to the creation of a Committee of Asian Solidarity in India, together with national Solidarity Committees in various other Asian countries. It was noted at the time that many officers of these various Solidarity Committees were also equally active in national Peace Committees affiliated to the WPC. At that stage the movement was entirely Asian but, in December 1957, 38 of these committees with African support, inspired the First Afro–Asian Solidarity Conference held in Cairo. AAPSO was formally constituted three years later at the second conference in this new series held in Conakry, Guinea, in April 1960, by the Afro–Asian Peoples' Solidarity Council in Cairo.

AAPSO is described by its sponsors as a 'bi-continental organisation'. They had originally intended it to be a tri-continental body, including the Latin Americans, but the latter are now served by a separate organisation, AALAPSO*.

The Cairo conference in 1957 reflected a temporary *mariage de convenance* between Soviet Communism, Arab nationalism, Chinese Communism and Asian neutralism. For a few years the new movement embraced all these disparate political trends. But from the early 1960s onwards, AAPSO, severely crippled by the long running Sino–Soviet dispute, never succeeded as the independent organisation which it purported to be. As a consequence of the deterioration of Soviet–Egyptian relations, it has in practice been controlled from Moscow by the Soviet Afro–Asian Solidarity Committee. Iraqis have also played a major role in its direction: numerous meetings have been held in Baghdad; for years the acting secretary-general was Iraqi and, in default of moving the international headquarters from Cairo to Baghdad, in the 1970s an Afro–Asian Development Centre under AAPSO control was established in the Iraqi capital. As for the Chinese, their official involvement with AAPSO ended over 20 years ago when, having failed to stage the Fifth Afro–Asian Solidarity Conference in Peking as a result of Soviet objections, they boycotted an AAPSO council meeting in Nicosia, Cyprus, in February 1967, never to return.

Declared Aims

According to the *Yearbook Of International Organisations* (1986–87), the aims of AAPSO are to

> Unite, coordinate and strengthen the struggle of the African and Asian peoples against imperialism and colonialism, accelerate the liberation of the peoples and ensure their economic, social and cultural development; implement and put into practice the resolutions and recommendations adopted towards these ends by the Conferences of Afro–Asian Peoples' Solidarity; promote and consolidate the Movement of Afro–Asian Solidarity in all countries of both continents and act as permanent liaison body between the different countries in the framework of the Solidarity movement.

These aims are also set out at considerably greater length in AAPSO's constitution, originally adopted in 1960, amended in 1974 and 1981 and readopted in its present form in 1984. This constitution makes clear that the 'liberation struggle' is against, not only imperialism and colonialism, but also 'racism, apartheid and all forms of discrimination, Zionism, fascism and reaction'; it specifically mentions AAPSO's support of the Non-Aligned Movement; it emphasises that 'the struggle . . . for . . . economic . . . development' includes opposition to 'Trans-National Corporations . . . and the struggle for the realisation of the New International Economic Order': and it stresses that, as part of its 'struggle for freedom, development, peace, security and disarmament', AAPSO aims at 'total nuclear disarmament in the world.'

Organisation and Membership

AAPSO's supreme organ of policy is its Congress (see below). In practice, as already explained, it is run from Moscow through a Council, consisting of representatives from all member organisations, which, every two years, elects an Executive Committee (which usually meet twice yearly). The Permanent Secretariat in Cairo controls business. A Presidium was established in 1974 primarily for the purpose of organising a programme of work. It has met on thirteen occasions so far and has set up special committees to deal with disarmament, 'non-alignment', development, Palestine, the Gulf, the Red Sea, the Indian Ocean, Southern African issues, Asian security, women and information.

The Presidium has 20 members. The Permanent Secretariat consists of a Secretary-General, 4 Deputy Secretaries-General and 19 Secretaries (seven from Africa, six from the Arab states, two from Asia, one from East Germany, one from Czechoslovakia and two from the Soviet Union).

AAPSO currently claims as its affiliates about 90 national Afro–Asian Solidarity Committees and 'national liberation movements'. There are also associate members in Europe and North America. In exceptional cases, countries 'may be represented by two organisations and not more'.

Office holders
The leading AAPSO officials are President: Dr Mourad GHALEB; (Egypt); Secretary General: Nuri Abdul Razzak HUSSEIN (Iraq); Deputy Secretaries-General: Facimo BANGURA (Guinea), Chitta BISWAS (India), Saleh El-Kheidr HAMZA (PDRY), Mirpasha ZEINALOV (USSR); Vice Presidents: Vasudev ACHARYA (India), Victor AGADZI (Ghana), Abu AL-SHAMAT (Syria), Abdel AZIZ (Sri Lanka), Vital BALLA (Congo), Kaddour BELGACEM (Algeria), Tarek CHEHAB (Lebanon), Abdullah EL-HOURANI (PLO), Abdel Wahab EL-ZINTANI (Libya), Pascal LUVUALU (Angola), Vassos LYSSARIDES (Cyprus), Ali Ameir MOHAMED (Tanzania), Hamid MOHTAT (Afghanistan), NGUYEN Thi Binh (Vietnam), Alfred NZO (ANC-South Africa), Johannes SELASSIE (Ethiopia), Aziz SHARIF (Iraq), K. M. SHEPANDE (Zambia), Aaron SHIHEPO (SWAPO-Namibia) and Vladimir TOLSTIKOV (USSR).

In 1984 the Secretary-General was awarded the Soviet Order of Friendship between Peoples for his work for AAPSO. His Egyptian predecessor, Yousef El-SIBAI, was assassinated while attending an AAPSO Presidium meeting in Nicosia in February 1978 by two Palestinian gunmen despatched by a dissident PLO group.

Publications and Information
AAPSO publishes a monthly review, *Solidarity*, in English and French and a quarterly, *Development and Socio-Economic Progress*, in English, Arabic and French, among many other smaller publications. Information and publicity about AAPSO's

joint ventures with the WPC are usually handled by the latter organisation from Helsinki.

Finance
AAPSO claims, in its Constitution, that it is funded by membership fees from its affiliates and by donations from 'friendly organisations or individuals'. Each affiliate pays 'a minimum annual subscription of two thousand US dollars or the equivalent' (although the National Liberation Movements are exempt from 'payment of annual subscriptions').

The Sub-Committee on Oversight of the US House of Representatives stated in February 1980 that, at that time, AAPSO was in receipt of a Soviet subsidy estimated at US$1,260,000. Large Soviet subsidies are doubtless essential because, as AAPSO officials admitted in 1975, many affiliation fees were not being paid, and, were it not for the Solidarity Committees in Egypt, Iraq and the Soviet Union, 'the Permanent Secretariat would not have been able to assume its duties and implement its programme of action', adding that other "Solidarity organisations in socialist countries'—particularly the GDR—had also produced considerable assistance in both money and kind. Four years later a Financial Committee was set up within AAPSO to handle its financial problems.

Relations with other bodies
(1) United Nations AAPSO has consultative status with ECOSOC (Category II), UNESCO (Category C), UNIDO and UNCTAD. When in 1981 it applied to ECOSCO for reclassification to Category I status (alongside the WPC), its application was deferred, as a result of western objections, on grounds that it was 'engaged in slanderous and unfounded accusations and subversive activities against certain States (which were) members of the United Nations'. A similar application in the following year was similarly deferred. AAPSO is, however, on the board of the unofficial Conference of Non Governmental Organisations (CONGO) which has consultative status with ECOSOC. AAPSO's European regional office in Geneva cooperates with various UN agencies and the organisation also had a so-called liaison officer, Jeanne Woods, stationed at UN headqarters in New York.

(2) Other International Front Organisations AAPSO has, of course, close working links with the WPC and it is represented

on the WPC Presidential Committee by the late Abdel Rahman
AL-SHARKAWI (Egypt) and Nuri Abdul Razzak HUSSEIN
(Iraq). Until 1973 most larger AAPSO events were jointly organ-
ised with the WPC but in recent years it has increasingly acted
on its own and, in the developing world, largely as a surrogate
for the WPC. AAPSO is also represented at all meetings of the
WPC and its subsidiary International Liaison Forum of Peace
Forces (ILF*).

AAPSO also has close working links with the other Soviet-
controlled front organisations and participates from time to time
in the bi-annual liaison meetings. AAPSO also has some contacts
with AALAPSO*.

(3) Non-Communist Organisations AAPSO is in contact with the
Organisation of African Unity (OAU), the League of Arab
States and has had observer status with the Non-Aligned Move-
ment since the 1970s.

Subsidiaries
AAPSO, which remained very much under the WPC's wing
until the early 1970s, has in turn, with the WPC's cooperation,
established a subsidiary organisation which is now almost an
international front organisation in its own right, namely the International Committee against Apartheid, Racism and Colonialism
in Southern Africa.

As a result of the AAPSO Conference on South Africa held
in Addis Ababa in October 1976, the so-called International
Commission of Enquiry into Crimes of the Racist Regimes in
Southern Africa was also set up. This has been based, since 1978,
in Brussels and was under the chairmanship of the late Sean
MacBRIDE, the former Irish politician and lawyer who was
also a former ILF vice-chairman; its secretary-general is Paulette
PIERSON-MATHY, a Belgian lawyer who belongs to both the
WPC and the International Association of Democratic Lawyers
(IADL)*, which also has its headquarters in Brussels.

Congresses
AAPSO is expected, under the terms of its Constitution, to hold
a Congress every three years. In practice Congresses have been
held irregularly as follows:

December	1957:	Cairo
April	1960:	Conakry
February	1963:	Moshi, Tanzania

May   1965: Winneba, Ghana
January   1972: Cairo
May   1984: Algiers

The sixth congress (Algiers, 1984) had been postponed for a decade for internal AAPSO reasons and was a troubled gathering. Although subsequently described by its Soviet sponsors as 'the most representative in the militant history of this organisation' (*New Times*, No. 24, June 1984), it was beset by arguments, including one which 'flared up over the question of the return of Chinese representatives, who themselves left the . . . movement in 1967' (a move strongly and successfully resisted by the Soviet delegates) and another major dispute over the nature of 'non-alignment'—the idea that the developing countries should keep an equal distance from both superpowers which, it was said, bear equal responsibility for the difficult economic situation of the African and Asian countries and for dangerous tension in the world', another concept highly distasteful to the Soviet Union and which AAPSO was compelled—but only after prolonged internal discussion—to reject. These dissident views did not survive the communiqué drafting session. Although it was only published many days later, the Congress's final communiqué gave no hint of disputes and contained no surprises.

A third issue was mentioned in a June 1984 issue of *La Révolution Africaine*, the Algerian FLN weekly newspaper—namely the role of associate AAPSO members representing countries outside Asia and Africa:

> While it is accepted by all that this Organisation is constituted of African and Asian national committees, attending in full right and with wide powers, the question—so controversial and the subject of a tumultuous debate— concerning the status of associate members (those who are not a part of the two continents) was given more precise definition. At the end of animated discussions in the organisational Commission it has been affirmed that this category will have an intermediate status, between that of full members and that of observers.

This reflected the determination of the pro-Communist representatives of the full member countries to retain their influence inside the organisation. There are five communist-controlled Afro–Asian Solidarity Committees in the principal communist countries of Eastern Europe. In most Western countries the associate bodies, if not under full communist control, are under strong communist influence. An example is the British associate, Liberation, which was founded by non-communists in 1954 as the

Movement for Colonial Freedom. Others are the Irish-Apartheid Movement, the Belgian Committee of Support for the Freedom Struggles against Colonialism and Apartheid, Canadians Concerned about Southern Africa, the Finnish Afro–Asian Solidarity Committee, the French Association of Friendship and Solidarity with the African Peoples, the West German Anti-Imperialist Solidarity Committee, the Greek Afro–Asian Solidarity Committee, the Italian Liberation and Development, and the US National Anti-Imperialist Movement in Solidarity with African Liberation.

3. Christian Peace Conference (CPC)

The Christian Peace Conference (CPC) is also known under its French, German and Spanish titles which are, respectively, *Conférence chrétienne pour la paix*, *Christliche Friedenskonferenz* and *Conferencia Cristiana por la Paz*. Its headquarters is at Jungmannova 9, Prague, Czechoslovakia.

Origins
The CPC also emerged from the aegis of the WPC in 1958 when the first CPC meeting was held in Prague on the 'ideological initiative' of the late Dr. Joseph Hromadka, a Lenin Peace Prize-winner and WPC member, and his colleagues on the Czechoslovak Ecumenical Council. Dr. Hromadka, a leading Czech Protestant theologian, was not a Communist but had long led the way towards dialogue between Christians and Marxist–Leninists. As a result of his initiative, the first All-Christian Peace Assembly was staged in Prague in June 1961 when the CPC as a permanent organisation was formally constituted.

Both the founding president (Hromadka) and the first secretary-general, J. Ondra, were Czechs. This was to have an unhappy sequel when in August 1968, Soviet tanks and troops entered Prague to foreclose the 'Prague Spring'. The invasion lead to a crisis in CPC: Ondra was forced to resign, followed swiftly by Hromadka, who added his own resignation in protest in 1969, after circulating an open letter opposing the invasion. 'And it was at this critical moment that His Eminence [the late] Metropolitan Nikodim [of Leningrad] took into his untiring hands the leadership of the movement and thanks to his boundless energy he was able to bring about not only the rebirth of the CPC, but also its metamorphosis into a fairly universal movement . . .' (the

Russian Metropolitan Yurenali of Krutitsy, writing in 1979 and quoted in *Religion in Communist Lands*, Vol. 13, No. 3 Winter 1985). A more critical view was expressed in the Amsterdam newspaper *De Telegraaf*, 17 April 1976:

> It is a fact that in 1968, during the Soviet occupation of Czechoslovakia, Nikodim with a heavy hand purged the churches of priests and pastors who under Dubcek had been able to come to the fore and obviously, were no friends of Moscow . . . Western observers who are familiar with the scene believe that . . . [Boris Georgiyevich] Rotov, alias Nikodim, is a KGB agent . . .

Nikodim's action followed a special CPC meeting held in Paris in October 1969 which had condemned the invasion of Czechoslovakia. By February 1970, when another CPC meeting was held in Warsaw, thanks to Nikodim Soviet control over the organisation had been restored. It was then agreed to create a collective leadership of the seven CPC vice-presidents, under Nikodim, and with the Polish Dr. J. Makowski as the new secretary-general (he was subsequently replaced by the present incumbent, the Hungarian Bishop Karoly Toth).

Brian Norris, one of the British delegates to the Fifth All-Christian Peace Assembly, held in Prague in 1978, subsequently reported on his experience:

> I sat in for an absent member of the drafting committee which helped draw up the many propaganda tracts issued by the Assembly. We sat in a back room of the Hotel Prinz and a patchwork of Kremlin-type policies was stitched together with pious words and a sprinkling of biblical peace texts. That the CPC is a pro-Communist movement seems to me to be self-evident. There is no need to wade through all the reports, statements, analysis and sermons emanating from the Prague headquarters to have any doubts about the CPC's Marxist stance . . . The word 'peace', as used by the CPC, cannot be taken at its face value. (*Religion in Communist Lands*, Vol. 7, No. 3, Autumn 1979).

Declared aims

According to the *Yearbook of International Organisations* (1986–87), the CPC aims to:

> dedicate itself to the service of friendship, reconciliation and the peaceful cooperation of nations, to concentrate the energies of Christian believers all over the world in united action for peace; to coordinate peace groups in individual churches, and facilitate their common effective participation in the peaceful development of human society.

There is nothing wrong with this, apart from the tell-tale

repetition of the word 'peace'. For the real aims of the CPC one has to examine the identity of the key office-holders and the way in which Communist control is exercised.

Organisation and Membership
The highest CPC organ is the approximately quinquennial All-Christian Peace Assembly, which elects a Committee for the Continuation of Work, with about 180 members, to run the organisation in the meantime. This Committee meets about every 18 months; a Working committee of 55 members meets about every six months and the International Secretariat, which has 26 members, meets three times a year. The Working Committee appoints a Study Department (to deal with long term policy) and various Study Commissions which concern themselves with specialised research. Currently there are Study Commissions, each with from twenty to fifty members, dealing with theology, economics, racism, youth, women and international affairs. There are sub-commissions on Indochina, European security, disarmament, the Middle East and the United Nations.

There are CPC affiliates or national committees in 78 countries. Membership is open to both the clergy and laity and cooperating churches or so-called 'Christian associations'.

Office holders
CPC's leading officials are (1987): President: Dr. Karoly TOTH (Hungary); Vice-Presidents: Dr. Richard ANDRIAMANJATO (Madagascar), Prof. Sergio ARCE-MARTINEZ (Cuba), Prof. Gerhard BASSARAK (GDR), Dr. Alexei BUYEVSKI (USSR), Metropolitan Paulos Mar GREGORIOS (India), Rev. Shoji HIRAYAMA (Japan), Dr. Jan MICHALKO (Czechoslovakia), Metropolitan NESTOR (Romania), Rev. Hans-Joachim OEFFLER (FRG), Metropolitan PANKRATI (Bulgaria), Prof. Luis RIVERA Pagan (Puerto Rico), Bernadeen SILVA (Sri Lanka), Rev. VO Tanh Trinh (Vietnam), Alice WIMER (USA), Canon Kenyon E. WRIGHT (UK); Honorary Presidium Members: Bishop Tibor BARTHA (Hungary), Nadeje HROMADKOVA (Czechoslovakia), Bishop Sergio MENDEZ Arceo (Mexico), Dr. Herbert MOCHALSKI (FRG), Pope SHENOUDA III (Egypt); Secretary-General: Dr. Lubomir MIREJOVSKY (Czechoslovakia); Deputy Secretaries-General: Archpriest Georgi GONCHAROV (USSR). Rev. Christie ROSA (Sri Lanka), Rev. Christoph SCHMAUCH (USA); Director of Central Office: Rev. Ferenc DUSICZA (Hungary).

Canon Wright, an active participant in the CPC's affairs, is Secretary of the Scottish Churches Council.

Publications
CPC has two main publications, namely the quarterly *Christian Peace Conference* (circulation at least 10,000) in English and German and a monthly bulletin, *CPC Information* (circulation about 3,000), in English and German. The Information Department also issues books and brochures as required.

Finance
The CPC statutes state that all activities and administrative costs

> shall be financed from voluntary current contributions and donations by the member churches, regional committees, groups and individuals adhering to the CPC. The financial resources of the movement are disposed of by the president, the chairperson of the Continuation Committee and the General Secretary in accordance with the budget approved by the Working Committee.

It is also recorded elsewhere in the statutes that all members, corporate or individual are expected 'to contribute financially' to CPC (voluntarily or otherwise). The Sub-Committee on Oversight of the US House of Representatives asserted in February 1980 that, at that time, CPC was in receipt of a Soviet subsidy estimated at US$ 210,000.

A report of the CPC's Finance Department of April 1987, which gives figures for the 1988 Budget, shows that, of a total local currency income of 3.65 billion Czech crowns, one third is expected from the Czech Committee and virtually all the remainder from East European and Soviet sources, and of a US dollar income of $80,000, half is due from Soviet and East European sources.

Relations with Other Bodies
(1) United Nations The CPC has consultative status with UNESCO and ECOSOC (both Category II) and is frequently represented at UN special committee meetings. It has a Permanent Liaison Office attached to UN headquarters in New York which is run by Dr. Philip OKE (US) and the Canadian Mrs. Winifred SEIGEL. It is also on the board of the unofficial Conference of Non-Governmental Organisations (CONGO) which has consultative status with ECOSOC.

(2) Other International Front Organisations The CPC has always maintained particularly close ties with the WPC and its president serves on the WPC Presidential Committee. It was actively involved in the WPC's World Congress of Peace Forces in Moscow in 1973, and, in September 1983, the CPC International Secretariat welcomed its involvement in the WPC's Prague Peace Assembly, held three months previously, which it opined 'had generated an enormous amount of ideas and propositions for peace work'.

CPC also has working links with the International Committee on European Security and Cooperation (ICESC)* and, more important, with the Berlin Conference of European Catholics (BC)* which was originally founded on CPC initiative, and the Asian Buddhist Conference for Peace ABCP*.

The CPC has close working links with the other Soviet-controlled front organisations and participates from time to time in the regular liaison meetings.

(3) Non-Communist Organisations CPC's posture is that of a genuine bridge-building organisation directly associated with all churchmen of goodwill in east and west. In its statutes, CPC claims that it:

> forms part of the worldwide ecumenical movement. In this sense it is prepared for neighbourly cooperation for peace and justice with all bodies and agencies of the World Council of Churches, with confessional world associations and other ecumenical organisations. Correspondingly, the continental CPC bodies may maintain relationships with their respective ecumenical counterparts.

In pursuit of these objectives the CPC makes every effort to increase its influence in, and enhance its status with, the World Council of Churches. CPC's overtures have also been particularly directed, in recent years, towards such groupings as the Conference of European Churches, the All-African Church Conference and Pax Christi International.

Assemblies

The 'highest CPC organ' is, under its statutes, the All-Christian Peace Assembly which, 'convoked by the Working Committee, shall meet every five to seven years. It shall determine the fundamental basis of the movement's work . . . Participants in the All-Christian Peace Assembly shall be delegates with the right to vote, observers, experts and guests'.

All such Assemblies since the First inaugural Assembly in 1961 have been held in Prague. There have been five so far since 1961—in 1964, 1968, 1971, 1978 and 1985. The Fourth Assembly in 1974 characterised 'western imperialism' as 'the greatest threat to the peaceful existence of mankind', rejected pacifism (since it 'does not distinguish between just and unjust peace'), and pledged support for liberation (*The Tablet*, London, 22 July 1978). The last—or sixth—Assembly in July 1985 was attended by over 500 people, about 360 of whom represented about 90 countries. On that occasion, half the delegates were non-European and, among 78 observers, there were two from China. The seventh Assembly, expected to be held in Prague between 1990 and 1992, has not so far been announced.

Other activities
The Soviet Union has made a major effort to extend CPC influence internationally, both on its own account and through such related organisations as the ABCP. The then secretary-general told the Fourth All Christian Peace Assembly in Prague in September 1971 that 'more militants' from the developing world 'should be recruited for the CPC . . . Representatives of the Third World have never been so numerous as today, when they constitute nearly 40 per cent of this Assembly.'

During the course of the 1970s, three 'Continental CPCs' were established, in Africa, Asia and Latin America and the Caribbean. In the same period a number of national regional committees, many of which had collapsed after 1968, were established or re-established (the British Regional Committee is run from London). A North American Regional CPC was set up in New York in October 1987.

In June 1977, the CPC helped the WPC to organise an International Peace Conference of Religious Figures, originally suggested at a meeting in Zagorsk, USSR, of religious delegates to the WPC's World Conference of Peace Forces in 1973 and eventually held in Moscow, ostensibly on the initiative of the Russian Orthodox Church. Subsequently the CPC was also involved in the preparations for the World Conference of Religious Leaders for Saving the Sacred Gift of Life from Nuclear Catastrophe, held in Moscow in May 1982. It cooperates with the continuing Working Presidium of the World Conference* which has held similar religious peace conferences in Moscow annually since that date.

In May 1983 the CPC organised a Consultation on Disarmament in Budapest and, in September 1984, an international theological seminar under the title Towards a Theology of Peace (this last arranged in conjunction with seven other non-communist organisations was repeated in December 1987). It also held symposia in Prague in December 1984 and November 1987 under the title, Global Threat to Humanity: Global Strategy for Peace.

In the words of a former CPC secretary-general, Bohuslav POSPISIL, in the CPC, 'Christians openly and sincerely march side by side with the progressive elements of society—the Communists' (quoted in *The Tablet*, London, 22 July 1978).

4. International Association of Democratic Lawyers

The International Association of Democratic Lawyers (IADL) is also known under its French, German and Spanish titles which are, respectively, *Association internationale des juristes démocrates, Internationale Vereinigung der Demokratischen Juristen* and *Asociación Internacional de Juristas Democráticas*. Its headquarters is at 263 Avenue Albert, 1180 Brussels, Belgium.

Origins
The IADL was founded in 1946, in Paris at an International Congress of Jurists convened by an organisation under strong communist influence, the Mouvement National Judiciaire, but attended by many non-communist lawyers. The latter were mostly unaware of the meeting's political origins but had been moved, partly as a result of the horrors discussed at the Nuremberg War Trials to support the idea, originally sponsored by the Soviet Professor Avon N. Trainin, of establishing an international group of this kind. The inaugural congress elected a bureau whose non-Communist members were some of the most widely respected lawyers in the democratic countries. But the Communists effectively controlled the fledgling organisation from the beginning and, by 1949, most of its non-Communist supporters had left, partly in reaction to the IADL's decision to expel its Yugoslav supporters solely in response to Stalin's breach with Tito (the Yugoslav IADL branch was found guilty of being 'active in the slanderous campaign against the Soviet Union, against the peoples' democracies and against the workers' movement in the whole world'). In 1950 the French Government formally expelled the organisation from France, where it had had its headquarters in Paris since 1946. The IADL thereupon moved

to Brussels (although for some years certain IADL activities were controlled from Warsaw).

The Communist group which controlled IADL from the start deliberately emphasised its links with its pre-war Comintern predecessor, the International Association of Red Jurists and the later International Juridical Association (IJA). In 1948 a Czechoslovak Communist lawyer is reported to have welcomed the Third IADL Congress held in Prague in 1948 as a direct continuation of the earlier movement, which had been sponsored by the Comintern and which had convened a celebrated international congress of lawyers in Moscow in November 1927. There were many direct links between the pre-war IJA and the post-war IADL, not least the fact that the IJA's former secretary, Hilde NEUMANN, reappeared in 1951 to serve as secretary to the IADL Bureau (and no doubt to serve as a living link with the Comintern).

The Stalinist character of the IADL during the Cold War years was undisguised. Its secretary-general, Joe NORDMANN, was a French lawyer who belonged to the French CP under Maurice THOREZ: even after Stalin's death, he was to attack the critics of the Soviet invasion of Hungary in 1956 as akin to:

> those pacifists whose petty bourgeois ideology may be sincere and responsible but [who] will always remain alien to the interests of the working class . . . We stand firmly on the positions of proletarian internationalism . . . The leaders of our party . . . incarnate the Marxist–Leninist vanguard of the French working class.

At that time the IADL president was the late D. N. PRITT, a well-known British barrister and sometime pro-Communist MP. Pritt was notorious for, among other testimonies, recording in August 1936, at the time of Stalin's show trials, 'I personally attended the trial in Moscow . . . I am satisfied that the case was properly conducted and the accused fairly and judicially treated . . . They voluntarily renounced counsel and addressed the court freely . . . I consider the whole procedure and treatment of the prisoners throughout the trial as an example to the world.' Subsequently Pritt, while IADL president, was to declare in Budapest in April 1950, six years before Moscow suppressed the Hungarian workers' revolution, 'those of us who work in western Europe have to face great difficulties . . . But I can assure you, colleagues from the countries of people's democracy, we shall not withdraw from the fight before we have secured victory.'

Declared aims

IADL's original statutes committed the organisation:

1. To develop mutual understanding among the lawyers of the world;
2. To support the aims of the United Nations, especially through common action for the defence of democratic liberties;
3. To cooperate with other groups to ensure respect for the rule of law in international relations and the establishment of a durable peace.

These apparently irreproachable views have recently been complemented in the annual *Yearbook of International Organisations* (1986–87), by the following aims:

> To facilitate contact and exchange among lawyers in order to develop a spirit of mutual understanding and fraternity; encourage study of legal science and international law, and support democratic principles favourable to maintenance of peace and cooperation between nations; promote independence of all peoples, and oppose any restriction thereof, whether by legislation or practice.

Organisation and Membership

The IADL, whose organisational links with the pre-war Comintern are more apparent than most of the current Soviet controlled international front organisations, is ultimately controlled by its Congress, which is supposed to meet at intervals of three years. Congress in turn elects the Council, which meets annually and consists of the officers and representatives of affiliated organisations, and the governing Bureau. There is also a Secretariat.

In 1958 the IADL claimed a total membership of 150,000, recruited through affiliated national groups and sections as well as individually, in 83 countries.

Office holders

The current IADL president (1987) is the aforementioned French Communist, Joe NORDMANN, who also represents IADL on the WPC. Other officials are Secretary-General: Amar BENTOUMI (Algeria); Secretaries: Eduardo BARCESAT (Argentina), Tudor DRAGANU (Romania), Ahmed EL HILALY (Egypt), Lennox S. HINDS (USA), Sergio INSUNZA (Chile), Lorand JOKAI (Hungary), Pierre LAVIGNE (France), M.V. MAZOV (USSR), Nelly MINYERSKI (Argentina), Ugo NATOLI (Italy), PHAN Anh (Vietnam), Kazuyoshi SAITO (Japan), Jitendra SHARMA (India), Roland WEYL (France); Treasurer; Heinrich TOEPLITZ (GDR).

Publications and Information
The IADL issues twice yearly a *Review of Contemporary Law* in English and French and also publishes, at irregular intervals, an *Information Bulletin*, as well as other pamphlets as required.

Finance
The IADL, which does not publish its accounts, claims, as do all the Soviet international front organisations, to be funded by its affiliation fees and by donations.

The Sub-Committee on Oversight of the US House of Representatives asserted in February 1980 that, at that time IADL was in receipt of a Soviet subsidy estimated at US$ 100,000.

Relations with other bodies
(1) United Nations The IADL had consultative status Category II with ECOSOC from its foundation until 1950, when this status was rescinded after the organisation had described 'the armed intervention of the UN in Korea as an act of aggression according to the international law . . . [and] in violation of all stipulations of the Charter referring to the use of armed force by the United Nations.' Subsequently, after many unsuccessful attempts to gain readmission to ECOSOC in the 1950s, the IADL was allowed back. It currently once again enjoys Category II status with ECOSOC and Category B status with UNESCO. Its Permanent Representative at the UN (New York) is Lennox HINDS (USA) and at the UN (Geneva) Mrs. Solange BOUVIER-AJAM (France), at the UN International Centre in Vienna, Dr. Heinrich DÜRMAYER (Austria) and at UNESCO, Armando URIBE (Chile). There are also two Assistant Representatives, Richard HARVEY (UK) and Leora MOSSTON (USA), in New York, and an Assistant Representative, Renee BRIDEL (Switzerland), in Geneva. In September 1985, the IADL was elected to the board of the unofficial Committee of Non-Governmental Organisations in Consultative Status with ECOSOC (CONGO).

(2) Other international front organisations The IADL has especially close links with the WPC. In the early 1950s it supported the WPC and the Women's International Democratic Federation (WIDF)* in concerted allegations that UN forces had committed war crimes, and had resorted to the use of germ warfare, in Korea. It also assisted the World Federation of Trade Unions (WFTU)* in its protest to the Austrian Government

against its expulsion from Vienna in 1956. More recently, the IADL and the WFTU Legal Commission jointly set up a Working Group on Labour Law (they have also co-sponsored three International Seminars for European Trade Union Lawyers), and the IADL and the International Organisation of Journalists (IOJ)* have jointly set up an International Committee for the Defence of Journalists' Rights (in October 1981).

The IADL has close working links with the other Soviet-controlled front organisations and participates from time to time in the regular liaison meetings.

(3) Non-Communist Organisations The IADL cooperated with the non-Communist International Commission of Jurists (ICJ) and the International Institute of Human Rights (Strasbourg) in organising a Conference on Human Rights in Namibia (Dakar, January 1976). It has also from time to time had working links with such bodies as the International Institute for Human Rights and the International Association of Catholic Lawyers.

National Affiliates
The IADL has a large number of national affiliates throughout the world, including the Haldane Society in the United Kingdom, which was originally founded in the 1930s as a society of British socialist lawyers, which was disaffiliated by the Labour Party in 1949 on account of its subservience to the Communist Party, and the National Lawyers' Guild in the US.

Subsidiaries
The IADL has over the course of time established a succession of specialist commissions in support of current Soviet propaganda themes, staffed mainly by Communist lawyers and intended to create an impression of impartiality. In 1952 there was a Commission of Enquiry on Korea, which visited that area from March to April of that year: it was composed of eight lawyers selected by the IADL, four of whom were known Communists. On March 2, before their inquiry had begun, the Soviet TASS agency announced that; 'The Commission was sent to Korea in accordance with the decision of the IADL to investigate and establish the crimes committed by interventionists in Korea.' As expected, the Commission subsequently announced in a telegram to the IADL President that it had gathered 'indisputable evidence' of germ warfare. Later, in its official report, the Commission claimed that its investigations had convinced it that

the facts, 'verified with all the vigour of judicial discipline', constituted 'an act of aggression committed by the United States, an
act of genocide and a particularly odious crime against humanity'.
(The campaign was later exposed by returning prisoners of war
as a fraud; the 'evidence' was based entirely on 'confessions'
signed by captured airmen under duress). This was followed in
1954 by the Commission on the Karlsruhe Trial 'to examine the
Karlsruhe trial of the organisers of the Referendum against the
remilitarisation of Western Germany'. The Referendum had in
fact been organised by the West German Communist Party; the
Commission consisted mainly of IADL officers and met twice in
Paris. It condemned the trial as 'a trial of opinion, worthy of . . .
Hitler and Mussolini'. In 1956 there followed the Commission
on WFTU Expulsion from Vienna, created at the request of the
WFTU, 'to study what action should be taken concerning the
publication and use of forged documents which were used as a
pretext by the Austrian Ministry of the Interior for expelling the
WFTU Headquarters from Vienna and for arbitrarily seizing its
goods'. The Commission consisted of the then Secretary-
General, Joe Nordmann, a Soviet lawyer and a Japanese
Professor of Law, Yoshitaro Hirano, who was an IADL Vice-
President and a WPC Bureau member.

In 1963, the IADL established an International Commission
for the Investigation of American War Crimes in Vietnam, later
supplanted by the Stockholm Conference on Vietnam, a WPC
subsidiary. An International Committee of Lawyers for Democracy and Human Rights in South Korea was set up in Paris
under the aegis of the IADL in October 1976; a Permanent
International Legal Commission on Palestine and on Peace in
the Middle East in October 1982: and an International
Commission of Enquiry into the Case of Sergei Antonov (a
Bulgarian implicated in the attempted assassination of the Pope)
was set up by the 12th Congress, October 1984.

Congresses
There have been twelve Congresses since the IADL's foundation
in Paris in October 1946. The second Congress was held in
Brussels in July 1947. Subsequent Congresses have been Prague
(September 1948), Rome (October 1949), East Berlin
(September 1951), Brussels (May 1956), Sofia (October 1960),
Budapest (March 1964), Helsinki (July 1970), Algiers (April
1975), Valletta (November 1980) and Athens (October 1984).

Other Activities
In August 1969 a Brazilian lawyer commenting on IADL protests against detention without trial in Brazil, stated in the Paris *Le Monde* that the Association had not made similar protests about events in the Soviet Union or Czechoslovakia, adding: 'I do not believe in the IADL's sincerity since it does nothing for political prisoners from Socialist countries, where it has great prestige'. Although the IADL has been represented by observers at trials in such countries as Morocco, Tunisia, Spain, Turkey, Paraguay, Chile and Iran, it has never sent one to a Communist country for a similar purpose. But it supported an International Tribunal on the British Presence in Ireland, called for the release of the late Bobby SANDS, while he was on hunger strike in Belfast, in May 1981, and in July 1981, approached the Special Committee of the Interparliamentary Union on Violations of the Rights of members of Parliaments, drawing attention to the plight of two Irishmen, Kieran DOHERTY and Patrick AGNEW, then imprisoned in Northern Ireland for offences connected with terrorism, on the grounds that having been elected to the Irish Dail in 1981, they were 'prevented from representing their constituents'. In December 1981, the IADL sent an observer to Dublin to attend the trial of demonstrators arrested outside the British Embassy in support of the Belfast prisoners' hunger strike: and in May 1986, it petitioned the Dutch Government not to extradite two IRA terrorists who had escaped from a British prison in 1983 and had been arrested in Amsterdam in 1986 (despite the IADL's efforts they were subsequently returned to British jurisdiction).

The IADL also organised an International Conference against the Threat of War and in Support of the Initiatives in Favour of Peace and International Detente (Moscow, June 1981), a Symposium on the Policy of Forced Disappearances [in Latin America] (Paris, January–February 1981), a Multi-disciplinary Conference on the Transition towards a New International Democratic Order (Mexico City, September 1981), an International Lawyers' Peace Conference (Frankfurt, March 1982), an International Conference on the Indian Ocean—a Zone of Peace (New Delhi, September 1982), an International Conference on The Mediterranean—a Zone of Peace (Algiers, December 1982): there was also a joint meeting with the International Federation of Resistance Fighters (FIR)* in Nuremberg in November 1985 to mark the 40th anniversary of the start of the Nuremberg trials. The IADL was also scheduled to hold an

International Seminar on the Arms Race in Space in Brussels in 1986.

IADL delegations also travel widely. Korea in 1952 was only a start; the Association was represented at the fifth anniversary celebrations of the 'Saharan Arab Democratic Republic' in March 1981: an IADL delegation visited the 'occupied Arab territories', and a joint IADL/WFTU fact-finding mission went to Turkey later in 1981. The Association was also represented at a law seminar, Justice in the Revolution, in Nicaragua in May 1981, organised by the Surpeme Court of Nicaragua, and at an international tribunal enquiring into Israel's Involvement in Lebanon, (Tokyo, March 1983).

The IADL has also taken a far from detached interest in the Soviet military occupation of Afghanistan. In March 1980, soon after Soviet troops invaded the country, an IADL delegation arrived in Kabul and was received by the then President, Babrak Karmal.

5. International Committee for European Security and Cooperation

The International Committee for European Security and Cooperation (ICESC) is also known under its French title, which is *Comité international pour la securité et la coopération européennes*. (It is also known more briefly as European Security and Cooperation or *Securité et coopération européennes*). Its headquarters is at 42 rue Dautzenberg B-1050 Brussels, Belgium.

Origins
When the Soviet Union began to press officially in the early 1960s for the convening of a European Security Conference at governmental level, it also launched in parallel a campaign to influence western public opinion in this sense. In 1963 the WPC was formally entrusted with the task of organising a non-governmental 'European Security Conference'. But, in order to disguise the WPC's hand in this project, an ostensibly independent Belgian group emerged and was given the task of organising the conference and issuing the invitations. Before the plan came to fruition, however, it was disrupted by the Soviet invasion of Czechoslovakia in 1968, and the relatively small meeting held in Vienna in 1969—much smaller than originally envisaged—made little public impact at the time. Plans were immediately

announced for a larger gathering, which, in addition to the WPC, were supported by the International Union of Students (IUS)*, the World Federation of Democratic Youth (WFDY)* and the World Federation of Trade Unions (WFTU)*, although balancing non-Communist support was slow to follow. In 1970 the Soviet Union intervened behind the scenes and, by using its own international contacts, caused a network of National Committees for European Security and Cooperation to be set up, thereby providing a broader base for the proposed international conference. And, in June 1971, a meeting nominally organised by the Belgian National Committee for European Security and Cooperation established an international preparatory committee for the forthcoming conference. That conference, eventually entitled the 'Assembly of Representatives of Public Opinion for European Security and Cooperation', was held in Brussels, 2–5 June 1972, and its working secretariat subsequently became a permanent international secretariat, the present ICESC, with headquarters in Brussels.

Declared Aims

According to the *Yearbook of International Organisations*, 1986–87, the ICESC aims to

> permit public opinion to express options and claims concerning a system of European security and cooperation; ensure representation of this public opinion; promote and support actions based on such ground principles as renunciation of resort to force, inviolability of existing frontiers, non-intervention in domestic affairs, respect of national independence, equality in rights, sovereignty and territorial integrity of European States, respect of the right of peoples to self-determination, peaceful coexistence and good-neighbourhood policy.

An ICESC pamphlet of October 1979 described the organisation's activities as follows:

> The movement of public opinion for European security and cooperation was formed on the initiative of people and pre-existing organisations belonging to different political, social, ideological and religious families from all over Europe. At that time, in various countries, groups and movements of opinion were springing up, which were decided (sic) to support the multilateral endeavours of States and governments aimed at achieving a concerted approach to overcome the 'cold war', and to replace it by one form or another of 'peaceful coexistence' on which could be founded a security other than that of arms, for all the countries of Europe. These endeavours, as is known, led in 1973, to the opening of the Conference on Security and Cooperation in Europe (CSCE) and to the signature by the heads of State

and government of the 35 participating countries on 1st August 1975, in Helsinki, of the Final Act of the Conference.

For their part, the movements of public opinion contributed towards the success of the inter-governmental Conference by supporting it through broad sectors of the population in all spheres and, before long, national committees and international organisations. It was the main *raison d'être* of the two Assemblies of Representatives of Public Opinion which were held in Brussels in 1972, and in Brussels and Liège in 1975, and which gave birth and life to the International Committee for European Security and Cooperation: ICESC. Whilst saluting the accomplishment of the CSCE, the ICESC does not feel, nevertheless, that its mission is over. On the contrary, it considers that it is most important to continue to work for the implementation and development of the Helsinki agreements in all their dimensions and in all respects. It coordinates the action of its own national committees, circles and forums, as well as other gatherings of public opinion, instituted in practically all the countries of Europe; it collaborates too, in various forms, with numerous non-governmental organisations, itself enjoying consultative status with the UN and UNESCO.

Organisation and Membership

The International Committee meets at least twice a year, usually in Brussels, the International Secretariat four times a year, and the Permanent Secretariat six times a year.

The ICESC has National Committees or National Groups in 26 European countries (including Cyprus).

Office Holders

Members of the Permanent Secretariat are:

DE GENDT, Robert	(Belgium) secretary-general
GOOR Canon, Raymond	(Belgium) former president
CLAEYS, Herman	(Belgium)
DE CONINCK, Albert	(Belgium)
DE SMAELE, Albert	(Belgium)
GALAND, Pierre	(Belgium)
GAILLARD, Albert	(France)
HAUCOTTE, André	(Belgium)
LEONARD, André	(Belgium)
LINDEMANS, Ignaas	(Belgium)
POLGAR, Denes	(Belgium)
SILIN, Yevgeni	(USSR)
VAN EYNDE, Jos	(Belgium)

Publications and Information

The ICESC publishes its *Internal Information Bulletin* quarterly, in English, French and German, and proceedings and reports also in those languages. In 1980 it published *From Helsinki to Madrid*.

Finance

No details are published of ICESC finances. But the Belgian newspaper, *Gazet Van Antwerpen* (27 February 1985) commented on the source of revenue for an *ad hoc* Forum which the Committee held in Brussels, 28 February to 3 March:

> The cost of organisation of the Forum is estimated at 5,390,000 BF of which only 900,000 BF is covered by the participation fees.
>
> Without wanting to insinuate anything, it is worthwhile to look into past statements on the financing of these congresses.
>
> The answer is near at hand: the head of the [CPSU] International Department is coming to Brussels on 28 February and it is this party body that controls the Soviet Peace Fund.
>
> This 'peace bank' is based at the Kropotskinskaya 10 in Moscow and served to finance the 'peace campaigns' in East and West. . . .
>
> As one recalls, the Belgian organisers of the Brussels Forum were in Moscow only last week. There they had talks with Vadim Zagladin, well known to them, who controls the activities and organisation of the Communist parties in the West. When this top official was himself still a member of the International Committee . . . he declared in the Austrian communist paper *Arbeiter Zeitung* (21 May 1982), in reply to the question about what happened to the money of the Soviet Peace Fund: There are several peace committees for 'European Security'. They issue newspapers and all Soviet participants to the peace demonstrations in Vienna, Amsterdam or Brussels are financed by the Fund.

Relations with Other Bodies

(1) United Nations The ICESC has category II Status with ECOSOC and Category C Status with UNESCO.

(2) Other International Front Organisations Most of the Soviet international front organisations send delegates to ICESC assemblies. Canon Raymond Goor (Belgium), until recently the ICESC president, served as an observer on the WPC's Presidental Committee.

(3) Non-Communist Organisations Although delegates from several non-Communist international organisations attend ICESC meetings, the ICESC's main aim is to make contact with delegations to meetings of the countries participating in the series of Conferences on Security and Cooperation in Europe, (the follow-up to the 1975 Helsinki Final Act) rather than the 'mass organisations'.

The ICESC also shares an address, telephone number with another organisation, Arms Reduction in Europe.

National Affiliates
There is a British Committee for European Security and Cooperation, which is under the chairmanship of Gordon Schaffer, a WPC Presidential Committee member. There is also a similar national committee in the Republic of Ireland. The dominant affiliate is, of course, the Soviet Committee for European Security and Cooperation (SCESC)*.

ICESC's Policies
The ICESC follows the Soviet Government's policies on European security and disarmament. At its meeting in Brussels in May 1987, it discussed prospects for European security in the light of the latest Soviet disarmament initiatives.

Assemblies
The ICESC has held Assemblies of Representatives of Public Opinion for European Security and Cooperation in Brussels, June 1972 and Brussels and Liege, April 1975. It held a European Forum for Disarmament and Security in De Haan (Ostend), Belgium in October 1979 and an International Forum for Peace and Security in Europe in Brussels in February–March 1985.

The first Assembly in 1972 was attended by about 1,000 participants from 28 countries, mainly East Europeans and their sympathisers or supporters in the West. According to Romesh Chandra, the WPC President, the WPC 'took a leading part' in its preparation and members of its Presidential Committee 'were among the principal organisers and leaders of activities in support of the Assembly'. Meetings of specialised groups were held—such as for women, young people, trade unionists and churchmen—and the final statement endorsed 'peaceful co-existence and good neighbourliness' as one of seven fundamental principles of security and cooperation. Other principles included renunciation of the use of force, the inviolability of existing frontiers and non-intervention in internal affairs of European states.

In an article in the *Gazet Van Antwerpen* (26 February 1985) published at the time of the ICESC forum held in Brussels February–March 1985, the ICESC was described as having served 'as a mouthpiece for Soviet proposals on "peace policy" for 13 years'. The Soviet delegation was reported to have included, in

addition to Vitaly Shaposhnikov, one of the deputy heads of the
International Department of the CPSU, members of the Central
Committee of the Supreme Soviet and Soviet officials of *Pravda*
and of the State press agency, *Novosti*.

The same newspaper reported on the following day that:

> The real initiators of the coming congress are seven Belgians working in the
> Brussels office of European Security . . . These are Jan De Brouwere
> (member of the Central Committee of the Belgian Communist party);
> Raymond Goor (international Lenin prize winner and member of the Presi-
> dential Committee of the communist led World Peace Council; Pierre Galand
> (president of the CNAPD, a peace organisation), Ignaas Lindemans (Pax
> Christi); Albert De Smaele (founder-administrator of the Belgium Soviet
> Union Association which according to *De Morgan* has good contacts with
> the Soviet capital); Robert De Gendt (secretary of the International
> Committee) and the aged Jos Van Eynde, who only gave his name and who
> did not take part in the meetings. The only foreigners in the Brussels office
> of the Committee are the French communist Albert Gaillard and the Soviet
> official Yevgeni Silin . . . The departments of the committee in other coun-
> tries have the same profile. Many of the top people of the Committee also
> represent their countries in the Communist World Peace Council. Most
> significant, however, are the close contacts of the International Committee
> with the two bureaux of the Central Committee of the Communist Party of
> the Soviet Union . . . The presence, on Thursday, of Vitaly Shaposhnikov
> (62) reveals, particularly, the intricate network through which Moscow is
> leading the Forum. At the International Department, Shaposhnikov is head
> of the geographic sector 'Scandinavia' and assistant head of the sector 'Latin
> Europe' to which Belgium belongs . . . In this function he monitors all the
> communist parties and undercover organisations in these areas. Also those
> in Belgium. The most interesting fact is that Shaposhnikov is in charge of
> the special sector of the so-called peace activities; he has to report directly
> to the party bureau in Moscow on the activities in the West under his
> supervision . . . For several years Shaposhnikov headed the Soviet section
> of the International Organisation for Security and Cooperation in Europe.

6. International Federation of Resistance Fighters (FIR)

The International Federation of Resistance Fighters (FIR) is
also known under its French title—*Fédération internationale des
résistants*, from which the acronym FIR is derived—and also
under its German and Spanish titles which are, respectively,
Internationale Föderation der Widerstandskämpfer and *Federación Internacional de Resistentes*. Its headquarters is at Alliierten-
strasse 2–4/5 A–1020, Vienna, Austria.

Origins

The FIR's origin is rather different from that of other post-war communist international front organisations. Originally, it was an organisation for former political prisoners of the Nazis (Stalin had no interest in the survivors, if any, from his own camps): it was founded in Warsaw in 1946 as the International Federation of Former Political Prisoners (FIAPP) and it was the first such body to try to group the survivors of Hitler's prisons and concentration camps in an organisation under Soviet control. In 1950, however, FIAPP suffered an internal crisis arising from Stalin's exclusion of Yugoslavia from the Cominform, an action echoed in all the Soviet-controlled front organisations at that time. FIAPP fell into line and expelled all former Yugoslav political prisoners for refusing to condemn Tito and 'his fascist clique'. The ensuing argument was resolved when, in June 1951, FIAPP was submerged in a new international front organisation which, for the first time, mainly included survivors of the wartime resistance movements, many of which had been under communist influence: the resulting body, founded on 3 July 1951 at a congress in Vienna, was the FIR. (The non-communists, who had hitherto supported FIAPP, had refused to join the new body and broke away to found, in November 1950, the World Veterans' Federation).

From the first, as intended by its Soviet sponsors, the communists dominated the new body. Their position was strengthened, by allowing the FIR to be managed, in the absence of the (communist) secretary-general, by the deputy secretary-general, 'collectively with one member of the Secretariat'.

In common with the other international front organisations, the FIR as a body never condemned violations of human rights in communist countries, defended the political prisoners who managed to obtain release from Soviet prisons, expressed any unease when the East German régime granted a general amnesty to former Nazis (in 1952) nor when the Soviet Union granted a free pardon to 'nearly 9,000 Nazi criminals'. Nor did FIR protest when the Soviet Red Army intervened in Hungary in 1956 or Czechoslovakia in 1968, although on the latter occasion the Italian president of FIR, Senator Arialdo BANFI, did attempt, without success, to persuade his Communist colleagues to register a protest (the official text subsequently issued by the FIR congress in Venice, in 1969, where doubts were expressed about the Soviet invasion of Czechoslovakia, did not even once mention the name of that country).

Declared Aims
The FIR's official aims are to

> unite resisters as in wartime resistance movements to secure the independence
> of their country, liberty and world peace; defend the spirit and values of the
> Resistance; make known its historical role and transmit its teaching to new
> generations; contribute to the defence of the material and moral interests of
> those having due rights and causes; create and develop social services in their
> aid; promote aims set out in the UN Charter and strengthen links of fraternity
> and solidarity between resisters in all countries; oppose racial, political,
> philosophical or religious discrimination, neofascism, imprescriptibility of war
> crimes and crimes against humanity; work for disarmament and détente.
> (*Yearbook of International Organisations*, 1986–87).

These bland aims intentionally conceal as much as they reveal
about the FIR's functions.

Organisation and Membership
As with other organisations of this stamp, the supreme FIR body
is the Congress, originally supposed to meet every three years
(amended in 1969 to 'not more than every four years'). The
General Council should meet annually. The Bureau, which is
convened by the Secretariat, is expected to meet 'at least once
a year'. It is the Secretariat, however, in which real power
resides. There are also a Financial Control Commission,
Commissions on Reparations and Fascism, and Historical,
Medical, Legal and Social Commissions.

The FIR claims an affiliated membership of over 5 million
members (three million of whom are 'full members') in 26 countries, all (with the exception of Israel) in Europe. Yugoslavia has
observer status.

Office holders
The leading officers, elected in 1982 for four years, were: Presi-
dent: Arialdo BANFI (Italy); Secretary-General: Alix LHOTE
(France); Vice-Presidents: Marcos ANA (Spain), Dr. Vladimir
BONEV (Bulgaria), Jean BRACK (Belgium), Otto FUNKE
(GDR), Maron ISPANOVITS (Hungary), Josef KAMINSKI
(Poland), Helge-Theil KIERULFF (Denmark), Spyros
KOTSAKIS (Greece), Alexei Petrovich MARESYEV (USSR),
Frantisek MISEJE (Czechoslovakia), Andrei NEAGU
(Romania), Dr. Josef ROSSAINT (FRG), Dr. Ludwig
SOSWINSKI (Austria), Mario VENANZI (Italy), Robert
VOLLET (France).

Publications and Information

The FIR publishes monthly, in French and German, *Résistance Unie/Service d'Information* (for which it used to claim a circulation of 15,000, now certainly considerably less) and, quarterly, *Cahiers d'Information Médicales, Sociales et Juridiques*, also in French and German. There are also reports and pamphlets published as required and, in 1958, the FIR exceptionally published a brief history, *Sept Années au service de la Résistance et de son idéal*.

Finance

The FIR does not regularly publish any accounts, but claims to be financed by affiliation fees, donations and other subventions of various kinds. The Sub-Committee on Oversight of the US House of Representatives asserted in February 1980 that, at that time, FIR was in receipt of a Soviet subsidy estimated at US$ 215,000.

Relations with other bodies

(1) United Nations The FIR has Category II status with ECOSOC and the corresponding Category B status with UNESCO.

(2) Other international front organisations The FIR has close working links with the other Soviet-controlled front organisations, and participates from time to time in the regular liaison meetings.

(3) Non-Communist Organisations In recent years the FIR has participated, with the non-communist World Veterans' Federation, the European Confederation of Ex-Servicemen and the International Confederation of Former Prisoners of War, in an *ad hoc* Coordinating Committee which now organises periodic 'world conferences on disarmament'. The International Union of Resistance and Deportee Movements, however, continues to reject the FIR's approaches for joint action: it has consistently maintained this line since FIR's inception, arguing that the FIR's national affiliates have always been governed by communists who, although undoubtedly resistance members, 'defended Communist interest and exploited the Resistance for Moscow's benefit' (*Résistance*, No. 140–141, October 1969, organ of the non-communist International Union of Resistance and Deportee Movements).

Congresses
The FIR's founding Congress was held in Vienna in June–July 1951, as were subsequent Congresses in November 1954 and March 1959. The fourth Congress was held in Warsaw (December, 1962), the fifth in Budapest (December 1965), the sixth in Venice (November 1969), the seventh in Paris (November 1973), the eighth in Minsk (May 1978), the ninth in East Berlin (September 1982) and the tenth in Athens (May 1987).

Other Activities
The FIR organised an International Conference on Legislation and the Rights of Resistance Fighters in Brussels in October 1955 and, two years later, an International Physicians' Conference in Moscow. FIR also held 'international symposia on Fascism' in Frankfurt, West Germany, in 1980 and in Perg, Austria, in 1984. In the past 'holiday camps' were regularly staged for the relief of the 'orphans of resistance fighters and other victims of Nazism'.

7. International Institute for Peace

The International Institute for Peace (IIP) is also known under its French, German and Spanish titles which are, respectively, *Institut international de la paix*, *Internationales Institut für den Frieden* and *Instituto Internacional pro Paz*. Its headquarters is at Estate Haus, Möllwaldplatz, 5, A–1040 Vienna, Austria.

Origins
Its address is the key to the origins of the IIP. It is that which from 1954–57 officially housed the WPC* and which in practice, from 1957–68 remained—clandestinely—the address from which the WPC was still being run.

The IIP was only established in July 1957 about three months after the WPC's official expulsion, to provide a convenient legal cover for the WPC. The WPC tries to pretend that the IIP was in fact founded by 'a decree of the Austrian Federal Ministry of the Interior' (*New Perspectives*, No. 1, 1973). It is, in fact, both a direct offshoot, and a subsidiary of the WPC, as well as having become in the intervening years an international front organisation in its own right. Since 1968 the IIP has concentrated on 'research' into peace and disarmament issues and on sustaining a dialogue between Marxism–Leninism and Christianity.

Declared Aims

The IIP held a constituent general meeting in July 1957 to agree to its articles of association. Officially, it is 'a forum where scientists from east and west can discuss the results of their research into all aspects of the peace problem, irrespective of their ideology of methodology . . . Its whole activity is oriented towards the study of the possibilities, principles and forms of peaceful co-existence and cooperation between the two social world systems . . .' (*New Perspectives*, No. 1, 1973).

Organisation and Membership

The IIP is governed by its General Assembly, which is supposed to meet at least once every three years and, between Assemblies, by its Presidential Committee, Executive Board and Scientific Council. The Presidential Committee includes a number of WPC members.

There are member organisations in Austria, Bulgaria, Czechoslovakia, Finland, the Federal Republic of Germany, the German Democratic Republic, Hungary, Poland and the Soviet Union.

IIP membership is open to both individuals and, corporately to societies and institutions. The IIP has members in 25 countries.

Office holders

The President (1987) is Dr. Georg FUCHS (Austria), who is a WPC member (representing the IIP); the office is under the control of the Administrative Director, Boris SHPEYER (USSR).

The WPC members of the Presidential Committee include: Professor Gerhard KADE (West Germany), the original administrator of Generals for Peace and Disarmament*, Dr. Josef MUDROCH (Czechoslovakia), Treasurer: Professor Marios NIKOLINAKOS (Greece), Professor Max SCHMIDT (German Democratic Republic), and Professor Janusz SYMONIDES (Poland).

The WPC President, Romesh Chandra, is a member of the Executive Committee.

Publication

The IIP publishes *Peace and Sciences* quarterly in English and German.

Finance

The IIP follows the common International Front Organisation practice; it does not usually publish accounts. An insight into the scale of its finances, however, was provided in 1973 when it was stated that:

> the scientific activity of the Institute is financed by its regular and honorary members in various countries. As of 1 January 1973 there were 26 honorary members (membership fee, five hundred US dollars per year) and 106 regular members (five US dollars per year). The budget for 1973 amounted to 1,056,000 Austrian Schillings (*New Perspectives*, No. 1, 1973).

It should be noted that since 1973, the scale of IIP operations has considerably expanded, with obvious implications for its finances.

The Sub-Committee on Oversight of the US House of Representatives asserted in February 1980 that, at that time, the IIP was in receipt of a Soviet subsidy estimated at US$ 260,000.

Relations with other bodies

(1) United Nations The IIP has Category B status with UNESCO and consultative status (roster) with ECOSOC.

(2) Other International Front Organisations The IIP is in one sense an adjunct of the WPC and in 1970 was described by a Czechoslovak professor, Josef LUKAS, who was then on the WPC Presidential Committee, as 'the scientific-theoretical workplace of the WPC' [in effect, the WPC's think tank]. It has frequently co-sponsored activities with the ILF*. It also now has especially close links with Generals for Peace and Disarmament. In 1979 the IIP staged a symposium at Tulbinger Kogel, Austria, in collaboration with the World Federation of Scientific Workers (WFSW)*, it has cooperated with the Christian Peace Conference (CPC)*. The IIP has close working links with the other Soviet-controlled front organisations and participates from time to time in the regular liaison meetings.

(3) Non-Communist Organisations The IIP claims to attach importance to its 'fruitful cooperation' with such 'national and international clerical organisations . . . as the World Council of Churches, the Conference of European Churches . . . and others'.

Other Activities

Its claim to academic status gives the IIP a better opportunity than the parent WPC to attract the participation of non-communist academics, theologians, peace researchers and scientists. In April 1978 it mounted a Symposium on Disarmament in Kishinev, Soviet Union. In January 1980 it held a disarmament symposium at Tampere, Finland (organised, it claimed, at UNESCO's request) and, in recent years, it has organised a series of meetings 'between Marxists and Christians', at least one of which (in 1981) was attended 'not only by representatives of different trends of Christianity but also by spokesmen for Judaism and Islam'. (*Twentieth Century and Peace*, Moscow, No. 7, 1981).

8. International Organisation of Journalists

The International Organisation of Journalists (IOJ) is also known under its French, German and Spanish titles which are, respectively, *Organisation internationale des journalistes, Internationale Organisation der Journalisten and Organización Internacional de Periodistas*. Its headquarters is at Parizska 9, 11001 Prague 1, Czechoslovakia; a regional centre was established in Mexico in 1987, and there are plans to open similar centres in Africa and Asia.

Origins

The IOJ originated from an organisation which existed before the start of World War II, the International Federation of Journalists (IFJ). This body joined with the similarly named but strongly communist-influenced International Federation of Journalists of Allied and Free Countries, which had been active in London and elsewhere since the early years of World War II, in promoting an international journalists' conference in Copenhagen in June 1946. At this conference the two earlier organisations were disbanded and replaced by a new body which was to become the IOJ. Although the new body was briefly representative of journalists everywhere, the communists predictably set out to capture the key posts, which they succeeded in doing, and turned it into an international front organisation subservient to Moscow as they had originally planned.

As a result of this development, by the end of 1949 all the non-communist journalists' unions had withdrawn from IOJ membership because it had obviously become, in the words of its founding president (Archibald Kenyon) 'a branch office of the Cominform' (an assertion confirmed by the IOJ's expulsion of its Yugoslav members on Stalin's instructions in 1949). The non-communist unions reconstituted the IFJ in 1952, whose leaders declared in *IFJ Information*, July–September 1955:

> we can say that we played a very considerable part in forming the IOJ at Copenhagen in 1946, and it was only because of the persistent use of its forum for political propaganda of a particularly virulent kind, that we were forced to conclude that no useful work could be done within its framework. We—that is to say most of the organisations now represented in the IFJ— left the IOJ for this reason.

From 1946–47, the IOJ was run from London, only moving to Prague in June 1947 where it has since remained.

Declared Aims
In 1956 the IOJ, which declared itself to be 'a union of progressive and anti-fascist journalists', listed its aims as:

> 1. The maintenance of peace and the broadening of friendship among the peoples, as well as international understanding through free, accurate, honest informing of public opinion. The struggle against the spreading of war psychosis and war propaganda, against nationalist or racial hatred and against the creation of international tension by means of falsehoods and calumnies.
> 2. The protection of freedom of the Press and of journalists against the influence of monopolist and financial groups. The defence of the right of every journalist to write according to his conscience and conviction. The protection of the rights of colonial peoples and of national minorities to publish in their native language. Support to journalists who have been persecuted for having taken up their pens in defence of peace, progress, justice, the liberty and independence of their countries.
> 3. The protection of all journalists' rights. The struggle for bettering material conditions of their existence. The gathering and dissemination of all information concerning the living conditions of journalists in all countries. (Collective agreements, salaries, right to organise). Support for the trade union movement in the struggle for journalists' demands.
> 4. The protection of the people's rights to receive free and honest information, the struggle against falsehood, calumnies and systematic misinformation by the Press, as well as against every form of journalistic activity in the service of individuals or particular groups of society whose interests are contrary to those of the working masses. (IOJ Booklet, April 1956)

In recent editions of the *Yearbook of International Organisations*, these aims have been summarised as being, 'by free and true information, to help maintain peace and friendship among nations; to defend freedom of the press and journalists, and fight for their better material and social position; and to support fully friendly cooperation of all journalists throughout the world and to help to achieve their unity.'

Organisation and Membership
The highest body of the IOJ is the Congress, supposed to meet at intervals of four years, at which the Presidium, which consists of the president, vice-presidents and secretary-general, and the Executive Committee are elected. Its policy-making functions may now have been taken over by the Bureau of the Presidium, established on Soviet initiative in 1987 as the main operative body of the organisation. The Executive Committee, although required to meet at least once a year in order to direct the organisation between Congresses, does not always do so.

Membership is open to all national journalists' unions and also to *ad hoc* groups and individual journalists. The organisation currently claims a membership of over 200,000 in 120 countries.

The IOJ maintains an International Information Centre in Paris which is closely associated with UNESCO headquarters.

Office holders
The IOJ's leading officials (1987) are Honorary President: Jean-Maurice HERMANN (France)[a]; President: Kaarle NORDEN-STRENG (Finland); Secretary-General: Jiri KUBKA (Czechoslovakia)[a]; Secretaries: Kosta ANDREEV (Bulgaria), Vladimir ARTEMOV (USSR), Luis BARRERA, Elson CONCEPCION (Cuba), Jamil HILAL (Palestine), Marek JURKOWICZ (Poland), Leena PAUKKU (Finland), Don ROJAS (Grenada), Constantin PRISCURU (Romania), Leopoldo VARGAS Fernandez (Colombia), Bernd RAYER (GDR); Treasurer: Karoly MEGYERI (Hungary). (Nordenstreng, the President, is publicly associated with the pro-Soviet wing of the Communist Party of Finland).

Publications and information
The IOJ issues a monthly magazine, *The Democratic Journalist*, edited by Rudolph PREVRATIL (Czechoslovakia) and published in English, French, Russian and Spanish; and also, fortnightly, *IOJ Newsletter* (which replaced *Journalists' Affairs* in June 1980), published in English and Spanish. Other publications

---

[a] HERMANN died June 1988. Dusan ULCAK (Czechoslovakia) replaced KUBKA April 1988.

are *Interpressgraphik*, quarterly, and *Interpressmagazin* (in Czech and Hungarian), monthly.

Finance
The IOJ claims to be financed by affiliation fees at rates established by the Executive Committee. In practice accounts are almost never published, although affiliation fees are believed to raise about US$ 75,000 annually. Some 10 per cent of these fees are devoted to an International Solidarity Fund (which also claims the proceeds of the IOJ's International Solidarity Lottery, as well as various undisclosed contributions; this lottery, while open in principle to all IOJ members, is, in practice, the preserve of journalists from the Soviet Union, Czechoslovakia, the German Democratic Republic, Hungary, Bulgaria, Mongolia and Vietnam).

The Solidarity Fund, which was originally established in 1953, is designed to support 'journalists, regardless of their nationality, religion or political beliefs who, for any reason, are discriminated against or persecuted for giving truthful information, for their stand in favour of cooperation among nations, or in defence of national sovereignty and the democratic rights of nations'; it has financed aid schemes for journalists from Vietnam and Chile and for those connected with 'national liberation movements', mainly in Africa. Its support is not, of course, extended to journalists in trouble with the authorities under communist regimes.

The Sub-Committee on Oversight of the US House of Representatives asserted in February 1980 that, as that time, the IOJ was in receipt of a Soviet subsidy estimated at US$ 515,000.

Relations with other bodies
(1) United Nations The IOJ has consultative status with ECOSOC (Category II) and with UNESCO (Category B). It works particularly closely with the latter. In June 1973, according to a report in the December issue of *The Democratic Journalist*, the IOJ organised, in co-operation with UNESCO, the first 'international colloquium on the development of communications media and new tendencies in the training of journalists'. This was held at the headquarters of the World Federation of Democratic Youth (WFDY)* in Budapest. Forty-one representatives from 16 countries were said to have attended. At the second international conference in December 1975, again organised by the IOJ with UNESCO in Budapest, attendance went up to 58 representatives from 24 countries, including 10 from the developing countries.

The Director of the Free Flow of Information and Development of Communication at UNESCO, Gunnar Naesselung, wrote subsequently to the IOJ welcoming the successful co-operation between the two organisations at this second conference, from which had emerged the draft of a 'Declaration of the basic principles regarding the use of the mass communication media for supporting peace and international understanding and for the combating of war propaganda, racism and racial discrimination'. This Soviet-inspired draft was approved and issued as a formal Declaration at the UNESCO Latin American Conference on the mass media, held in San José in July 1976. The Declaration, adopted as the standard UNESCO guidelines, contained detailed recommendations for operational and ideological regulations to be exercised by governments over the flow of views within and between countries. In a key passage, directly reflecting Soviet views channelled through the IOJ, it stated:

> The new international economic and social order will be best served by a balanced flow of messages between nations. There must be new national policies for the Sovereign determination by governments with regard to the international flow of messages. Governments must have an equal footing in the control over the use of international channels of dissemination.

In other words, governments should exercise complete control over information handled and transmitted by the media. A series of IOJ-orgnaised meetings have been held under UNESCO auspices in the decade since this Declaration was adopted. The ultimate aims of the IOJ, in which it evidently has full support from UNESCO, appears to be to establish a World Journalists' Council, whose purpose would be to restrict, rather than to ease, the free flow of ideas and comments, which is so highly prized by western journalists and upheld by their governments. In *The Democratic Journalist* for February, 1976, the western concept of the 'free flow of information' was dismissed as 'nothing but the free flow of information for imperialist ideas'.

(2) Other International Front Organisations The IOJ works closely with the other international front organisations. The delegate of the World Federation of Trade Unions (WFTU) to the IOJ's Seventh Congress, Lazaro PENA (Cuba), said that 'the IOJ and the WFTU have common aspirations, concerns, hopes and tasks'. The Secretary-General usually represents the IOJ on the WPC Presidential Committee.

The IOJ has close working links with the other Soviet-controlled front organisations and participates from time to time in the regular liaison meetings.

In 1985 it was agreed at a meeting of representatives of AAPSO*, CPC*, IOJ*, IUS*, WIDF*, WFDY*, WFTU*, WPC* and the Afro–Asian–Latin American Peoples' Solidarity Organisation (AALAPSO*), held under IOJ auspices, to establish a 'consultative commission', to oversee the output in official publications of the individual organisations. This accords with the clause in the IOJ constitution which records that, 'in pursuit of the struggle for peace', the IOJ must 'cooperate with other international organisations which fight for peace'.

The IOJ has especially close links with the Latin American Federation of Journalists, known as FELAP and with the new Journalists for Peace*.

(3) Non-communist organisations Under cover of its UNESCO links, the IOJ has occasional links with a number of non-communist journalists' organisations and also with the pool of the news agencies of the Non-Aligned Movement. The IFJ, which resumed its pre-war independence in 1952 after the breach with the IOJ in 1949, eventually resumed minimal contacts with the IOJ in 1973, within the framework of meetings organised biennially by the independent Italian Federation of Journalists. These meetings have now been put into suspense, although IOJ/IFJ contacts continue for purposes connected with UNESCO: for example, the IOJ and the IFJ planned to sponsor a symposium on the Mass Media, under UNESCO auspices, in Helsinki in March 1988.

Subsidiaries
There are two Permanent Commissions, the Social Commission (1967) and a Professional Commission (1968), as well as two 'auxiliary service organisations', Videopress (Prague) and Interpress (Budapest). Other offshoots are the International Photo-Section (1962), Interpress Auto Club (1965), Interpress Graphic Club (1967), International Club of Agricultural Journalists (1970) and International Club of Science and Technology. An International Journalism Institute to deal with mass communication media was set up in Prague in 1986.

Congresses
Ten IOJ Congresses have so far been held as follows:

Copenhagen	(June 1946)
Prague	(June 1947)
Helsinki	(September 1950)
Bucharest	(May 1958)
Budapest	(August 1962)
East Berlin	(October 1966)
Havana	(January 1971)
Helsinki	(September 1976)
Moscow	(October 1981)
Sofia	(October 1986)

Other activities

While publicising cases of alleged persecution of journalists and writers in non-communist countries, the IOJ made no protest about the expulsion of Alexander SOLZHENITSYN from the Soviet Writers' Union in 1969, the trials and imprisonment of other Soviet Writers, the arrest by the KGB in August 1982 of Zoya KRAKHMALNIKOVA, editor of a religious publication, *Nadezhda*, or even about the arrest and expulsion from Czechoslovakia of one of its own Secretaries, Ferdinando ZIDAR (Italy) in February 1972.

The IOJ supports the Soviet campaign to regulate the use of new technical equipment, insisting that broadcasting by satellite must be 'devoid of everything that could interfere in the internal affairs of other countries'. It believes that only the 'Socialist States' are capable of controlling and administering the 'research, production and educational application' of new techniques (*The Democratic Journalist* No. 1, 1976). Putting it another way, R. OVSEPYAN, a Soviet Candidate of Historical Sciences, stated in *The Democratic Journalist* No. 1 1975, that 'the suppression of the reactionary Press marked an important stage in the development of Socialist journalism. Within the peoples' democratic States there no longer existed bourgeois and anti-Communist Press organs . . .'

The IOJ is now mainly concerned with cultivating journalists in the developing world, either by providing equipment or financing courses at 'schools of journalism' held in the communist countries and by providing courses in the developing countries themselves. The importance of this activity was described in a speech by Kubka, the Secretary-General, to the Presidium in October 1987 as follows:

The most important area of our actions of solidarity is, of course, systematic training of journalists from developing countries. In 1986 alone, the courses in IOJ schools were attended by some 400 journalists from 70 countries. (*The Democratic Journalist*, No. 1, January 1988.)

Regional Activities

In Africa the IOJ has a friendship and cooperation agreement with the Union of African Journalists. It has had talks with national organisations in Ghana, Algeria, Nigeria, Mali and Zambia and has offered aid to Ethiopian journalists. The Tanzanian Minister of Information visited the IOJ in Prague in May 1979 and Tanzania has been given material aid by GDR journalists, who sent two lecturers to the Tanzanian School of Journalism in 1981; in 1981 the IOJ President NORDEN-STRENG, also worked in Tanzania, 'for at least a year' on a UNESCO project to promote the 'new world information and communication order'. The IOJ attended the first conference of journalists from Front Line States, Mozambique, August 1985.

In Asia the IOJ has given financial assistance to the Association of Vietnamese journalists and has constructed and equipped a Press centre in Hanoi. It is considering setting up a permanent IOJ office in India.

A World Conference of Journalists against Imperialism and for Friendship and Peace, held in Pyongyang in July 1983, was organised by the IOJ (and several other regional journalists' organisations); it was attended by a delegation of Chinese journalists (the first time any Chinese delegation had attended an international front meeting for 20 years).

In Europe the IOJ has been involved in a series of 'Jablonna meetings' of journalists from Eastern and Western Europe, organised by the Polish Journalists' Association. The series, suspended in 1979, was resumed in 1984.

The Czechoslovak IOJ Secretary-General, Jiri KUBKA, wrote in *The Democratic Journalist* No. 1, January 1985, that the [WPC] World Assembly for Peace and Life (Prague, 1983) had enabled journalists

> for the first time to meet at their own forum and it brought surprising results: new groups of journalists for peace and against nuclear death from Sweden, Denmark, Great Britain, the FRG and other countries met there for the first time. These groups today have thousands of members . . . I am sure that this process will continue. In this regard, the almost snowballing development of democratic journalism in North America deserves, in my opinion, special attention.

The WPC's World Congress Devoted to the International Year

of Peace, held in Copenhagen in October 1986, provided the venue for the fifth meeting of Journalists for Peace*.

The IOJ sent observers to the First Congress of West European Journalists for Peace, held in Finland in October 1983 at the invitation of its associate, the Union of Journalists in Finland (SSL), and organised its own Forum of Journalists for Peace in Paris, November 1983. An international seminar on new technologies and the journalistic profession was held in Hungary in May 1985.

The IOJ also held a seminar on Women and the Mass Media, in Warsaw, October 1984, under UNESCO auspices. It also planned to hold a training course in journalism for women, in cooperation with UNESCO and the International Programme for the Development of Communication (IPDC).

In Latin America, FELAP was set up at the First Congress of Latin American Journalists (Mexico City, June 1976), with a Peruvian IOJ Executive Committee member, the late Genaro CARNERO Checa, as its Secretary-General. The IOJ signed cooperation agreements with FELAP and the Latin American Institute of Transnational Studies (ILET) in November 1978 (FELAP also has agreements with the WPC and the WFTU).

The IOJ has had a Latin American Information Centre in Lima since 1974.

A conference of Journalists of Central America and the Caribbean was held in Managua in June 1984, and a seminar of Latin American and Caribbean Journalists in Havana in July 1984.

In the Middle East the IOJ cooperates with the Federation of Arab Journalists (FAJ) and the General Union of Palestinian Writers and Journalists (GUPWJ). It plans to open a new Secretariat for the Middle East (it established a regional office in Cairo in 1979 but, owing to Egypt's changed relations with the USSR, announced in 1980 that this had been closed). The IOJ's International Committee for the Protection of Journalists decided at a meeting with the FAJ and GUPWJ in Cyprus, in July 1983, to set up an initiative committee in Nicosia to prepare for a meeting of journalists from the Middle East and Mediterranean. A delegation of Tunisian journalists visited the IOJ Secretariat in January 1985 to discuss closer cooperation.

Training Schools and Courses
Several IOJ-sponsored schools have been opened since 1961 in Eastern Europe to train journalists from developing countries. These include:

IOJ Centre of Professional Education of Journalists, Budapest, principally for radio and television journalists;

Werner Lamberz Institute (formerly School of Solidarity of GDR Union of Journalists), East Berlin, which concentrates on newspaper and magazine journalists;

Georgi Dimitrov International Institute of Journalists, Bankia, near Sofia, established in 1978, which trains journalists in agriculture and economics;

Julius Fucik School of Solidarity, Prague, opened in 1983 to train qualified journalists in newscasting;

Jose Marti International Institute of Journalism, Havana, opened in 1983;

The IOJ also has schools in Pyongyang (1985) and Hanoi.

Training courses have also been held in Afghanistan, Algeria, Cuba, Egypt, Ethiopia, Ghana, Guinea, Iraq, Peru, Somalia, Syria and the PDRY (South Yemen). The IOJ has cooperated in the organisation of a Journalists' School in Bucharest, an International School of Solidarity in Havana, and a training centre for Arab journalists in Baghdad. As the IOJ's principal Soviet mentor, Viktor AFANASIEV, Chairman of the USSR Union of Journalists* and an IOJ Vice-President, said at his Union's Fifth Congress in March 1982, that the Russians were 'assisting, within the framework of the IOJ', the training of journalists from the developing world.

Rest Homes
The IOJ runs International Rest Homes for Journalists in Varna, Bulgaria, and near Lake Balaton, Hungary, which also serve as conference and holiday centres.

9. International Radio and Television Organisation

The International Radio and Television Organisation is more commonly known by its French title, *Organisation internationale de radiodiffusion et télévision* (OIRT); it is also known under its German and Spanish titles as, respectively, *Internationale Rundfunk und Fernsehorganisation*, and *Organización Internacional de Radiodifusión y Televisión*. Its headquarters is at 1 Skokanska 169, 56, Prague 6, Czechoslovakia.

Origins
The OIRT was founded, as the International Radio Organisation or Organisation internationale de radiodiffusion (OIR), in Brussels in June 1946. Although dominated by communists from the start a number of western radio organisations were originally included in it. In 1949, as happened about the same time in other Soviet international front organisations, the European non-communist national radio organisations (being no longer prepared to endure the constant pressures to conform with Soviet policies) decided to withdraw. In 1950, under the leadership of the British Broadcasting Corporation (BBC), they set up their own European Broadcasting Union (EBU). In the same year, 1950, the OIR moved its headquarters to Prague and, in July 1959, added television to its title.

Declared Aims
The OIRT's ostensible aims, as a primarily technical body of communist radio and television broadcasts, are apparently non-political, the mutual assistance of broadcasting stations in exchanging technical knowledge and programmes.

Organisation and Membership
The highest body in the OIRT is its General Assembly, which meets annually and which represents all member organisations. There is also an Administrative Council or Board, which must meet at least twice each year, consisting of about twelve members, and a Bureau which meets as required and consists of the President, the three Vice Presidents, the Secretary-General, the Deputy Secretaries-General and two other representatives.

There are also a Technical Commission and *ad hoc* committees (e.g. the Radio Programme Commission and the Economic and Legal Commission) concerned with various aspects of radio and television broadcasting.

Membership is open to any broadcasting organisation. In 1981 the OIR claimed no more than 25 corporate members, drawn from the USSR and a number of its constituent Socialist Republics separately, Algeria, Bulgaria, Cuba, Czechoslovakia, Finland, the German Democratic Republic, Hungary, Iraq, North Korea, Mali, Mongolia, Poland, Romania and Vietnam.

Office holders
President: Sakari KIURU (Finland); Secretary-General: Dr. Gennadij CODR (Czechoslovakia); Deputy Secretaries-General: Alexander EVSTAFIEV (USSR), H. ZIELINSKI (Poland), Hans URBITSCH (GDR); Vice-Presidents: N. F. OKHMAKIE-VICH (USSR), Maciej SZCZEPANSKI (Poland), Stefan TIKH-CHEV (Bulgaria).

Publications and Information
The OIRT publishes bi-monthly *Radio and Television*, in a joint French and English edition and also in German and Russian; it also publishes, monthly, *OIRT Information* in English, German and Russian.

Finance
The OIRT is apparently financed by its affiliation fees but accounts are never published. The Sub-Committee on Oversight of the US House of Representatives asserted in February 1980 that, at that time, OIRT was in receipt of a Soviet subsidy estimated at US$50,000.

Relations with other bodies
(1) United Nations The OIRT has links with several UN agencies, including ECOSOC, UNESCO and the ITU (International Tele-communications Union).

(2) Other International Front Organisations The OIRT, histori-cally, has always collaborated with the WPC and for some years after 1957, it sponsored the broadcasting from Prague, in col-laboration with the World Federation of Scientific Workers (WFSW)* of a series of communist propagandist broadcasts under the general title of 'Science in the Service of Peace'.
   The OIRT has close working links with the other Soviet-controlled front organisations and participates from time to time in the regular liaison meetings.

(3) Non-communist Organisations In addition to having been admitted, since the late 1950s, to the International Telecommuni-cations Union's administrative conferences, the OIRT now belongs, along with the European Broadcasting Union and other regional broadcasting organisations, to the World Conference of Broadcasting Unions. As a consequence, in February 1986, it played host in Prague to the Fifth World Conference of Broad-

casting Unions, which was attended by 175 representatives of nine such organisations. This was described at the time as:

> the first time in history that the site of deliberations of this representative forum was a socialist country and the conference organiser was OIRT . . . The conference . . . recognised the exceptional responsibility of mass communication media in the work to ensure a lasting peace and to avert the threat of nuclear war. (*IOJ Newsletter*, No. 5, March 1986).

Subsidiary

The OIRT's major subsidiary is Intervision, essentially an East European version of Eurovision. The Intervision Council meets at frequent intervals: uniquely in this area, it does not merely conduct technical discussions but also involves itself in supporting the activities of the WPC and other Soviet-controlled organisations (e.g. according to the *OIRT Information*, No. 2, 1973, the 53rd session of the Intervision Council met in Dresden, GDR in February 1973 and was attended by WPC representatives who 'informed the Intervision Council about the forthcoming World Peace Congress to be held in Moscow in October 1973').

10. International Union of Students

The International Union of Students (IUS) is also known under its French, German and Spanish titles which are, respectively, *Union internationale des étudiants, Internationaler Studentenbund* and *Unión Internacional de Estudiantes*. Its headquarters is at 17 November Street, POB 58, 110 01, Prague 01, Czechoslovakia.

Origins

The IUS was founded at a World Student Congress in Prague in August 1946. The Congress was attended by students of wide-ranging political and religious persuasions who (apart from the communists) thought they were creating a non-political and universal student body, described in the constitution as 'the representative organisation of the democratic students of the whole world who work for progress'. The communists, however, managed to gain control of the organisation by capturing the key posts at the outset and by providing not only the headquarters (in Prague), which became a communist capital in 1948, but also most of the money. A former president of the British National Union of Students once described the IUS as 'the Student Section of the Cominform'.

Most of the non-communist students had left the organisation by 1950 in protest against its policies, in particular its expulsion of the Yugoslav Union of Student Youth in 1950 without a hearing, at the time of the Stalin–Tito quarrel.

Most of the non-communist unions which had left the IUS originally formed the Co-ordinating Secretariat of National Unions of Students (COSEC) (later called the International Student Conference—ISC), with its headquarters in Leiden, Holland, but that was dissolved as a result of internal dissension in 1969.

Declared Aims

According to the *Yearbook of International organisations* (1986–87) the IUS 'strives for the right and possibility of all young people to enjoy primary, secondary and higher education, regardless of sex, economic circumstances, social standing, political conviction, religion, colour or race, promote world peace, international friendship among all peoples and the employment of advances in science and culture for the benefit of humanity'.

According to its Constitution the IUS aims to promote 'the struggle for freedom and genuine national independence, economic and social progress, democracy, national sovereignty and self-determination . . . and against imperialism, colonialism and neo-colonialism, reaction, fascism and all forms of discrimination, in particular racial discrimination'.

Organisation and Membership

The Congress, the highest body of the IUS, is supposed to meet at least every three years. It decides policy, adopts a work programme, approves the budget, confirms new affiliations and elects the Executive and Finance Committees. All affiliated and associated member organisations may send delegates to Congress (observers have no voting rights).

The Executive Committee implements the policies, decisions and projects adopted by the Congress. It supervises the work of the Secretariat and meets at least once a year. National student organisations are elected to it by the Congress; each organisation nominates its own representative. Daily business is conducted by the Secretariat. There are also subordinate departments for Student Action on Peace and Disarmament, Education and Students' Rights, Cooperation with International Organisations, Student Struggle for Development, Physical Education and

Sports, Student Tourism and Exchange, Press and Information, Student Solidarity Actions and Student Cultural Activities, together with four regional commissions, a Festival Commission and an Arab working group.

Full IUS membership is open to national student unions and national coordinating committees, or to one or more student organisations in countries where neither of these categories exist, and also to representative national student organisations. Provision is also made for associate corporate membership and for observer status. The IUS claims to have 111 full or associate members in 109 countries or territories. The bulk of its membership, said to total 10 million, predictably comes from communist countries.

Office Holders
The IUS' leading officials (1987) are: President: Josef SKALA (Czechoslovakia); Secretary-General: Georgios MICHAE-LIDES (Cyprus); Vice-Presidents: José CASTILLO (Panama), Leonardo Candieiro CELANO (Mozambique), Sergei CHEL-NOKOV (USSR), Georgi GEORGIEV (Bulgaria), Pallab Sen GUPTA (India), KIM Gwang-hub (North Korea), Ravane KONE (Senegal), Jerzy KOZMINSKI (Poland), Jorge MATU-RANA (Chile), ONG Dung (Vietnam), Antonio PARDO (Cuba), Petrus SCHMIDT (Namibia), Vesselin VALCHEV (Bulgaria), and a representative from 'Palestine'; Secretaries Faysel AL-MEKDAD (Syria), Ahmed AL-WAHISHI (PDRY), Manuel COSS ('Puerto Rico'), Nicolai DARAVOINEA (Romania), Philip GARDINER (Ghana), Karoly GYORGY (Hungary), Abebe HANKORE (Ethiopia), Burkhard HERRMAN (GDR), Peter KRPATA (Czechoslovakia), Benjamin LIBEROFF (Uruguay), Andrei MOROZOV (USSR), Victor PAREDES Lara (El Salvador), Norbert RANDRIAM-AMPIANINA (Madagascar), Mohammed SHAKIR; Treasurer: Rainer ARZINGER (GDR).

Publications and Information
The IUS publishes *World Student News* monthly in English, French, German and Spanish; *Democratisation of Education*, quarterly, in English, French and Spanish; *Secretariat Reports*, 10 times a year, in English and Spanish. There are also three special bulletins—on disarmament, on the democratisation of education and on sport—and five regional information bulletins. *Solidarity Newsletter* was started in 1986.

Finance
Although the IUS claims to be financed by affiliation fees and
by fund-raising activities, it is dependent on support from the
Soviet Union and the other communist countries.

The Sub-Committee on Oversight of the US House of
Representatives stated in February 1980 that, at that time, the
IUS was in receipt of a Soviet subsidy estimated at US$905,000.

Relations with Other Bodies
(1) United Nations The IUS has Category B status with UNESCO
and Category II with ECOSOC (it was not re-elected to the
board of the unofficial Conference of Non-Governmental Organisations in Consultative Status with ECOSOC, known as
CONGO, in 1985).

(2) Other International Front Organisations The IUS works
particularly closely with the World Federation of Democratic
Youth (WFDY)* with which it jointly sponsors the periodic
World Youth Festivals. The IUS President is usually a member
of the Presidential Committee of the World Peace Council
(WPC). The IUS and the WFDY have cooperation agreements
with the World Federation of Trade unions (WFTU)*.

The IUS has close working links with the other Soviet-
controlled international front organisations and participates from
time to time in the regular liaison meetings.

(3) Non-communist organisations The IUS cooperates with three
regional student organisations—the All-Africa Students' Union
(AASU), the General Union of Arab Students (GUAS) and
the Continental Organisation of Latin American Students
(OCLAE). It also has contacts with the Asian Students' Information Centre (ASIC), the International Youth and Student
Movement for the United Nations (ISMUN), the World Student
Christian Federation (WSCF) and the International Federation
of Medical Students' Associations (IFMSA). A delegation from
the World Organisation of Esperanto Youth (TEJO) visited the
IUS headquarters in January 1985.

In recent years the IUS and the WFDY have joined with a
number of non-communist youth and student organisations—
such as the International Union of Socialist Youth (IUSY), the
Council of European National Youth Committees (CENYC),
the Democrat Youth Community of Europe (DEMYC) and the
International Federation of Liberal and Radical Youth (IFLRY),

in establishing the Framework for All-European Youth and Student Cooperation (AEYSC), officially set up at a meeting in Budapest in October 1980. Its various bodies met regularly until December 1982 when, owing to internal disagreement fired by the communists' policy on 'Zionism', its activities were suspended; they were resumed in July 1986.

The possible establishment at some future date of a separate student movement by the non-aligned countries has caused both the IUS and the WFDY some concern. As the Soviet *Radio Peace and Progress* said on 27 October 1978, such a body could be influenced by 'imperialist and Maoist propaganda' attempting to persuade young people in the developing countries that they were 'in a dependent position' on such organisations as the WFDY and IUS, and that 'their interests are allegedly disregarded when youth forums and such are held'. Although little so far has come of this project, the IUS was represented at the first Conference of Non-Aligned Student Organisations held in Valletta, Malta in January 1979. The IUS denounced attempts to set up a rival international students' organisation by representatives of some 30 national student unions who met in Paris in June 1981 (this was the International Students' Association, which condemned the IUS for its 'ideological alignment with the USSR').

National Affiliates
Although the IUS claims to have 111 full or associate member organisations in 109 countries or territories, its only West European members come from France, Spain, Portugal and an associate member in Finland. The Union of Irish Students (USI) became an associate member in 1967. Fom 1971 till 1984 the USI provided the IUS with a Secretary.

The British National Union of Students (NUS), although not a member, has for some years maintained formal relations with the IUS short of corporate membership (the IUS regularly sends observers to NUS national conferences in the United Kingdom) and the two organisations signed a joint agreement in the autumn in 1983. But the IUS has no affiliate in the USA. So the bulk of its membership comes from the Third World and from communist countries.

Subsidiaries
IUS subsidiary organisations include an International Student Research Centre (ISRC) and an International Student Travel Bureau (ISTB).

IUS Policies
IUS activities and public statements consistently echo Soviet foreign policy. The IUS has condemned Western, not Soviet, nuclear tests; it campaigns against NATO, not against the Warsaw Pact; it protested about alleged violations of students' rights in non-communist countries, but ignored the expulsion of Chinese and Albanian students from the Soviet Union in 1962, demonstrations by African students in Sofia and Moscow in 1963, the imprisonment of Polish students in 1968 and the widespread arrest of students in East Germany in 1969.

In recent years the IUS has met increasing opposition from rival 'broad Left' groups. The (Trotskyist) League for a Workers' Republic, quoted by the *Irish Times* (Dublin, 13 January 1976), said that the IUS 'devotes more attention to endorsing the foreign policies of the Kremlin than to discussing the problems of students'.

The IUS, with its headquarters in Prague and with a Czechoslovak President, Zbynek VOKROUHLICKY, was adversely affected by the Soviet invasion of Czechoslovakia in 1968; the Congress due to have been held in 1969 was delayed until 1971. VOKROUHLICKY, in a letter to the youth and student organisations of the Warsaw Pact countries, spoke of 'absolutely unfounded aggression against my home and my country . . .' and it was no surprise when both he and the Secretary-General, an Iraqi communist, were subsequently replaced.

Jiri Pelikan (Czechoslovakia), formerly both Secretary-General and President of the IUS, subsequently revealed in an interview with the British *New Left Review*, Janaury–February 1972, that 'the Soviet Union was always trying to impose its tactical policy of the moment on the organisation'. The Soviet members 'saw the IUS and similar organisations merely as unofficial instruments of Soviet foreign policy'. Even before the Soviet invasion of Czechoslovakia in 1968, Soviet control of the IUS led to a dispute following Vokrouhlicky's speech at the ninth IUS Congress. The Swiss newspaper, *Basler Nachrichten*, April 27, 1967, reported that 'a sharp discussion arose when several delegations, led by the Romanians, vehemently attacked the IUS leadership because of its policy and demanded an amendment of the statutes, as well as strict regard to the independence of the member organisations. They accused the Prague Secretariat of using undemocratic methods to enforce its will on the member organisations.' Swedish and Finnish observers at the Congress reported that 'the Congress was controlled by the Soviet and pro-Soviet delegations from Eastern Europe and from the Arab countries . . . ' (*Student Mirror*, No. 332, 16 September 1967).

An article in *The Irish Press* (Dublin), 30 January 1980, about a recent congress of the Union of Students in Ireland (USI), outlined the USI's controversial relationship with the IUS since 1967. It said that Paul Tansey, a former USI representative on the IUS Secretariat in Prague, explained after relinquishing his post in the early 1970s that the USI had enjoyed a privileged position within the IUS although it was only an associate member, because the IUS was eager to gain credibiility in Western Europe where it had a few affiliates. One reason why Tansey left his IUS post was because he felt that no proposal of his had a chance of success unless it was in line with official policy, which was usually laid down by Vladimir PONOMAREV, the (then) Soviet student's union representative to the Secretariat. Tansey felt that Ponomarev, who held no official position on the Secretariat, was in fact its most important member and that, although the Secretariat met twice weekly, the most important meetings 'took place elsewhere'.

Patrick Buckley, another Irish representative on the IUS Secretariat, was also critical of the way the IUS was run, complaining in particular of 'undemocratic procedures' in the preparation of an IUS Congress [Budapest, May 1974]. In his report, he stated that

> several sections of the Constitution have been violated on the grounds of practicality by those who view any infringements of 'tradition' as sacrilege. Their arrogance has to be seen to be believed—it bodes ill for the running of the Congress and any dissenters. Also in relation to the Congress, I have been informed that quite an amount of corruption can be expected—offering of scholarships in certain countries, money etc. Little can be expected from any of the Latin Americans, the Arabs, most Africans and the paper organisations. (*Irish Press*, 30 January 1980)

Congresses
Fifteen IUS Congresses have so far been held:

Prague	(August 1946)
Prague	(August 1950)

Warsaw	(August 1953)
Prague	(August 1956)
Peking	(September 1958)
Baghdad	(October 1960)
Leningrad	(August 1962)
Sofia	(November/December 1964)
Ulan Bator	(March/April 1967)
Bratislava	(February 1971)
Budapest	(May 1974)
Sofia	(November 1980)
East Berlin	(November 1980)
Sofia	(April 1984)
Havana	(November 1987)

Other Campaigns and Activities
Dusan ULCAK, former IUS President, told the Czech youth newspaper *Mlada Fronta* (6 May 1974) that without IUS influence 'no single major international or regional student event takes place, regardless of whether it is organised within the framework of the IUS, its member organisations or organisations that are not IUS members'.

The 'democratisation and reform' of education is a recurring theme in IUS activities, taking its inspiration from the alleged situation in communist countries. Demands include 'the elimination of all reactionary, fascist, chauvinist, militarist and other similar ideas from educational curricula'. IUS campaigns also include 'Education: A Right not a Privilege', launched in 1977, and 'Students for Peace, against Nuclear War', launched in 1984.

Since the IUS started its scholarship scheme in 1956, over 3,000 students from developing countries have studied in Bulgaria, Czechoslovakia, GDR, Hungary, Poland, the USSR and also Finland (and, for a time in the 1970s, in Syria and Iraq). Scholarships are awarded annually for periods of four to seven years. According to *Mlada Fronta* (6 May 1974), students are expected to 'provide a guarantee that after finishing their schooling they will become not only good specialists but also propagators of progressive ideas formulated by the IUS'.

In an article on 'mass sport and physical education', which appeared in *World Student News* No. 2, February 1983, Mikhail VARTOSU (Romania), head of the IUS Physical Education and Sports Department, stated that, for the IUS, these activities are 'an effective means of promoting friendship, fruitful cooperation and militant solidarity among students and their organisations in their struggle for peace, security and cooperation, national independence, democracy, social progress and a better, just world'. The Union's sports camps, of which more than 100 have been organised in different countries, have become 'a platform for the struggle for peace, detente and disarmament'. Solidarity events, 'part and parcel' of some of the camps, have been aimed at promoting Soviet policy in relation to El Salvador, Chile, Nicaragua, Angola, Palestine, Cyprus and other countries of Soviet concern.

The IUS celebrates several anniversaries, notably International Students' Day, 17 November. It is also co-sponsor, with the World Federation of Democratic youth (WFDY), of the series of World Youth Festivals, of which there have so far been 12:

Prague	(July 1947)	(attended by some 17,000 participants)
Budapest	(August 1949)	10,000
East Berlin	(August 1951)	26,000
Bucharest	(August 1953)	30,000
Warsaw	(July 1985)	30,000
Moscow	(July 1957)	34,000
Vienna	(July 1959)	18,000
Helsinki	(July 1962)	10,800
Sofia	(July 1968)	10,000
East Berlin	(July 1973)	25,600
Havana	(July 1978)	18,500
Moscow	(July 1985)	20,500

The next Festival, the 13th, will be held in Pyongyang, North Korea, in July–August 1989. It will be the first to be held in Asia (and only the second to be held outside Europe) and will reflect the Soviet Union's current efforts to extend its propagandist activities to Asia and Oceania on a greater scale than hitherto.

At the constituent meeting of the Tenth Festival's International Preparatory Committee (IPC), held in East Berlin in February 1973, new prospects were envisaged for the 'festival movement' because of international detente, a trend attributed to the 'consistent and constructive' foreign policies of the Soviet Union and other communist countries. Twelve years later, in 1985, Vladimir Aksyonov, Chairman of the Soviet Committee of Youth Organisations and Deputy Chairman of the National Preparatory Committee for the 12th Festival, told the Soviet current affairs journal, *New Times* (No. 21 May 1985), that the 'festival movement' had become a 'powerful means of drawing broad masses of the young generation into vigorous social and political activity'. In practice, on such occasions the selection of participants is, in most countries, controlled by national Preparatory Committees directed by communists. Historically, the need to maintain complete political control has caused most festivals to be staged in communist capitals. The original Festival slogan of 'Peace and Friendship' was broadened to 'Anti-imperialist Solidarity, Peace and Friendship' in 1973.

Regional Activities

Africa The IUS supports the African 'national liberation movements' and cooperates with the Pan-African Student Movement (PASM) and the All-Africa Students' Union (AASU). In February 1979 it cooperated with the UN Special Committee against Apartheid, the WFDY and others in organising an International Youth and Student Conference of Solidarity with the Peoples, Youth and Students of Southern Africa, at UNESCO Headquarters in Paris (a second was held in Luanda in November 1981). It has organised a variety of meetings in Africa on such subjects as Neo-Colonialism in African Universities, Democratic Education, the Student Press, Disarmament, the Struggle for National and Social Liberation, Illiteracy, and Education under Apartheid. It held an Executive Committee meeting in Addis Ababa in January 1987.

The IUS has sent solidarity delegations to Africa, arranged tours of Europe by delegations from 'liberation movements', helped to build schools in 'liberated areas of southern Africa', and sent medical brigades.

Asia and Pacific The IUS has appealed for stronger solidarity with the struggle of the peoples of Vietnam, Laos and Cambodia. A delegation visited those countries in 1983. The IUS supports the idea of a 'zone of peace' in the Indian Ocean. On the initiative of the IUS Indian affiliate, the All-India Students' Federation (AISF), an Asian Student Information Centre was set up in New Delhi in 1981. In conjunction with the WFDY and with Indian organisations, the IUS organised a seminar on the Socio-Economic Impact of Imperialist Economic Aid to the Developing Countries and its Political Consequences, in Trivandrum, India, in July 1972. In December 1978, it organised an International Student Conference on the Struggle against Illiteracy, in New Delhi.

An IUS group visited Afghanistan in May 1979, and a

delegation of student journalists, organised by the IUS, went there in August 1980.

The IUS held the first regional meeting entitled For Peace, National Independence and a Nuclear-free Pacific, in Sydney, Australia, in October 1985, and an Executive Committee meeting in Pyongyang, North Korea, in January 1986.

Europe The IUS has consistently supported Soviet policy on European security, disarmament and the deployment of new US nuclear missiles in Europe. With the WFDY, and with certain non-Communist bodies, it helped to organise the World Forum of Youth and Students for Peace, Detente and Disarmament in Helsinki in January 1981 (at which the communist elements by no means had everything their way). It held a round-table on Students for Disarmament, in Nicosia, in April 1982, and supported a tribunal against US Missiles and US Intervention held by the VDS (the National Union of Students in the Federal Republic of Germany), in Cologne in June 1982.

The IUS organised a World Student Forum on 'Education is a Right, not a Privilege', in Weimar in January 1980, a seminar on the Social Situation of Students in Europe, in Espoo, Finland, in February 1983, and a World Student Forum on Education and Society, in Prague in November 1986.

The Union awarded its 17 November Medal to the Cypriot Federation of Students and Young Scientists (POFNE) in 1983. It organised an international seminar, The Mediterranean—Zone of Peace, in Nicosia in August 1983 and an international student meeting, Learning from History—Never Again Fascism!, in Hamburg, May 1985. Other activities have included a European Students' Forum on Education, Technology and Society, in Dublin in May 1980, and visits to Northern Ireland by the IUS, the (British) National Union of Students and the Union of Students in Ireland (USI) in October 1979 and May 1980.

Latin America Since the death of President ALLENDE of Chile in September 1973, the IUS has run a campaign entitled; 'Every University a Centre of Solidarity with Chile'. Together with the British National Union of Students and the Chilean union, CPFUCH, the IUS organised a World Student Seminar of Solidarity with Chile, in London in November 1975.

The IUS is also involved in the 'anti-imperialist struggles' of the Caribbean and Central America. It held an International Student Meeting for Peace, Disarmament and Anti-Imperialist

Solidarity in Mexico in May 1982; a Central American University Seminar, in Costa Rica in August 1982; an International Student Conference against Imperialism, in Mexico in September 1984; an international seminar on Sandino's Deeds and their Validity for the Students' and Peoples' Struggle, in Managua, in September 1984; and a seminar on The Caribbean—A Zone of Peace, in Puerto Rico, February 1985.

Under IUS auspices, the Oliverio Casteneda de Leon International Solidarity Brigade went to Nicaragua in 1980 to help in the campaign against illiteracy. The IUS and the WFDY organised a solidarity tour of European countries by AGEUS, the student organisation in El Salvador, in 1981, and a tour of Eastern Europe by a delegation of Central American students in January–February 1983. An IUS delegation visited Argentina in August 1984.

Middle East The IUS seeks to promote support for 'the Arab peoples and students against imperialism, Zionism, Israeli aggression and local reaction'. Together with the National Union of Syrian Students, it organised meetings in support of Arab 'liberation movements', in Damascus in 1975 and 1978. The IUS held an International Student Conference for Solidarity with Palestine, in Athens in January 1983 and a similar gathering in Solidarity with the Struggle of the People and Students of the Syrian Arab Republic, in Damascus in November 1983. In March 1983 it awarded 17 November Medals to the General Union of Palestinian Students (GUPS) and the National Union of Syrian Students (NUSS).

The IUS has also organised an International Seminar on the Role of Students in the Struggle against Racism and Zionism (Tripoli, October 1978); an International Seminar on the Role of Students in the Struggle for the Establishment of a New International Economic Order (Benghazi, July 1979); an International Seminar on the Contribution of Youth and Students to the Struggle for National Independence in the Developing Counties (Aden, May 1980); an International Student Forum on Unity of Action and Solidarity in the Anti-Imperialist Struggle (Damascus, May 1980); and an International Student Seminar on the Imperialist Military Build-up in the Middle East as a Threat to Peace (Damascus, November 1983).

11. Women's International Democratic Federation

The Women's International Democratic Federation (WIDF) is also known under its French, German and Spanish titles which are, respectively, *Fédération démocratique internationale des femmes, Internationale Demokratische Frauenföderation* and *Federación Democrática Internacional de Mujeres*. Its headquarters is at Unter den Linden 13, Berlin 108, East Germany.

Origins

The WIDF was founded in November 1945 at a Congress of Women in Paris organised by a French communist-dominated organisation, Union des femmes françaises. Unlike most of the other Soviet international front organisations, it was never disrupted by mass resignations in the 1950s because, as it had been almost totally under communist control from the start, no significant non-communist women's organisation has ever joined it (although the important Italian affiliate did withdraw from the Federation in 1964).

In 1951, together with the World Federation of Democratic Youth (WFDY)* and the World Federation of Trade Unions (WFTU)* the WIDF was expelled from Paris by the French Government for 'fifth column activities'. It thereupon settled in the Soviet sector of Berlin—East Berlin—where it has ever since remained.

Declared Aims

According to the *Yearbook of International Organisations 1986–87*, the WIDF's aims are to

> unite women regardless of race, nationality, religion and political opinions, so that they may work together to win, implement and defend their rights as mothers, workers and citizens; defend the rights of children to life, well-being and education; win and defend national independence and democratic freedoms, eliminate apartheid, racial discrimination and fascism; work for peace and universal disarmament.

Organisation and membership

Under the WIDF constitution, the Federation's highest authority is the World Congress of Women, which now meets every six years. The Council, which is elected by the Congress and meets annually, elects the Bureau and the Secretariat and appoints members of the Finance Control Commission.

The WIDF claims to have 136 affiliated organisations in 117

countries. In 1966 it claimed a total membership of 'over 200 million' (most of whom resided in communist countries).

Office Holders
The leading officials are: President: Freda BROWN (Australia), a Lenin Peace Prize Winner (1978); Secretary-General: Mirjam VIRE-TUOMINEN (Finland); Vice Presidents: Luisa AMORIM (Portugal), Fatima AOUFI (Algeria), Fanny EDELMAN (Argentina), Vilma ESPIN de Castro (Cuba), Issam Abdul HADI ('Palestine'), Fuki KUSHIDA (Japan), Salome MOIANE (Mozambique), NGUYEN Thi Dinh (Vietnam), Zoya PUKHOVA (USSR), Dr. Nirupama RATH (India), Ilse THIELE (GDR); Secretaries: Norma HIDALGO (Chile), Valeria KALMYK (USSR), Irena KARSKA (Poland), Prima LOOMBA (India), Azza el Horr MROUE (Lebanon), Vesselina PEYTCHEVA (Bulgaria), Nancy RUIZ (Cuba), Mittah SEPEREPERE (ANC-South Africa), and representatives from Greece, Japan, Canada and Congo; Organising Secretary: Sabine HAGER (GDR); President of Finance Control Commission: Maria DUSHCHEK (Hungary).

Publications and Information
Women of the Whole World is published quarterly in Arabic. English, French, German, Russian and Spanish. Bulletins and pamphlets also appear from time to time.

Finance
WIDF claims to be financed by affiliation fees and 'special contributions'.

The sub-committee on Oversight of the US House of Representatives stated in February 1980 that, at that time, the WIDF was in receipt of a Soviet subsidy estimated at US$ 390,000.

Relations with other bodies
(1) United Nations The WIDF has Category B status with UNESCO and Category I status with ECOSOC, and maintains permanent representatives at both organisations: it also has consultative status with UNICEF and is on the ILO Special List. In common with other such Soviet-controlled organisations, the WIDF has in recent years sought to widen its influence inside the UN and its agencies and it was on an initiative of the WIDF that the UN designated 1975 as International Women's Year.

The WIDF was elected to the board of the unofficial Conference of Non-Governmental Organisations in Consultative Status with ECOSOC (CONGO) in September 1985.

(2) Other international front organisations The WIDF has close relations with other international front organisations, particularly the World Peace Council (WPC) on which it is represented by Freda BROWN and Mirjam VIRE-TUOMINEN (members of the WPC Presidential Committee, Freda BROWN being a Vice President).

The WIDF has close working links with the other international Soviet-controlled front organisations and participates from time to time in the regular liaison meetings.

(3) Non-communist organisations The Federation closely collaborates with the Women's International League for Peace and Freedom (WILPF)* It participated in the STAR (Stop the Arms Race) campaign launched by the WILPF's US section in March 1982, and the WILPF participates in the WIDF's peace events— and also with the Pan-African Women's Organisation (PAWO). Representatives of 40 national and 43 regional and international organisations, including eight UN specialised agencies, were associated with the preparations for the WIDF's World Congress of Women in Prague in 1981, and representatives of 133 countries, 96 regional and international organisations and 18 UN organisations, took part in the Congress itself.

National Affiliates
Among the WIDF's 143 affiliates in 124 countries is the British National Assembly of Women (NAW). The NAW nominates one of the WIDF Bureau members. An Honorary Vice President (formerly Vice President) is Mrs. Marie Pritt, widow of D. N. Pritt who was sometime president of the International Association of Democratic Lawyers (IADL)*.

The Communist journal, *World News and Views* wrote on 22 March 1953, with reference to the NAW, that

> The rising movement among the women demonstrates that for our women cadres nothing can be more important than to become mass leaders of the women; that we need to pay special attention to these comrades and help them to develop, and that not only do we need many more women members, but that they are there for the asking, fresh militant fighters who are already playing an active part in the movement and who must and can be won for membership of the Communist Party.

Subsidiaries

The WIDF has from time to time established a number of committees usually to organise and publicise particular campaigns or a forthcoming congress.

In 1960 the WIDF set up an International Liaison Bureau to secure cooperation with other women's organisations, with its headquarters in Copenhagen and an office in Brussels. The WIDF also set up a Permanent Committee for Women's Questions in Colonial Territories in 1947, an International Committee for the Defence of Children in 1951, a Permanent Committee of Mothers in 1955, a Committee for Problems of the Child and the Family which was first publicised in June 1964, and an International Solidarity Committee with South Vietnam in 1964.

There have also been WIDF Commissions on International Relations, Peace, Solidarity and Independence, Propaganda and Women's Rights.

WIDF's policies

In practice the WIDF has faithfully followed Soviet policies and has supported propaganda campaigns inspired by Moscow or other international front organisations. The Federation's essential theme that only in communist countries can women enjoy a full and happy life was repeated by the then President Hertta Kuusinen, member of the Politburo of the Finnish Communist Party, in an article in *World Marxist Review* in March 1971, when she wrote that 'only Socialism [communism] leads to women's complete liberation and offers the most favourable conditions for maximum use of her rights as mother, worker and citizen'.

Opposition to Soviet control of the WIDF led to the withdrawal from full membership of the Italian affiliate, the Union of Italian Women (UDI), in 1964. When the Sino–Soviet dispute disrupted the Congress in 1963, the Chinese and their allies sought to expose Soviet control of the organisation, in line with their criticism of all the Soviet front organisations in which they had previously participated.

Although the Union of French Women, the WIDF affiliate from which the WIDF had originally sprung, condemned the Soviet invasion of Czechoslovakia in 1968 as contrary to the principles of sovereignty and non-interference, no such protest came from the WIDF itself. At the Congress in 1969, however, French delegates were, for the first time, not elected to the post of either President or Secretary-General, one or both of which had always been previously filled by representatives of the French affiliate.

An observer at this Congress from the WILPF, writing in *Call to Women* (July 1969), commented that

> although the final appeal for joint action by the [Sixth] Congress called for a spirit of peace, friendship and mutual understanding, little mention of these essential themes was made in the speeches . . . rather did so many of the contributions tend to build up hatred and the cold war . . . Certainly we would all condemn imperialism, neo-colonialism and aggression, but to reiterate continuously that such evils emanate from one side only cannot further the cause of peace.

The Belgrade weekly *NIN* (quoted by the Yugoslav news agency, *Tanyug*, 23 October 1981) noted that only those who had been chosen beforehand had the chance to speak in plenum at the World Congress in Prague, in October 1981. *NIN* said that all those who were likely to blame both blocs for strained international relations were prevented from addressing the plenum; such views were denounced by the President, Freda BROWN, who said that the notion of the guilt of both sides was 'the falsehood of the century' (according to *NIN*, many countries said in the commission that the crisis in detente was as much the fault of the East as the West). The Japanese representative stated that her organisation, Fundaren, disagreed with the condemnation of China and the Soviet line in Afghanistan and Cambodia; when she wished to say so in plenum, she was pushed out of the hall by a steward. Subsequently, representatives of other countries tried to take the floor (including Algeria, France, Iraq, Italy, Denmark, Norway, Romania and Yugoslavia), but the microphones were switched off, the 'peace march' was played loudly and the meeting brought to an end.

Congresses

Since its first Congress in Paris in November 1945, the WIDF has held Congresses as follows—Budapest (December 1948), Copenhagen (June 1953), Vienna (June 1958), Moscow (June 1963), Helsinki (June 1969), East Berlin (October 1975), Prague (October 1981) and Moscow (June 1987).

According to Freda Brown, writing in *Women of the Whole World* (No. 1, 1987), before the June 1987 Congress was held

> . . . For the first time a thematic centre 'Women and Socialism' will be functioning at a World Congress of Women. This will be all the more

important, since many women's organisations, above all of the developing countries are showing great interest in the experience of socialist society in solving the women's question.

It should be noted, that the Congress will be taking place in the 70th year of the Great October Socialist Revolution. We hope that Soviet women will acquaint the participants and guests of the Congress with the concerted achievements of socialism in the host-country . . .

Other activities

The WIDF has organised two conferences in Copenhagen in support of Soviet policy, one in May 1979 on 'disarmament and against the neutron bomb' and a second in April 1983 on the arms race. In 1982 it launched a Women's World Campaign for Peace and Disarmament. It also runs a campaign with the title 'No to Star Wars. Yes to Peace on Earth and in Outer Space'. It has held numerous seminars—e.g. Panama (June 1980—with UNESCO), New York (June 1980), Antananarivo (summer 1980), Aden (November 1980), Kabul (December 1980), Mexico (June 1983), Warsaw (September 1984). It organised a peace school in June 1984 and a 'peace work-shop' in May 1985, both in Bulgaria; a peace school in Leningrad in May 1986; and subsequently a peace school in Australia.

A WIDF regional centre for Latin America was opened in Havana in 1987. The Federation, together with UNESCO, has also helped to establish an orphanage in Beirut. It has set up a welfare centre in Hanoi and a literacy centre in Afghanistan, and held a training course for African women in Sofia in October 1982.

Freda Brown represented the WIDF at the 26th Soviet Party Congress in Moscow in February 1981. The WIDF was also represented at the Fifth National Congress of the Vietnamese Women's Union in Hanoi in May 1982, and at a women's peace festival in Dusseldorf (FRG) in September 1982. The Federation sent a message of solidarity to the wives and mothers of British miners on strike in 1984, and a WIDF Secretary addressed a meeting of women at the Greenham Common peace camp.

The WIDF held an emergency women's meeting in solidarity with the Libyan People and for a Mediterranean Peace Zone, in Athens in June 1986 and an International Conference in Solidarity with the Women of South Africa, Namibia and the Front-Line States, in London January–February 1987. It organised a tour of Europe by representatives of the women's section of the African National Congress (ANC).

WIDF delegations have also visited Nicaragua (September

1979), Cambodia and Vietnam (November 1979), Lebanon (May 1982), Syria and Lebanon (October 1982), Lebanon again (February 1983), Mozambique (spring 1983) and India (September 1983), Libya (1986) and the UK including Northern Ireland (1986).

International Women's Year and Decade

Despite its role in inspiring the UN Year of Women in 1975, the year of its own 30th anniversary, the Federation almost completely ignored the UN Conference on International Women's Year, held in Mexico in June, maintaining that its own Congress in East Berlin in October was the year's most important event. Subsequently there was a change of course and the WIDF took part in the World Conference on the UN Decade for Women (1976–85) in Copenhagen in July 1980, and in the concluding UN conference in Nairobi, in July 1985, which ended the Decade.

The Continuing Committee set up by the 1975 WIDF Congress was named the International Committee for the UN Decade for Women (President, Freda Brown). This Committee organised a World Conference in the International Year of the Child (Moscow, September 1979).

The WIDF also marks 8 March each year as International Women's Day. This anniversary was originally a celebration kept by the Second International Conference of Socialist Women (the Socialist International's Women's organisation) to commemorate the first major women's demonstration which took place in New York, 8 March 1857: it was only after the Russian Revolution, for which the date was also significant, that the communists tried to take over the anniversary for their own ends.

12. World Federation of Democratic Youth

The World Federation of Democratic Youth (WFDY) is also known under its French, German and Spanish titles which are, respectively, *Fédération mondiale de la jeunesse démocratique, Weltbund der Demokratischen Jugend* and *Federación Mundial de la Juventud Democrática*. Its headquarters is at Ady Endre Utca 19, Budapest 11, Hungary (during the Hungarian uprising in 1956, however, the headquarters was temporarily removed, for safety's sake, to Prague).

Origins

The WFDY was founded in November 1945 at a World Youth Conference convened in London by the World Youth Council, an existing international front organisation subsequently disbanded. Many other youth organisations then joined what was alleged to be a non-political movement but, as was foreseeable, communists soon captured the key posts in the new international body and turned it into another of Stalin's new Soviet-controlled propaganda organisations. By 1949 most of its non-communist members had left, many of whom thereupon formed their own organisation, the World Assembly of Youth (WAY). Their departure was hardly surprising; the WFDY was by then fully aligned with the Cominform: as the Cominform Journal commented in 1950:

> The WFDY and the organisations affiliated to it more and more persistently place the struggle for peace in the forefront of their activities—pointing out to youth that, in view of the criminal manifestations of the warmongers, the struggle for democracy, for the national independence of peoples, for a better life is bound up with the struggle for peace. (*For a Lasting Peace, For a People's Democracy*, Bucharest, 9 June 1950)

There was further disruption in January, 1950, when (following Tito's break with the Cominform) the WFDY expelled the Yugoslav 'People's Youth' organisation. The executive committee's resolution described the Yugoslav youth 'leaders as traitors to the cause of peace and democracy, and deserters into the camp of the imperialist warmongers.'

Such strictures echoed the Moscow broadcasts to mark International Youth Day on November 10, 1949. One radio commentator spoke of 'the criminal Tito clique striving to educate Yugoslav youth in the spirit of Fascist ideology' and thus 'serving the interests of the American imperialists'. Another commentator spoke of 'Judas Tito and his agents', who were training young Yugoslavs in a spirit of 'hatred for the USSR, the People's Democracies and the democratic youth movement throughout the World'.

Although the WFDY was founded in London, its headquarters was originally in Paris, like those of a number of Soviet international organisations, until expulsion by the French Government in 1951. Since then it has been in Budapest (apart from a brief period at the time of the Hungarian uprising).

Declared Aims

According to the *Yearbook of International Organisations* (1986–87) the WFDY aims to

contribute to the education of youth in the spirit of freedom, democracy and solidarity; end imperialism, colonialism and neocolonialism; end racist and fascist regimes; ensure peace and security in the world . . . ; promote active participation of youth in economic, social, cultural and political life by acting against all restriction and discrimination connected with age, sex, methods of education, domicile, property, social status, religion, political convictions, colour and race, so as to ensure full . . . freedom of speech, of the Press, of religious belief, assembly and organisation; support the struggle of youth for higher living standards, for better conditions of education, work and leisure . . . , further development . . . in the spirit of peace and international friendship . . .

Organisation and Membership

The WFDY has 270 affiliates and observers in 115 countries, most of its membership being from communist countries. Affiliated organisations from non-communist countries generally represent small groups associated with national communist Parties.

The highest organ of the WFDY is the Assembly which meets at least every four years. The Executive Committee, elected by the Assembly, is responsible for implementing its decisions; it has 72 members and meets annually. The Bureau, responsible for routine business, has 33 members and controls the activities of the Secretariat, departments and commissions at headquarters. The departments deal with such matters as disarmament, international solidarity, peace, national independence, the rights of youth, young women, culture, children, students and sport: each commission covers a major geographical region.

Office Holders

The officers are (1987) President: Walid MASRI (Lebanon); Secretary-General: Vilmos CSERVENY (Hungary);[a] Deputy Secretaries-General: Miguel GONZALEZ Reyes (Colombia), Turay SAIDU (Sierra Leone); Vice-Presidents: Luis CARDOSO (Portugal); Alfredo JUNIOR (Angola), LI Jong-gun (North Korea), NGUYEN Van Ky (Vietnam), Abdel Basit MOUSA (Sudan), Tomas MOYA (Cuba), Vsevolod NAKHODKIN (USSR), Cesar NAVARRO (Chile), Jorge PRIGOSHIN (Argentina), Mathew RAJAJI (India); Secretaries: Saleem Obaid ALTAMIMI (PDRY), Henrik ANDERSON (Denmark), Mihai BOTOROG (Romania), Uli BROCKMEYER (GDR), Freddy FERNANDEZ (Venezuela), Andrzej GERHARDT

[a] Replaced by Gyorgy SZABO (Hungary), September 1988.

(Poland), Vladimir JOHANNES (Czechoslovakia), Tadaaki KAWATA (Japan), Michel NKOLI (Congo), Atanas RUPCHEV (Bulgaria), Jackie SELIBI (ANC-South Africa), Markku SOPPELA (Finland), Konstantin STATHIS (Greece); Treasurer: Jorge CEZANNE (FRG). Other officers 'represent' El Salvador, France, Italy, 'Palestine' and the US.

The Italians and the French were Presidents and Secretaries-General respectively for 28 years until 1978 when the former Italian President, Pietro LAPICCIRELLA, was replaced by Ernesto OTTONE of Chile, and the French Secretary-General, Jean-Charles NEGRE, by Miklos BARABAS (Hungary). The Italian Communist newspaper, *l'Unità*, 10 March 1978, stated that the Italians wished to ensure a rotation of posts in a body having an increasingly universal character and to reflect the Italian communists' changing international policy; although the Italian communist youth organisation, FGCI, wished to remain within the WFDY, it wanted to 'be free to develop independent initiatives'. OTTONE was subsequently replaced by MASRI, and BARABAS by CSERVENY.

Publications
The WFDY regularly publishes *World Youth*, a monthly magazine; *WFDY News*, a monthly news bulletin (both published in English, French and Spanish); and *Disarmament Bulletin*. It also publishes booklets and pamphlets and its main subsidiary bodies—International Committee of Children's and Adolescents' Movements (CIMEA)*, International Bureau of Tourism and Exchanges of Youth (BITEJ) and International Voluntary Service for Friendship and Solidarity of Youth (SIVSAJ)—also publish information bulletins of their own.

Finance
The WFDY publishes no accounts. In practice, of course, most of its resources, whether affiliation fees, subsidies, voluntary donations, the provision of air tickets or conference facilities, come from Communist countries.

In 1980, the Sub-Committee on Oversight of the US House of Representatives stated that, at that time, it was calculated that the WFDY received a concealed Soviet subsidy of about US$ 1,575,000.

Relations with Other Bodies

(1) United Nations The WFDY has Category B status with UNESCO, Category I with ECOSOC, liaison status with the FAO and Special List status with the ILO. It is also an associate member of the Co-ordinating Committee for Voluntary Work Camps under the aegis of UNESCO (the WFDY Medal and Diploma were given to Amadou Mahtar M'BOW, UNESCO Director-General, when he visited the WFDY headquarters in June 1979). The WFDY was not re-elected to the board of the unofficial Conference of Non-Governmental Organisations in Consultative Status with ECOSOC (CONGO), in September 1985.

(2) Other International Front Organisations The WFDY has 'close and fraternal cooperation' with the International Union of Students (IUS)*, particularly in organising the World Youth Festivals. Its President and Secretary-General are usually members of the Presidential Committee of the World Peace Council (WPC)*.

Jointly with the WFDY and the IUS, the Commission of the Soviet Communist theoretical journal, *World Marxist Review*, which is published in Prague, sponsored an international symposium in Prague in 1985 on the theme 'Working Youth and Students against the Threat of Nuclear War'.

The WFDY has close working links with the other Soviet-controlled international front organisations and participates from time to time in the regular meetings.

(3) Non-communist Organisations The WFDY cooperates with the Pan-African Youth Movement (PAYM), the Continental Organisation of Latin American Students (OCLAE) and the All-Africa Students' Union (AASU) in the sphere of 'anti-imperialist solidarity, peace and disarmament'; and with such organisations as the International Union of Socialist Youth (IUSY), the Council of European National Youth Committees (CENYC), the International Federation of Liberal and Radical Youth (IFLRY), the Nordic Centre Youth (NCY), the Ecumenical Youth Council in Europe (EYCE), the International Student Movement for the United Nations (ISMUN) and others in 'the struggle for peace and activity for disarmament, solidarity and youth rights'.

The WFDY is also associated with the IUS in the work of the Framework for All-European Youth and Student Cooperation (AEYSC).

National Affiliates
The WFDY has national affiliates in most countries including the UK, Ireland and the USA. They are respectively the British 'Young Communist League', the Connolly Youth Movement of Ireland and the 'Young Communist League' in the USA (all three countries are regularly represented on the Executive Committee).

Subsidiaries
The WFDY's specialised bodies include the International Committee of Children's and Adolescents' Movements (ICCAM) (also known by its French initials—CIMEA)*, which was founded in Kiev in 1957 (its Secretary-General is Sandor MOLNARI of Hungary): the International Bureau of Tourism and Exchanges of Youth (BITEJ), founded in March 1960 (its Director is Andrzej CHECINSKI (Poland) and the Bureau's links include membership of the Co-ordinating Committee for International Voluntary Service which works under aegis of UNESCO): and the International Voluntary Service for Friendship and Solidarity of Youth (SIVSAJ), founded in Moscow in February 1967 to increase WFDY influence in the developing countries and to counter the US Peace Corps (its Director is Atanas RUPCHEV of Bulgaria). The WFDY also has bureaux directed towards students, culture, young women, and children.

Assemblies
The Assembly has met as follows:

London	(November 1945)
Budapest	(September 1949)
Bucharest	(July 1953)
Kiev	(August 1957)
Prague	(August 1959)
Warsaw	(August 1962)
Sofia	(June 1966)
Budapest	(October 1970)
Varna	(November 1974)
East Berlin	(February 1978)
Prague	(June 1982)
Budapest	(November 1986)

WFDY's Policies
The WFDY consistently supports Soviet policies. Having expelled the Yugoslav affiliate following Stalin's quarrel with Tito

in 1949, its leaders made no criticism of the Soviet suppression of the Hungarian uprising in 1956 or the Soviet invasion of Czechoslovakia in 1968. They even supported the Soviet invasion of Afghanistan in December 1979. China left the organisation in 1967, declaring that it had become an instrument for 'the Soviet revisionist leading clique'.

As non-communist critics of the WFDY stated in an article in the organ of the International Union of Socialist Youth, *IUSY Survey* (No. 3 of 1965), commenting on the granting of scholarships by the WFDY:

> We do not mind WFDY distributing 100 scholarships on behalf of eight Communist governments. We think it is, in some cases at least a very good thing for Africa. But we in IUSY object to the hypocrisy of trying to conceal that WFDY is the Communist Youth International. IUSY openly states that it is the International of the Socialist Youth and Students. Why does not WFDY openly admit that it is the Communist Youth International? Do the leaders of WFDY consider it 'bad' or 'dirty' in any way to be Communist?

An Italian delegate to the Seventh WFDY Assembly, in June 1966, writing in the Italian youth periodical, *Nuova Sinistra*, July 1966, made a different point: he was 'surprised and shocked that youth movements in socialist countries were also party and State organisations, so that it was impossible for enthusiastic Western youth delegates to discuss fruitfully economic or political problems on a national, regional or world scale with these ill-prepared fellow delegates.'

In *World Marxist Review*, January 1970, Raymond GUYOT (France), then a member of the WPC Presidential Committee, wrote that 'the torch of proletarian internationalism, freedom and peace, held aloft by the Socialist Youth International at the time of its founding, later picked up and carried forward with glory by the Young Communist International, is now in the new conditions borne with merit and in different ways by the WFDY.' (The comment is interesting as being a rare communist admission that the post-war WFDY directly descends, through the World Youth Council of the 1940s, from the Comintern).

The WFDY was represented by its President at the Twenty-seventh Soviet Party Congress in Moscow in February–March 1986, and by its Secretary-General at the 26th in February 1981.

Unfortunately, however, the British 'Young Communist League' (YCL) expressed concern over some of the conclusions reached at the WFDY's 11th Assembly in Prague in June 1982. Stating that it was totally opposed to the imposition of martial law in Poland and to the Soviet intervention in Afghanistan, the YCL criticised the manner in which peace issues were dealt with in the Executive Committee's report. The YCL did not agree that 'the US and its allies were the sole source of world tension' and, although deeply concerned by some aspects of Chinese foreign policy, it said it was opposed to 'collective condemnation of China' (The Communist daily newspaper, *Morning Star*, London, 21 June 1982).

Other Campaigns and Activities
The WFDY has from time to time launched numerous *ad hoc* campaigns, such as the 'Youth Accuses Imperialism' campaign inaugurated by the Eighth Assembly in 1970, 'World Campaign of Common Actions—Youth for Anti-imperialist Solidarity, Peace and Progress' and 'The Youth of the World with Chile' inaugurated at the Ninth Assembly in 1974, a campaign for peace and disarmament and against the production of the so-called 'neutron bomb' at the Tenth Assembly in 1978 and a 'World Campaign of Youth Actions against the Nuclear Threat, for Peace and Disarmament' at the Eleventh in 1982. The Twelfth Assembly in 1986 called for participation by young people in an 'Anti-Nuclear Youth Coalition'.

The WFDY awards scholarships regularly for study in East European countries, usually to leaders from developing countries.

Regional Activities
Africa The WFDY campaigns on behalf of what the Soviet Union recognises as 'national liberation movements'. An International Conference in Solidarity with the People and Youth of Africa Stuggling against Colonialism, held in Mogadishu in April 1974, was organised jointly with the PAYM and the Somali Youth Union. In 1979, the WFDY's 'Julio Antonio Mella Brigade' sent teams of doctors to Ethiopia and Angola. A delegation of the youth section of the ANC-South Africa visited the WFDY in 1980 and 1981, as did an Angolan youth delegation in mid-1980 and a PAYM delegation in February 1983.

An international seminar on The Role of Youth in the Struggle for the Consolidation of National Independence and Socio-economic Development was held in February 1981 in Addis Ababa. A WFDY delegation toured Africa in 1984.

The Americas The WFDY organised an International Work

Brigade to build a school in Cuba. (This 'Julio Antonio Mella Brigade' was established as a permanent body by the WFDY Executive Committee in December 1972). Fidel CASTRO visited WFDY headquarters in June 1972, when he received the WFDY's Medal.

The WFDY, IUS and other bodies organised a Youth Meeting on National Independence of Latin America, in Caracas in September 1975. An international seminar on The Struggle against Fascist Regimes and Violations of Human Rights in Latin America was held in Bogota in November 1979, and a conference on The New International Economic Order was held in Oaxtepec, Mexico, in September 1980. A Caribbean Youth Anti-Imperialist Seminar was held in Jamaica in July 1980; a meeting of Latin American and Caribbean Youth against Imperialist Intervention, in Managua, Nicaragua, in September 1981; a consultative meeting of Latin American and Caribbean affiliates, in Buenos Aires in December 1984, and a meeting of Latin American and Caribbean Youth against Imperialist Intervention, in Cuba in March 1985.

OTTONE, then WFDY President, led a delegation to Nicaragua in October 1979, and delegates of the Nicaraguan Sandinista Youth visited WFDY headquarters in November 1979 and in October 1980. The WFDY sent an International Medical Brigade to Nicaragua in 1979 and an International Brigade to help with the coffee harvest there, from December 1984 to February 1985 and early in 1987.

A youth delegation from Mexico visited the WFDY in November 1979. In May and June 1980, delegations from Guatemala, Panama, El Salvador, Argentina and Brazil made similar visits. OTTONE led a delegation to Brazil, Argentina, Uruguay and Paraguay in May 1980, and another delegation is reported to have gone to Bolivia, Panama, Jamaica, Mexico, Nicaragua and the Dominican Republic at about the same time. A WFDY delegation visited Chile in December 1981.

Asia A joint WFDY/IUS delegation, together with representatives of the Tenth World Youth Festival Permanent Commission, visited Hanoi in April 1973. In 1977, Vietnam awarded the WFDY the 'Order of Friendship' for its support and assistance. The WFDY supported the Soviet line by condemning Chinese intervention in Vietnam in February 1979. OTTONE led a delegation to North Korea in September 1979. Delegations of WFDY journalists visited Afghanistan in June 1980 and Indochina in April 1982. Other delegations visited Korea in April 1985, and Laos and Cambodia in February 1986.

Meetings organised by the WFDY in Asia have included a conference on Peace in the Indian Ocean, in Madras in October 1976, and another in Trivandrum in August 1981 (jointly with the IUS); an International Youth and Student Conference in Solidarity with Vietnam, in Hyderabad in May 1979 (jointly with the IUS); and an International Conference of Solidarity with Afghanistan, in Kabul in September 1980. A consultative meeting of WFDY member organisations from Asia and Oceania was held in Tashkent in February 1982, a conference For Peace, Security and Cooperation in Asia and the Pacific Region in Ulan Bator in August 1984, and an international youth meeting on Peace, Security, Development and Cooperation in Asia and the Pacific, in Hanoi in May 1986.

Europe The Eleventh Assembly, in June 1982, launched a World Campaign of Youth Actions against the Nuclear Threat, for Peace and Disarmament. The Campaign's organisers publish *Disarmament Bulletin*. A WFDY Executive Committee meeting in West Berlin, 21–23 April 1983, was followed by an international conference: Youth Peace Work—News and Views, on 23–24 April, the first of three in this series, the other two having been held in Copenhagen, April 1984 and Mlada Boleslav, Czechoslovakia, May 1985. A Peace Meeting of Youth Organisations of the Socialist Countries was held in Potsdam in May 1983, and an international seminar on Young People's Contribution to Peace and Disarmament in Warsaw in October 1983. A Youth Peace Festival was held in Portugal in July 1983.

The WFDY held an Executive Committee meeting in Nicosia in December 1981, followed by an international conference for Solidarity with the Youth and People of Cyprus; and a conference of Mediterranean Youth Organisations in Athens in January 1982. The WFDY organised a seminar on Transnationals and the Mass Media in Geneva in March 1980, a Youth Press Seminar in West Berlin in October 1981, an international meeting on Solidarity with Turkey, in Athens, September 1984, and a seminar on the fortieth anniversary of the 'Victory over Fascism' in Sofia, March 1985.

The WFDY campaigns against British policy in Northern Ireland (a WFDY delegation visited Dublin in October 1972). It promoted a Round Table Conference on Ireland in Dublin in February 1981 in conjunction with two of its national affiliates, the British 'Young Communist League' and the Irish Connolly Youth Association.

In October 1984, a WFDY journalists' delegation visited the United Kingdom to show solidarity with the miners' strike. The WFDY held a special meeting on a 'new international economic order', in Budapest in May 1984.

Middle East The WFDY follows the Soviet line on the Arab–Israeli dispute and on Lebanese affairs and OTTONE led a delegation to Lebanon in October 1979. Visits to WFDY headquarters have been made by delegations from the People's Liberation Front of Oman in July 1980, from the General Union of Palestinian Students in February 1983, and from Egyptian Youth in January 1984. Yasser ARAFAT, the Chairman of the Palestine Liberation Organisation (PLO), met WFDY leaders in Budapest in February 1982 and April 1983.

The WFDY held an Executive Committee meeting in Beirut in March 1981 and sent a fact-finding delegation to Lebanon in March 1982. It organised a meeting on the Role of the Arab National, Progressive, Youth and Student Organisations in the Struggle against Imperialism, Zionism and Reaction, for a Just and Lasting Peace in the Middle East in Aden in March 1985, and a session of the Tripoli-based International Secretariat of Solidarity with the Arab Peoples and their Central Cause—Palestine, in Budapest in January 1985.

13. World Federation of Scientific Workers

The World Federation of Scientific Workers (WFSW) is also known under its French, German and Spanish titles which are, respectively, *Fédération mondiale des travailleurs scientifiques, Welt Föderation der Wissenschaftler, Federación Mundial de Trabajadores Científicos*. Its headquarters is at 6 Endsleigh Street, London WC1 (and also 10 rue Vauquelin, Paris 5e, France). There are also a number of Regional Centres; those in Prague, Calcutta and Peking have been closed over the years, but those that survive include Algiers (transferred in 1980 from Cairo), East Berlin and New Delhi.

Origins
A number of Stalin's postwar international front organisations were founded in London in 1945–46 but most of them

subsequently established their headquarters in Paris (before being asked to move on by the French authorities, usually to communist capitals in eastern Europe). The WFSW was exceptional in both being founded in London and electing to establish its base in London, where it has always remained (although in recent years an alternative head office has also been established, for practical reasons, in Paris). The link with London survived because the WFSW was founded at the instigation of a British trade union, the Association of Scientific Workers, which then and for many years after was under Communist control, but which no longer exists in this form. The founding conference, at which scientists representing eighteen organisations in fourteen countries were present, took place in London in 1946 and, as intended by the sponsors, communists soon secured most, if not all, of the key posts in the new international organisation.

Declared Aims
The WFSW claims to exist to link organisations whose purpose is to safeguard scientific rights, to improve scientists' working conditions and status and to promote 'the use of science for peaceful purposes'. In practice, in common with its sister international front organisations, the WFSW has always functioned as a mouthpiece for Soviet foreign policy.

Organisation and Membership
The WFSW is controlled by its General Assembly which is supposed to meet every two years, and in which all affiliated organisations are represented. It is governed between Assemblies by an Executive Council of 40 representatives of these member organisations, elected individually by the Assembly but subject to replacement from time to time by the organisation which they represent. There is also a Bureau, consisting of the President, five Vice Presidents, the Secretary-General, the Deputy Secretary-General, three Assistant Secretaries and the heads of the WFSW Regional Centres, which transacts the ordinary daily business of the organisation.

The WFSW claims a membership of about 750,000 scientific workers representing some 57 national organisations in about 40 'capitalist, socialist and developing states, and also a great number of individual members from many countries' (*Pravda*, 20 July 1986).

Office holders
The leading WFSW officials are (1987) the President: Professor Jean-Marie LEGAY (France), who was awarded the Lenin Peace Prize in 1983; Vice Presidents: Nikolai BASOV (USA), Pierre BIQUARD (France), Kiril BRATANOV (Bulgaria), Narendra GUPTA (India), Tokutaro HIRONE (Japan); and Secretary-General Stanley DAVISON (UK). The Deputy Secretary-General is Len WELLS (UK) and the Treasurer is Andre JAEGLE (France).

Publications and Information
Scientific World is produced quarterly, in English, Esperanto, French, German and Russian (some 24,000 copies in all). WFSW also produces a *Bulletin ad hoc* about every two months and such pamphlets as *Human Progress Depends on Peace* (about disarmament) and *The Earth Must not Become a Desert* (about ecology)—both of which were published jointly with the World Federation of Trade Unions (WFTU)—and such brochures as *Ending the Arms Race: The Task of the Scientist, An Arms Race in Space Must be Prevented*, as well as brochures about the WFSW itself and catalogues of all the articles published in *Scientific World* and in other WFSW publications. It has also published a *Charter for Scientific and Technical Cooperation and Technology Transfer*.

Finance
The WFSW claims that it is financed by subscriptions from member organisations, calculated as a percentage of their members' subscriptions. In practice, as with all the international front organisations, about 90 per cent of this income comes from communist sources, mainly the Soviet Union (and in this case East Germany) and any shortfalls are met by communist affiliates either in cash or in kind (e.g. the Romanian affiliate prints the French language edition of the magazine *Scientific World*). As usual, no accounts are circulated.

In 1980 the Sub-committee on Oversight of the US House of Representatives stated that, at that time, it was calculated that the WFSW received a concealed Soviet subsidy of about US$100,000.

Relations with other bodies
(1) United Nations The WFSW has Category A status with UNESCO, consultative status with ECOSOC and maintains

contact with the ILO. The association with UNESCO dates from 1950; 'international cooperation in science and technology . . . through close cooperation with UNESCO' is among the WFSW's original aims.

(2) Other International Front Organisations Even since its former president, the French Communist scientist Frédéric JOLIOT-CURIE, was also president of the WPC, the WFSW has always worked closely with that organisation, especially on joint campaigns against the West's nuclear weapons. It has also collaborated with the WFTU: in 1949 the two organisations issued a statement agreeing on 'joint activity in those fields in which they have a common ground'. It has also cooperated with the International Radio and Television Organisation (OIRT) in producing the series of broadcasts called 'Science in the Service of Peace' which emanated from Prague before 1968.

In March 1979, the Federation collaborated with the International Institute for Peace (IIP) in holding, in Vienna, an international conference on Problems of Conversion from War to Peace Production.

The WFSW has close working links with the other Soviet-controlled international front organisations and participates from time to time in the regular liaison meetings.

(3) Non-communist Organisations The WFSW and WFSW members individually have links with the Pugwash Movement and also with the Non-Aligned Movement (NAM): a WFSW delegation visited India in August 1985, had talks with the Indian Prime Minister, Rajiv GANDHI (India then being the incumbent President of the NAM). LEGAY, its leader, stressed the 'common stands' of the WFSW and the NAM on questions of war and peace; and both sides noted the importance of expanding and cementing contacts 'in the field of disarmament'.

Subsidiaries The WFSW has four Permanent Standing Committees on science policy, disarmament, socio-economics and publications. In addition, its members benefit from the facilities offered by the Rest Home which the Bulgarian Union of Scientific Workers runs, on behalf of the WFSW, at Druzhba, near Varna on the Black Sea.

General Assemblies

The General Assembly has met on fifteen occasions, namely

London	(July 1946)
Dobris (Czechoslovakia)	(September 1948)
Paris & Prague	(April 1951)
Budapest	(September 1953)
East Berlin	(September 1955)
Helsinki	(August/September 1957)
Warsaw	(September 1959)
Moscow	(September 1962)
Budapest	(September 1965)
Paris	(April 1969)
Varna	(September 1973)
London	(September 1976)
East Berlin	(May 1980)
Paris	(September 1983)
Moscow	(July 1986)

The next Assembly will be held in the GDR, probably in East Berlin, in 1989.

Other activities

According to *Pravda*, 20 July 1986, the WFSW was among the first organisations 'to declare against the US [when it] unleashed chemical warfare in Vietnam, against neutron weapons, against American plans of militarisation of outer space. . . . '

In other words, the WFSW has faithfully carried out its role as a front organisation. It has invariably attacked the 'imperialist' countries and praised the Communist ones (with the exception of Yugoslavia during the Stalin–Tito quarrel). It has waxed indignant at the 'victimisation' of scientists in the United States when from time to time Communist scientists have been refused passports or removed from jobs on security grounds: it has said nothing about the purges, trials and continual restrictions on scientists in the Soviet orbit, from which most of its members come.

Some idea of the WFSW's real attitude to scientific truth may be gained from an illuminating speech made by General Hruska at a scientific conference organised in Brno, in February, 1952, by the WFSW's Czech affiliate. He said, *inter alia*:

It is essential that Marxism–Leninism should penetrate into every branch of science . . . A particularly strong attack must be delivered on cosmopolitanism . . . An attack must also be launched on the deliberately misleading reactionary hypothesis of the 'non-political' nature of science and its position 'above party'. The fight against cosmopolitanism must be stepped up and an end put to scientific objectivism. (*Prague Radio*, 26 February, 1952)

WFSW activities have included the holding of symposia on the Higher Training of Scientists and Engineers (East Berlin, May 1980), Disarmament and Development (Varna, October 1980), Science and the Crises of Development (Paris, September 1983) and Scientific, Technical and Socio-economic Evolution: the Responsibility of Scientists (East Berlin, November 1984); Science, Technology and Development (New Delhi, March 1987). The WFSW also sponsored a forum (Science, Technology, Peace) in Moscow in July 1986.

As *Pravda* has indicated, the WFSW instigated campaigns against nuclear tests (American, French and British, but not Soviet) in the early 1960s. It held a conference on the Dangers of ABC [i.e. atomic, biological and chemical] Weapons in Europe, in East Berlin in November 1971, and in May 1972 issued an appeal for progress towards disarmament and the abolition of nuclear weapons. It held an international round-table on the Qualitative Arms Race, in East Berlin in April 1983 and a symposium on the Arms Race in Outer Space in Prague, October 1985.

At its Executive Council meeting held in Budapest in April 1981, a resolution was adopted supporting the proposals made by the late President BREZHNEV for 'an international commission of scientists', and expressing the WFSW's willingness to participate. Total and uncritical support has also been given to his successors' various disarmament initiatives, including those of Mikhail Gorbachev.

14. World Federation of Teachers' Unions

The World Federation of Teachers' Union (FISE) is best known by the acronym derived from its French title, *Fédération internationale syndicale de l'enseignement*; it is also known under its German and Spanish titles namely *Internationale Vereinigung Lehrergewerkschaften* and *Federación Internacional Sindical de la Enseñanza*. Its headquarters is at Wilhelm-Wolff-Strasse 21, BP 176, 1110 Berlin, GDR.

Origins
Technically, FISE is one of eleven trade union internationals (TUIs) which function both as ostensibly autonomous international trade union organisations each for a particular industry and as trade departments of the WFTU*.

In fact, FISE was founded in Paris in 1946 and existed for three years before, in 1949, it became a WFTU trade department.

FISE was based in Paris until 1952, when it was expelled by the French Government for 'fifth column activity'. It then joined its parent body, the WFTU, in what was at that time the Soviet Sector of Vienna until, in February 1956, it was in turn expelled by the Austrian Government as infringing the new Austrian Government's neutrality. It eventually settled in Prague in November 1959 but in July 1977, in part to emphasise its separate identity, it left Prague (where the WFTU has its own headquarters) and removed to East Berlin.

FISE has never enjoyed any significant non-communist support. But it is notably more independent than other WFTU trade union internationals, and functions more as an international professional association than as a TUI.

Declared Aims
FISE's declared aims are to 'Build a democratic educational system in all countries of the world; fight against illiteracy and for peace and disarmament; unite teachers' trade unions and promote teachers' trade union and professional rights' (*Yearbook of International Organisations*, 1986–87). According to a resolution of its World Conference in Warsaw in 1949, it originally existed to establish universal free education, outlaw the militarist or racialist textbooks, oppose military training and corporal punishment, train teachers in a 'democratic spirit . . . and to struggle actively against reaction' and to eliminate religious influence in schools.

Organisation and Membership
FISE is controlled by World Conferences—held at intervals of one or, more recently, usually two years—and is run by an Administrative Committee. There is also an Auditing Commission.

It claims a membership of 26 million teachers, organised in national affiliates active in 78 countries.

Office holders
FISE's leading officers (1987) are; President: Lesturuge ARIYA-
WANSA (Sri Lanka); Vice-Presidents: Michele BARACAT
(France), Abani BORAL (India), Antonio JAIMES (Mexico),
Helga LABS (GDR), Mamadou N'DOYE (Senegal), Dr. Rimm
PAPILOV (USSR), Jamil SBIBADA ('Palestine'); Secretary-
General: Gerard MONTANT (France); Secretaries: Hans
CHRISTOPH (GDR), Mikhail KOLESNIKOV (USSR),
Eulogio SUAREZ (Chile).

Publications and information
FISE publishes—*Teachers of the World* quarterly (in English,
French, German and Spanish), *International Teachers' News*
eight times a year (in English, French, German, Spanish,
Russian, Arabic and Portuguese) and occasional brochures and
reports.

Finance
FISE seldom publishes accounts. It claims to be financed by
contributions from its affiliated member organisations and by
'subventions from UNESCO'. Its annual budget is said to total
$130,000 (in convertible currency) and $225,000 (in non-convert-
ible currency).

Relations with other bodies
(1) United Nations FISE has Category A status with UNESCO
and Roster Status with ECOSOC.

(2) Other International Front Organisations Apart from its organisational ties with the WFTU, FISE has also had especially close
links with the WPC. As early as 1956, the FISE Administrative
Committee ordained that:

> It is important that teachers' trade unions in different countries should play
> a significant part in the peace movement, and should extend their activity
> among students and parents. The Administrative Committee notes that the
> FISE has in the past collaborated with the WPC and considers that this
> collaboration must be further strengthened in future. (*Teachers of the World,*
> *March 1956*)

The FISE has close working links with the other Soviet-
controlled international front organisations and participates from
time to time in the regular liaison meetings.

(3) Non-communist Organisations FISE has signed agreements with the Confederation of American Educators (CEA) and the Federation of Arab Teachers (FAT). It is a member of the International Teachers' Trade Union Cooperation Committee (ITTCC), which was established in Paris in 1971.

Despite the fact that the non-communist World Confederation of Organisations of the Teaching Profession (WCOTP) agreed in 1958 to cooperate with FISE on 'the basis of mutual respect', their relationship has not proved particularly harmonious. In November 1977, FISE and the three non-communist teachers' international groups (WCOTP, the International Federation of Free Teachers' Unions and the World Confederation of Teachers) met together in Copenhagen, but a second such meeting, scheduled to be held in Helsinki in 1981, was cancelled because of objections to FISE's support of the Soviet invasion of Afghanistan.

World Conferences
Fifteen FISE World Conferences have been held as follows: Paris (1946), Brussels (1947), Budapest (1948), Warsaw (1949), Vienna (1950), Vienna (1953), Warsaw (1957), Conakry (1960), Algiers (1965), Damascus (1969), Bucharest (1973), Moscow (1977), Budapest (1981), Lisbon (1983), Sofia (1985).

Other campaigns
FISE has historically played a major role in the campaign against 'colonialism' (not, of course, in Soviet Asia) and, in the post-colonial era, has devoted much energy to campaigning in the developing world. In 1957 the Warsaw Conference recorded that the 'constant assistance' which FISE had given to trade union organisations in the 'colonial, semi-colonial and recently liberated countries' had resulted in the participation of numerous delegations from Africa, Asia and the Middle East in its activities.

In its propaganda, FISE has held out the system of education in the Soviet Union and other communist countries as an example to be followed by others. It has also advocated 'education for peace'. It handed over the results of its campaign, 'Millions of Signatures by Teachers for Peace', to the UN in 1986, the International Year of Peace (IYP).

At a meeting in Cologne in April 1985, 33 members of 18 national Teachers for Peace organisations, peace movements and teachers' Unions, together with FISE representatives, participated on the initiative of the Teachers for Peace organisations of the Nordic countries, when it was decided to hold an International Conference on Peace Education (Copenhagen, August 1986).

15. World Federation of Trade Unions

The World Federation of Trade Unions (WFTU), is also known under its French, German and Spanish titles which are, respectively, *Fédération syndicale mondial*, *Weltgewerkschaftsbund* and *Federación Sindical Mundial*. Its headquarters is at Vinohradska 10, 12147, Prague 2.

Origins

Historically it was the British Trades Union Congress (TUC) which originally launched the initiative for setting up the WFTU. In November 1943 at the height of the Anglo–Soviet wartime rapprochement the TUC issued invitations to 71 trade union organisations in 31 countries to appoint delegates to a world trade union conference, the first such event intended to heal the earlier split between the Comintern's Red Labour Unions and the Second International's socialist labour union movement. A preparatory conference, held in London in February 1945, set up a provisional Administrative Committee to draft a constitution; when their work was complete, the Foundation Congress was convened in Paris in October 1945, with permanent headquarters there.

Thus, the origin of the WFTU differs from that of most Soviet-controlled organisations in that the intention at least of its non-communist founders was to make it a genuine international trade union organisation. But it was not long before the communists asserted their control. Although, in recognition of the TUC's initiative its chairman Sir Walter CITRINE had been elected the first President, the Russians insisted, as the price of their cooperation, in having their nominee, the Frenchman Louis SAILLANT, as General Secretary. Saillant, ostensibly a socialist, was in fact a Stalinist and, as a full-time official was soon more powerful than the President. He filled the Secretariat with his allies, later became a WPC Bureau member, then Honorary President and was awarded a Lenin Peace Prize in 1957. Moreover it was not difficult at that time to maximise the communist element in WFTU as one by one the trade union groups in Eastern Europe and China fell to the communists.

In 1948, the British trade union leader, Arthur DEAKIN, who had succeeded Sir Walter Citrine as President, said 'The WFTU is rapidly becoming nothing more than another platform and instrument for the furtherance of Soviet policy'. By January 1949 the position of the non-communists in the WFTU had become so intolerable that, led by the TUC, the American CIO and the Dutch trades union organisation, the NVV, they left the organisation and later that year set up their own International Confederation of Free Trade Unions (ICFTU) with its headquarters in Brussels. In the foreword to a TUC pamphlet entitled *Free Trade Unions leave the WFTU*, representatives of the three above mentioned trade unions said that the WFTU was ' . . . completely dominated by communist organisations, which are themselves controlled by the Kremlin and the Cominform'. As Deakin said to the TUC Congress in September 1949, 'We started with an honest intention, but we were not dealing with honest men'.

Deakin was succeeded as WFTU President by an Italian Communist Giuseppe Di VITTORIO.

On 5 January 1951, the French Ministry of the Interior ordered the dissolution of the Paris headquarters of the WFTU as well as those of two other international front organisations—the World Federation of Democratic Youth (WFDY) and the Women's International Democratic Federation (WIDF) (see above). According to *The Times*, London, of 27 January 1951:

> The order was issued in accordance with a decree law of 1939 empowering the Minister of the Interior to withdraw authorisation for the existence of all foreign organisations if he judged it necessary. A foreign organisation is described in the law as one which either has its headquarters abroad, or, having headquarters in France, is in fact controlled by foreigners.
>
> It is officially stated that the three organisations concerned have carried out activities in complete contradiction of the aims stated in their statutes. They have been prominent instruments of Communist 'peace' propaganda and have been used as information services of the Cominform. Although the precise nature of their fifth column activity has not been revealed, this seems to have become more prominent in the last three months.

The Times added that the Ministry of the Interior 'is determined to take the necessary steps against foreign associations which try to undermine public security.'

The headquarters was then transferred to what was at that time the Soviet sector of Vienna where it remained until February

1956 when the Austrian Government, as a consequence of the Austrian State Treaty of the previous year, expelled it on the grounds that it had both broken its own statutes and endangered Austrian neutrality. The then Austrian Minister for the Interior, H. Helmer, explained that:

> The so-called World Federation of Trade Unions is a collection of Communist trade union organisations of various countries. During the Four Power occupation it transferred its headquarters to Vienna, after being expelled from France owing to its activities being against the interests of other States. In Vienna, a Secretariat of very large size was set up and developed into a centre for the direction of propaganda abroad. I hoped that, after the conclusion of the State Treaty and the withdrawal of the occupation troops, the WFTU leaders would take note of the changed situation in Austria. In this expectation, I gave the organisation the chance to work as an officially recognised association. However, only a short time later, the security authorities came into possession of unequivocal evidence that the WFTU officials are not prepared to respect the obligations arising from Austrian neutrality. The activities of the Vienna Secretariat of WFTU evoked the danger of conflicts with other States with whom Austria has friendly relations. These abuses could be tolerated no longer. I decided, therefore, after mature consideration, to give the order for the dissolution, with immediate effect, of the association World Federation of Trade Unions in Vienna. ('*Wiener Zeitung*' and '*Arbeiter-Zeitung*', 5 February, 1956).

The WFTU thereupon settled in Prague where it has since remained. There were abortive attempts to return the organisation to Paris in 1984: as the General Secretary of Force Ouvrière, the French affiliate of the ICFTU, told President Mitterand, his organisation would regard the re-establishment of the WFTU in France as

> an extremely disruptive element, which would have serious consequences for the international free trade union movement's action for social progress, and above all for democracy, freedom and peace: action prompted by the WFTU and its members against the installation of American missiles in Europe, in reply to the USSR's SS20s, is the most recent example of the objectives and the general attitude of this organisation, which is at the service of the Soviet Bloc.

The fact that the WFTU headquarters is in Prague caused serious internal problems in August 1968, at the time of the Soviet invasion of Czechoslovakia. The organisation's critical view of the invasion led to the removal from office of the ailing Louis SAILLANT and Renato BITOSSI, the Italian Communist, who had replaced Di Vittorio, and their eventual replacement by, respectively, Pierre GENSOUS (France) Deputy General

Secretary, and Enrique PASTORINO (Uruguay), both of whom were loyal communists. (Saillant, as a face saver, was made Honorary President).

Declared Aims

According to the *Yearbrook of International Organisations* (1986–87) the aims of the WFTU are

> To consolidate and unite the trade unions of the world, irrespective of race, nationality, religion or political opinion: strengthen the solidarity of the international trade union movement by encouraging systematic exchanges of information and experience in trade union work; help the workers in organising trade unions, promote their training in questions of international unity, increase their class consciousness; represent the interests of the workers in the international organisations and institutions.

Taken at their face value these declared aims differ little from the aims of the non-communist ICFTU, taken from the same source:

> Promote the interests of working people everywhere; work for constantly rising living standards, full employment, social security; reduce the gap between rich and poor, both within and between nations; work for international understanding, for disarmament and for the establishment of peace; help to organise the workers everywhere and secure recognition of their organisations as free bargaining agents; fight against oppression and dictatorship everywhere and against discrimination of any kind on the grounds of race, colour, creed or sex; defend the fundamental human and trade union rights. These aims are summarised in its motto 'Bread, Peace and Freedom'.

As usual, the difference lies in the membership, control and actual policies pursued.

Organisation and Membership

The WFTU's highest authority is its Congress, which meets every four years and which last met in East Berlin in September 1986.

Between Congresses the WFTU is administered by the General Council and the Bureau: the Council, which meets once a year, has 184 members from 92 countries (the places reserved for China and Albania have not been filled since 1966) and from the 10 Trade Union Internationals (TUIs)* plus FISE*. The Bureau, a more restricted body, guides the organisation between Council sessions and meets at least twice a year. It includes the President, the 13 Vice-Presidents, the General Secretary and 74 members from 37 countries, plus representatives of three TUIs.

The WFTU claims a total membership of 214 million. Almost 90 per cent come from communist Countries, 130 million living in the Soviet Union alone.

Membership of the WFTU is usually restricted to one national trade union organisation in each country, although affiliation may, according to the Constitution, be granted 'in exceptional circumstances to more than one national centre or more than one trade union'. Non-member organisations may also 'take part in the discussion of all problems and the adoption of resolutions concerning action with which they have been associated'. The 1973 Congress amended the Statutes to allow for 'associate membership' (on an Italian initiative, intended not so much to encourage new contacts as to loosen the Italian (communist) CGIL's ties with the WFTU, enabling it to apply for membership of the European Trade Union Confederation (ETUC), which it subsequently joined). In 1978 the CGIL formally disaffiliated from the WFTU, taking advantage of these new conditions.

Office Holders

The leading WFTU officials (1987) are President: Sandor GASPAR (Hungary); Vice Presidents: Ernest BOATSWAIN (Australia), Elias EL HABRE (Lebanon), Romain Vilon GUEZO (Benin), Indrajit GUPTA (India), Henri KRASUCKI (France), B. LUVSATSEREN (Mongolia), Izzedine NASSER (Syria), Valentin PACHO (Peru), Stepan SHALAYEV (USSR), Tadesse TAMERAT (Ethiopia), Roberto VEIGA (Cuba), Miroslav ZAVADIL (Czechoslovakia), Andreas ZIARTIDES (Cyprus); General Secretary: Ibrahim ZAKARIA (Sudan); Secretaries: Marie FRYBORTOVA (Czecholosvakia), Debkumar GANGULI (India), Siegfried KATZSCHMANN (GDR), Vsevolod MOZHAEV (USSR), Mario NAVARRO (Chile), Jan NEMOUDRY (Poland), Alain STERN (France).

Gaspar is a member of the Politburo of the Hungarian Socialist Workers' [communist] Party and Zakaria a member of the Central Committee of the Sudanese Communist Party.

The most important other officials in the Secretariat, are Vladimir PANCHEKHIN (USSR), head of the Asia and Oceania Department; Julio REYES, head of the Americas Department; Ali SABRA (country unknown), head of the Near and Middle East Department; Cassien GBAGUIDI (Benin) head of the African Department; Brian PRICE (UK), head of the West European Department (a former President of the communist-dominated British trade union TASS); (Technical,

Administrative and Supervisory Staffs); Siegfried KATZSCH-
MANN (GDR) head of the Solidarity and Education Department; R. URMANTSEV (USSR), head of Press and Propaganda
Department; Jean Dominique SIMONPOLI (France), Chairman
of the Young Workers' Commission; Ferenc BAKOS (Hungary),
head of the TUI Department; Emilian HAMERNIK (Czechoslo-
vakia), head of the Inter-governmental Organisations Depart-
ment; Alain OBADIA (France), head of the Committee for
Engineers, Managerial Staffs and Technicians; Daniela KUBA-
TOVA (Czechoslovakia), head of the Department for Working
Women and Peace; Maurice GASTAUD (France), permanent
WFTU representative for Africa (based in Paris).

Publications and Information
The WFTU has two main publications: *World Trade Union
Movement* published monthly in English, French, Russian,
Spanish, Arabic, Japanese, German, Portuguese and Romanian
(about 75,000 copies) and *Flashes from the Trade Unions*
(formerly *News in Brief*), weekly in English, French, Russian,
Spanish and Arabic. Other publications include *Opinions*, a
monthly journal on Africa, in English and French; *Asian Worker*,
monthly in English: and *WFTU–Arab Workers*, quarterly in
French, English, Russian, Arabic and Spanish. Bulletins entitled
Solidarity with Korea, *Solidarity with Chile*, *European Trade
Union Contacts*, *Dialogo Sindical* and *Economic Bulletin* are also
published. There are now WFTU publishing houses in Prague,
Mexico City, Tokyo, East Berlin, Moscow, Bucharest and
Almada (Portugal). A broadcasting service *WFTU Calling*, was
started in April 1981.

Finance
Details of the WFTU's finances have not been disclosed since
the communists took control and, although figures are sometimes
circulated for internal consumption, they do not reveal the full
extent of financial support from Communist sources. The WFTU
claims to be financed by its affiliation fees, sales of publications
and special donations, but the Soviet Union and other East
European countries provide most of these 'special donations',
together with free travel and free conference facilities. This was
acknowledged by the General Secretary of the Dockworkers'
Union of Dahomey, a Transport TUI affiliate, in an article in
the TUI publication, *Transport Workers of the World* (No. 4,
1971): he wrote that

The transport workers of Dahomey and the rest of Africa welcome the considerable efforts and the active assistance of friendly countries who are making a positive contribution in paying our air fares to and from each Administrative Committee session of the TUI. Bulgaria, Hungary and the Soviet Union are but a few of those countries that have done the maximum to assist us in this respect.

The Sub-Committee on Oversight of the US House of Representatives asserted in February 1980 that, at that time, WFTU was in receipt of a Soviet subsidy estimated at US$ 8,575,000.

Relations with Other Bodies

(1) United Nations The WFTU has consultative status with ECOSOC(1), the ILO, the FAO, UNESCO(A), UNCTAD and UNIDO. It has permanent representatives at the UN and its agencies, namely Ivan MITYAYEV (USSR) and Lucien LABRUNE (France)—ILO and other bodies, Geneva; Gerhard WETZEL (GDR) and Michèle LOMBARDO (France)—UNESCO, Paris; Giuseppe CASADEI (Italy)—FAO, Rome; Fred GABOURY (USA)—UN, New York. WFTU was elected to the board of the unofficial Conference on Non-Governmental Organisations in Consultative Status with ECOSOC (CONGO) in September 1985. Currently, the WFTU is seeking to expand its activities inside the UN network, particularly in the ILO. In May 1984, the WFTU launched a series of seminars to 'provide trade unionists with information on ILO activities' (the first two have been held in Moscow, the second in October 1985).

(2) Other International Front Organisations The WFTU cooperates closely with the other Soviet-controlled international front organisations. ZAKARIA, its General Secretary, is a Vice President of the WPC. The WFTU works closely with the WIDF and the World Federation of Democratic Youth (WFDY) on issues affecting working youth and women and also collaborates with the World Federation of Scientific Workers (WFSW). The WFTU Legal Commission and the International Association of Democratic Lawyers (IADL) also have a joint working group and together organise seminars.

The WFTU cooperates closely with the WPC on issues of 'peace and disarmament', and at its Ninth Congress in 1978, decided to hold a World Conference on the Socio-economic Aspects of Disarmament, a project which was revived at a round-table meeting of trade unionists at the WPC's World Parliament of the Peoples for Peace, Sofia, September 1980. The Conference was finally held in Paris in December 1981. In May 1982, at a meeting in Dublin, the continuing committee was transformed into a permanent body, the International Trade Union Committee for Peace and Disarmament (also known as the 'Dublin Committee')*. This Committee headed by Brian PRICE and Campbell CHRISTIE, both British trade unionists, is run from Prague, where PRICE has been on the WFTU staff since 1981.

The WFTU participates from time to time in the regular liaison meetings and hosted one which took place in September 1987 in Prague.

(3) Non-communist Organisations WFTU's attempts to renew contacts with genuine international trade union organisations, such as the ICFTU and the World Confederation of Labour (WCL), have so far met with little success. ZAKARIA, commenting in *World Trade Union Movement* No. 4, 1981, on the ICFTU's document, *Priorities for the '80s—Programme of Action*, said:

> The ICFTU is prepared to resume the dialogue with the WCL 'on the understanding that this must be a conscious step towards unity'. He dismissed as a lame excuse, the ICTFU's requirement that 'as long as the WFTU continues to act as a tool for promoting the foreign policy objectives of the USSR, rather than for advancing the interests of the world's workers, the ICFTU can have no truck with it'.

H. O. VETTER, President of the Federal German Trade Union Movement (DBE/ICFTU), said in May 1976 that 'we . . . know enough to realise that an organisation whose members, at the time of its foundation, could agree only on an aim that had already been more or less achieved, namely the destruction of Hitlerian Fascism, but not on any real common economic and social objectives, that such an organisation does not constitute an adequate basis on which to fight for improvement in living and working conditions' (Free Labour World, June 1976). Nevertheless, the WFTU and ICFTU General Secretaries met for the first time at an East–West Consultative Meeting, held under the auspices of the ILO Workers' Group in Geneva, in January 1974 and further meetings under ILO auspices were held in February–March 1975, March 1977, October 1979 and November 1981. ICFTU participated only on the understanding that the meetings were unofficial, non-political and held on the neutral ground (i.e. the ILO) and has now withdrawn from these encounters. When, therefore in 1982 the WFTU Bureau, meeting in Prague, appealed to the ICFTU, WCL and regional trade union organisations to take part in 'joint action to stop the arms race', the ICFTU ignored this appeal, being well aware of the political motivation of its authors.

(4) National Affiliates Although WFTU has no affiliate in the United Kingdom, Tom Sibley has been WFTU's London representative since at least 1984. His predecessor-in the 1970s— was Gerry Pocock, a CPGB official, and before him, Tom McWhinnie who in the 1960s was English editor of the *World Trade Union Movement*. Sibley, a British communist, was expelled from his Party for being too pro-Moscow in sympathy. (*Morning Star*, 15 July 1985; *The Times*, same date.) In February 1985, Sibley was the secretary of *ad hoc* '40th Anniversary Unity Committee' which organised WFTU's Anniversary conference in London. This event was supported by a small minority of British and Irish trade unionists, among them Brian Price, who combines his post as secretary of the 'Dublin Committee'* with being head of the WFTU's West European Department in Prague and Noel Harris (Ireland) who headed the WFTU's Social and Economic Department in Prague in 1979–80 but who is now on the staff of the British Association of Cinematograph, TV and Allied Technicians (ACT). The WFTU's only major West European affiliate is the French Communist Trade Union, the CGT.

The WFTU's affiliate in the Soviet Union is the All-Union Central Council of Trade Unions of the USSR (AUCCTU)*, and in the US is the Labor Research Association.

Subsidiaries
The WFTU has set up a number of subsidiary bodies, mostly short-lived. These have included the International Trade Union Committee for Social Tourism and Leisure (which the WFTU turned into an 'autonomous' organisation in the autumn of 1983); International Trade Union Committee for Solidarity with the People and Workers of Palestine; Commission on Trade Union Education; WFTU-International Confederation of Arab Trade Unions (ICATU) Joint Committee; International Trade Union Committee for Solidarity with the People and the Workers of Africa; Young Workers' Commission; History Commission; Advisory Committee on Socio-economic Affairs; International Trade Union Committee for Solidarity with the People and

Workers of Chile; Commission on Engineers, Managerial Staffs and Technicians; Permanent Committee for Printing Industry Trade Unions; Legal Commission; Commission on Transnational Corporations; Environment Commission; Commission on the Constitution; International Trade Union Committee for Solidarity with the People and Workers of Korea; European Commission; Working Women's Commission. In addition, there are the permanent Trade Union Internationals*.

WFTU's Policies

The WFTU's ultimate purpose is to establish a single, unified international trade union organisation under communist control. It has however, vocal critics on the democratic left in Western countries, who are not fooled by its pretentions; it was, for instance, described as being 'controlled by the KGB' in the British magazine *The Leveller*, No. 32, November 1979. The essential point is that trade unions in communist countries discharge managerial roles inimical to free trade unionism: the nature of Soviet trade unionism, for instance, was explained in *World Trade Union Movement* (No. 11, November 1972), when a Secretary of the Soviet All-Union Central Council of Trade Unions (AUCCTU)*, V. PROKHOROV, said that 'the unions of the USSR are part of the State power; they are the organisers and educators of the builders of Communism . . .'. Or, as Piotr PIMENOV, AUCCTU Secretary, phrased it in an article in *World Trade Union Movement*, No. 3, March 1973 'the Soviet trade Unions unreservedly support the Leninist foreign policy of the Communist Party'. Pierre GENSOUS (France), the WFTU's General Secretary from 1969 to 1978, spelled out their role in the West when he told the Soviet trade union newspaper, *Trud*, 18 June 1976, that trade unions in communist countries exert 'considerable influence on the development of the international trade union movement, helping the working people of the capitalist countries in their struggle for democratic rights and liberties against the dominance of the monopolies'.

The fact is that the WFTU campaigns for unity of the 'working class' only for Soviet ends. As GENSOUS put it: 'the struggle against imperialism . . . cannot be effectively conceived except on the basis of the coming together of the three main forces; the Socialist countries, the working class of the capitalist countries and the movement for national liberation' (Czechoslovak news agency, *CTK*, 14 May 1974). But while preaching 'unity', the WFTU tries to undermine its non-communist rivals, particularly the ICFTU, by attempting to subvert their members and by supporting regional bodies sympathetic to its own policies. In the London *Times'* obituary of Louis SAILLANT, the first Secretary-General on 30 October 1974 it was recalled that his 'chief function seemed to be to arouse industrial strife in the Western democracies and in the emerging countries of Africa and Asia, for whose workers he demanded better pay and conditions than obtained behind the Iron Curtain'.

The WFTU early ceased to be either an all-embracing body or a champion of workers' rights. Soon after STALIN's quarrel with TITO, the Yugoslavs were expelled from the WFTU (in 1950), which gave no support to the workers' strikes in East Germany in 1953 or to subsequent strikes in Poland, which were subdued by force. On the other hand WFTU supported in 1956 the Soviet suppression of the uprising in Hungary and although the WFTU Secretariat criticised the Soviet invasion of Czechoslovakia in 1968, French and Italian communist insistence on full Soviet control over the organisations was swiftly reasserted. In 1981, WFTU backed measures taken by the Polish Government against the independent Polish trade union organisation, Solidarity.

Official strikes are not allowed under communist rule in Eastern Europe; by contrast, the WFTU encourages and gives virtual blanket support to strikes in Western countries. This one-sided approach was admitted in a *Moscow Radio* commentary on 3 October 1967, to mark the WFTU's Twenty-second Anniversary: '. . . as a class organisation of the workers, the Federation is doing a great deal to develop the strike movement, and if the strike movement in capitalist countries has been growing recently, much of the credit must go to the Federation . . .'. It was in this selective spirit that, to mark WFTU's Thirtieth Anniversary in October 1975, the USSR Supreme Soviet awarded it the Order of Friendship Among Peoples. GASPAR and ZAKARIA subsequently attended the 26th Soviet Party Congress in Moscow in February 1981 and GASPAR addressed the 27th Soviet Party Congress in February–March 1986.

Congresses

The Congress, the highest WFTU authority, held every four years, has met as follows: in Paris (October 1945), Milan (June 1949), Vienna (October 1953), Leipzig (October 1957), Moscow (December 1961), Warsaw (October 1965), Budapest (October

1969), Varna (Romania) (October 1973), Havana (February 1982), East Berlin (September 1986).

Each Congress is described as a 'World Trade Union Congress', doubtless in order to mislead the unwary. Each is in fact merely a routine WFTU Congress, but staged as a major propaganda event designed to attract as many non-communist or uncommitted trade unionists as possible. With the WPC's 'world peace congresses' and the Soviet-controlled youth and student organisations' successive 'world youth festivals', these Congresses are among the largest periodic gatherings in the international front organisations' calendar.

The East Berlin Congress (the 11th) was, according to WFTU, attended by 1,014 delegates, observers and guests from 432 national regional and international trade union organisations (of differing affiliation or none) from 145 countries. There were also representatives of nine other Soviet international front organisations and from the ILO, UNESCO, the Christian World Confederation of Labour (WCL) and such WFTU-related organisations as the Paris-based International Mineworkers Organisations (IMO)* and the 'Dublin Committee'*. Special guests on that occasion included Erich HONECKER, General Secretary of the East German Socialist Unity (Communist) Party, and Daniel ORTEGA President of Nicaragua, both of whom, addressed the Congress, as did Romesh CHANDRA, the WPC President. Messages of greetings were sent by Libya's Colonel QADHAFI, Poland's General JARUZELSKI, Syria's President Hafez ASSAD, and Z. BATMUNKH, General Secretary of the Central Committee of the Monogolian People's Revolutionary Party.

The slogan of the East Berlin Congress was 'United Action and Solidarity between all Workers for Jobs, Peace and Social Progress'. GASPAR, the Hungarian President said that participation 'showed that the WFTU's influence goes far beyond its own member organisations and that the WFTU has thus become stronger . . . '. The Sudanese Communist General Secretary, Ibrahim ZAKARIA, also spoke at length about the struggle for 'peace' (Soviet style) and delivered the Congress introductory report. Soviet trade unionism was also, of course, represented in force. Stepan SHALAYEV, Chairman of the All-Union Central Council of Trade Unions of the USSR (AUCCTU), said that the WFTU and the TUIs could use their potential more actively for broadening 'the anti-war movement' and went on to say that it 'should search for new things, should think flexibly and strive for new approaches to analysing and solving present day issues'.

The Congress reiterated its appeal for cooperation to the ICFTU, the WCL and other international and regional trade union organisations. Some speeches suggested that the WFTU was in the mood for change, as evidenced, for example, by the return of CGT representatives to the main bodies of the organisation after an absence of eight years. CGT's General Secretary, Henri KRASUCKI, in his turn referred to the need for change in their approach to union independence and autonomy; he even hinted in a special congress article, that unions from East European countries may soon be able to support workers' economic demands independently of their respective Communist parties.

Other Campaigns and Activities

The WFTU has conducted numerous campaigns in support of Soviet policy on such subjects as Indochina, the Middle East, European security, anti-colonialism, apartheid, the arms race and multinational companies. In its time it has campaigned, always with great urgency, against the Marshall Plan, the North Atlantic Alliance and the European Community.

Africa The WFTU aspires to influence and, if possible, ultimately to control the African trade union movement originally centred on the All-African Trade Union Federation (AATUF), which it helped to establish in 1961. Until 1966, the AATUF was based in Accra and financed largely from communist funds. After its headquarters were moved to Tanzania, it continued to be dominated by officials sympathetic to WFTU but its prestige suffered from the exposure of its influence on the ailing AATUF through a Liaison and Co-ordinating Committee, set up in 1969; although the AATUF was eventually disbanded, it tried to ensure that AATUF-affiliated unions dominated the new Organisation of African Trade Union Unity (OATUU), set up under the auspices of the Organisation of African Unity (OAU) in April 1973. Cooperation agreements were signed between the WFTU and the OATUU in August 1976 and January 1987.

Asia and Oceaina In November 1978, a WFTU Asian Liaison Office was opened in Ho Chi Minh City (Saigon), Vietnam, and later moved to Hanoi. The WFTU organised the Fourth Asian

Trade Union Seminar in Nagpur, India, in September 1975 and a further one in New Delhi in March 1979.

In February 1979, the WFTU arranged a meeting of front organisations in Prague to discuss the situation in South-East Asia in the light of the Chinese military campaign in Vietnam which, following the Soviet line, they condemned.

More recently all Soviet international front organisations have mounted renewed campaigns in Asia and the Pacific. As a result of its efforts—mostly in the form of regional conferences—to increase its influence in the Pacific area, the WFTU finally established an Asian and Oceanic Coordination Committee at a Conference in New Delhi, February 1985. The new Committee, based in New Delhi, had as President Jim KNOX, a New Zealander and a WPC member; the Secretary is K.G. SRIWASTAVA (India), a former WFTU Secretary. KNOX has since been replaced by an Australian Ernie BOATSWAIN, a new WFTU Vice President and Chairman of the Australian-Czechoslovak Friendship Society. The Second Asian and Pacific Trade Union Conference was in Manila in August 1987, when Bonifacio TUPAZ (Philippines) was elected as its president. And, while attending WFTU's East Berlin Congress in September 1986, WFTU Secretary Debkumar GANGULI (India) 'assured the assembly of full and firm support of the WFTU in the activities of the AOTUCC'.

Europe The WFTU's main short-term aim in Europe is to undermine the ICFTU, partly by trying to infiltrate communist-controlled unions into the ETUC, and by encouraging bilateral contacts between Western and Eastern Europe. When the Italian CGIL left the WFTU in March 1978 a CGIL Secretary, Aldo BONACCINI, explained that 'the WFTU had become obsolete and behaved more like a propaganda centre than one geared to possible action': its reports gave an 'uncritically idyllic picture' of the unions in Eastern Europe and a gloomy one of the workers' movements in the West. The French CGT, however, has remained in the WFTU throughout most of the post war period although according to the CGT Secretary Johannes GALAND, the organisation withdrew from the WFTU leadership in 1978 'to mark our disagreement with a WFTU whose activities were raising doubts as well as its autonomy of initiative'.

Galand listed the following changes in WFTU as responsible for CGT's eventual return: the establishment of a WFTU commission on transnational corporations (TNCs) oriented towards activities at plant level in liaison with the TUIs, the establishment of 'a European Commission with our Soviet comrades', the coordination of regional activities against the TNCs and on questions related to the New International Economic Order, and the fact that WFTU is the only organisation 'pressing for unitarian development'.

Latin America Attacks on the present régime in Chile are prominent in WFTU propaganda, which is also directed against other Latin American governments, particularly Uruguay. After closure in 1964 of its Latin American regional organisation, the Confederation of Latin American Workers (CTAL), the WFTU set up a new 'united centre', the Permanent Congress for the Trade Union Unity of Latin American Workers (CPUSTAL), in Chile. Efforts to secure the cooperation of the Latin American Christian Trade Union Organisation (CLASC) and other non-communist bodies failed, however, because the communist aims of the CPUSTAL became evident. The overthrow of the Chilean government under ALLENDE, in September 1973, destroyed, at least for the time being, the WFTU's hopes of establishing a permanent base in Chile. The CPUSTAL eventually set up new headquarters in Mexico City in March 1978. The WFTU also has an agreement with the Latin American Federation of Journalists (FELAP).

Near and Middle East WFTU's activity in the Near and Middle East concentrates on echoing Soviet policy on the Arab–Israeli dispute. It cooperates closely with the International Confederation of Arab Trade Unions (ICATU), set up in 1956 and based in Damascus and the two bodies established a joint working committee in March 1968. Support for the WFTU in the area suffered a setback in 1971 when the communist-controlled Sudanese Trade Union Federation was outlawed (as President NUMEIRY said, 'We soon found out that the leadership of the Labour trade unions was but a front for the Communist Party').

Training Schools and Courses Since 1953 a number of trade union schools have been set up by the WFTU, mainly in Eastern Europe. One of their objectives is to indoctrinate trade union officials in communism; students return home, often with promises of financial assistance, to help secure the support of national groups for the WFTU—or to form splinter groups. The WFTU has a permanent Consultative Group of experts on trade union education in Asia, Africa and Latin America to co-ordinate policy. Currently the main schools are the Higher Trade Union School, Moscow; the Georgi Dimitrov Trade Union School, Sofia; and the Fritz Heckert Trade Union College, Bernau, East Germany (courses vary from four to 18 months).

Training has also been organised in developing countries, and seminars usually lasting about a month are held regularly in Czechoslovakia.

Anniversaries The WFTU celebrates a number of 'solidarity days', most of which are also supported by the other major front organisations. 1 September has been designated 'Day of Trade Union Action for Peace'.

PART B

SUBSIDIARIES

1. Asian Buddhist Conference for Peace

The Asian Buddhist Conference for Peace (ABCP) is also known under its French and Russian titles which are, respectively, *Conférence pour la paix asiatique bouddhiste* and *Aziatskaya Buddiyskaya Konferentsiya za mir*. Its headquarters is at Gangdantekchenling Monastery, Ulan Bator, Mongolia.

Origins
The ABCP is related, as are the Christian Peace Conference (CPC)* in Prague, the Berlin Conference of European Catholics (BC)* in East Berlin and the Asian Christian Conference for Peace, itself a CPC offshoot, to the Soviet peace movement. The ABCP was founded in 1979.

As was stated by an ABCP spokesman in the Soviet journal *New Times* (No. 3, January 1985):

> the ABCP does not confine itself to Buddhists in its peacemaking effort; we also actively cooperate with other organisations working for peace such as the United Nations—specifically, its Department for Disarmament Affairs— the World Peace Council, the Afro–Asian Peoples' Solidarity Organisation, the Women's International Democratic Federation . . . the Christian Peace Conference, the Berlin Conference of European Catholics . . . we have been cooperating with these organisations for years . . . After all, the Buddhists of the Soviet Union were among the founders of the ABCP . . .

Declared Aims
The ABCP seeks to 'attain the Lord Buddha's ideals on peace and tranquility' and, by working 'in close collaboration' with such organisations as the WPC, 'to safeguard and consolidate international peace and universal security'.

Organisation and Membership
The ABCP has General Conferences at regular intervals—the Seventh General Conference was held in Ulan Bator in 1986—and is directed by a President, Vice-Presidents and an Executive Council of 15 members, which includes the General Secretary *ex-officio*. There are also a number of subordinate Commissions on such themes as Disarmament, the Promotion of Pancha Sila in International Relations, Peace Education and the Indian Ocean as a Zone of Peace.

The ABCP has 15 national centres in 12 countries, namely Bangladesh, India, Kampuchea, Japan, Laos, Mongolia, North Korea, Nepal, Soviet Union, Sri Lanka, Thailand and Vietnam.

Office holders
The ABCP President is the Mongolian Buddhist Lama, the Most Venerable Kharkhuu GAADAN. ABCP Vice-Presidents include T. ANANTASOUTHONE (Laos), Kushok BAKULA (India), Shojun MIBU (Japan), THICH Minh Chan (Vietnam) and Mapalagama WIPULASARA (Sri Lanka). The Executive Council elected in 1986 also includes D. P. BANIA (Bangladesh), CHANG Tae Song (Japan), J. ERDYNEYER (USSR), KHAMTUL Jamyang Dhondup of the Dalai Lama's Council, N. KHEMPALI (Thailand), PAK Tae-ho (North Korea), and TEP Vong (Kampuchea). The Secretary-General is Gelegjamtsyn LUVSANTSEREN (Mongolia): V.B. TSYBIKDORJIEV (USSR) is Deputy Secretary-General.

Publications
The ABCP publishes monthly, in English, the *Asian Buddhist Conference for Peace Bulletin* and quarterly, also in English, *Buddhists for Peace*.

Finance
The ABCP does not publish details of its finances, but its dependence on WPC, CPC and Mongolian sources is obvious from the nature of its activities.

Relations with Other Bodies
(1) United Nations The ABCP claims to work closely with the UN and its General Conferences usually receive messages of greeting from UNESCO, but it has not so far been successful in obtaining formal links with ECOSOC.

(2) Other International Front Organisations The ABCP states that it works closely with the WPC, AAPSO*, CPC, WIDF* and the Berlin Conference of European Catholics: in addition it is known to have fraternal links with WFDY* and IUS*. The ABCP also has close working links with the other Soviet-controlled front organisations and participates from time to time in their regular liaison meetings.

General Conferences
There have so far been seven ABCP General Conferences, usually held in Ulan Bator. The latest was held, in February 1986, in Vientiane, Laos.

2. Berlin Conference of European Catholics

The Berlin Conference of European Catholics (BC) is also known under its French, German and Esperanto titles which are, respectively, *Conférence de Berlin des catholiques européens*, *Berliner Konferenz Europäischer Katholiken* and *Berlinskaja Konferencija Katolikov Evropy*. Previously it was known as Berlin Conference of Catholic Christians in European Countries, *Conférence de Berlin des catholiques des etats européens*, *Berliner Konferenz Katholischer Christen aus Europäischen Staaten*. Its headquarters is at Postrasse 4–5, 1020 Berlin, East Germany.

Origins
The BC was founded as the result of an initiative of the second All-Christian Peace Assembly convened by the Christian Peace Conference (CPC)* in Prague in June 1964. Subsequently, an East German Catholic group which advocated cooperation with the communist régime sponsored the 'First International Meeting of Catholics for the Application of the Encyclical Pacem in Terris in International Life' in East Berlin in November 1964. Its organisers were known more for their participation in World Peace Council (WPC) events than for church activities. (Significantly, all of them were lay men and women.) That meeting, which was attended by 140 delegates from 12 countries, was in practice only concerned with political issues and passed resolutions on the lines of those adopted at WPC meetings.

Delegates at the WPC's World Peace Congress in Helsinki in July 1965 decided to hold a second meeting in the same series. In its preparatory stages it was renamed the Berlin Conference of Catholic Christians, and was held in East Berlin in March 1966, being attended by some 200 delegates from 18 countries, as well as by representatives of the WPC and CPC. The Catholic rank and file and the official government-controlled Church in East Germany paid little attention to these two meetings, nor did they receive favourable comment from Catholic circles in West Germany.

In an article in the West German *Frankfurter Rundschau* (12 June 1968) about the third meeting, which was also held in East Berlin at that time, Klaus Kreppel wrote that

> During the week after Whitsuntide the capital of the GDR harbored some rather unusual guests: 300 delegates, thrown together on an equal basis from East and West, gathered for the third Conference of the 'Berlin Conference of Catholic Christians in European States'. . . .

The BC is the Roman Catholic wing of the Communist religious peace movement, complementing the CPC, which mainly recruits Protestants and Orthodox Christians, and the Asian Buddhist Conference for Peace (ABCP)*.

Declared Aims
According to the *Yearbook of International Organisations* 1986–87, the BC aims to establish and safeguard lasting peace founded on truth, justice, love and freedom; to contribute to social justice.

Organisation and Membership
The first BC President acted as Chairman of its Presidium and of a larger International Continuation Committee. The Presidium has held nine plenary meetings at two to three yearly intervals. The International Continuation Committee meets much more frequently. In 1973 it launched an appeal in support of the WPC's World Congress of Peace Forces, held in Moscow in that year.

The BC has supporters and 'co-workers' in 45 countries, almost half of them outside Europe (whereas as recently as 1982 it was active only in 25 European countries). The non-European countries where BC is active are Australia, Egypt, Argentina, Brazil, Canada, Chile, Colombia, Cuba, El Salvador, Guatemala, Haiti, Nicaragua, Peru, USA, Jordan, Lebanon, Mongolia, Syria, Vietnam. Its European members are in Austria, Belgium, Bulgaria, Czechoslovakia, Denmark, Finland, France, German Democratic Republic, German Federal Republic,

Hungary, Iceland, Ireland, Italy, Luxembourg, Malta, Netherlands, Norway, Poland, Portugal, Romania, Spain, Sweden, Switzerland, USSR, Vatican, Yugoslavia.

Office Holders
The BC's founder, who died in April 1987, was Otto Hartmut FUCHS (GDR). After Fuchs' death, Hubertus GUSKE, a member of the BC Presidium and editor-in-chief of *Begegnung* (an East German monthly Catholic publication) 'complied with the suggestion of the Presidium members and many other members of the BC and took up the Secretary Generalship of the BC on 1 August 1987'. (*Neues Deutschland* 15 January 1988). Franco LEONORI (Italy) succeeded Fuchs as Chairman of the Presidium.

Relations with Other Bodies
(1) Other International Front Organisations The BC has close relations with the WPC and the CPC. It is represented on the WPC Presidential Committee by a member of its Presidium, Yves Grenet. The BC's former President, the late Otto Hartmut Fuchs, was a member until his death. The BC also has five other representatives on the WPC. In November 1986 it held a joint meeting in Prague with the CPC, at which both sides discussed future international cooperation (particularly with regard to disarmament), as well as closer cooperation with other religious and peace movements. The BC also has close working links with the other Soviet-controlled front organisations and participates from time to time in their regular liaison meetings.

(2) Non-communist Organisations The BC has links with the Roman Catholic pacifist organisation Pax Christi International: they jointly held a consultative conference in Budapest in April 1979. The BC also claims to have support in the Vatican.

Plenary Meetings
There have been nine BC Plenary Meetings so far, all held in the GDR and mostly in East Berlin; in November 1964, March 1966, June 1968, November 1971, November 1974, November 1977, June 1980, November 1982 and November 1985.

Activities
The *Frankfurter Rundschau*, 12 June 1968, reporting the third meeting in Berlin, said:

The initiators of this 'Berlin Conference' are Catholic representatives of the East German Christian Union who for the past eight years have been publishing the magazine *Begegnung*. The conference is mainly accused of following in the wake of the German Socialist Unity Party because the latter in the final analysis puts its stamp of approval on the existence and content of the 'Berlin Conference'. In its 11 May [1968] edition, *Osservatore Romano* expressed the fear that the sponsors of the conference were trying to degrade Catholicism to the 'slave of a definite, specific line.' The Catholic News Agency, on the other hand, appears to be inclined to grant [the East German] organizers Fuchs, Guske, and Grobbel some 'mitigating circumstances', because 'we are quite familiar with their by no means enviable position in a state that is totally dominated by the German Socialist Unity Party.' This time, the Catholic News Agency did not repeat its earlier blanket judgements, such as 'fellow travellers of the Communists', because in addition to the Vatican the Dutch primate, Cardinal Alfrink, and Cardinal König, Archbishop of Vienna, despatched 'silent observers' to Berlin: the Bishop of Mainz likewise maintained indirect contact with the sponsors of the 'Berlin Conference'.

Discussing the intentions of the 'Berlin Conference', Otto Fuchs, Chairman of the Working Committee, indicated that the Conference is to be understood as a 'political initiative' which 'consciously tries to continue the work of the Catholic avantgardists of the past.' It tries to help in the implementation of the peace and social programmes of the Popes and all of the various positions on individual issues. In this connection there is no chance at all of 'Catholicism being enslaved by a political line' because there is no more uniform official opinion within Catholicism. But with this remark Fuchs did not yet refute the accusation made by *Osservatore Romano* as to the issue of 'enslavement'. A brief glance at the course of this year's 'Berlin Conference' leads to the conclusion that the Conference of Catholics has achieved a certain degree of independence . . .

In addition to holding nine plenary meetings, it has staged several colloquia on the theme of 'peace', as defined by Soviet apologists, and has also held a meeting for Roman Catholic publicists and journalists.

3. Esperantist World Peace Movement

The Esperantist World Peace Movement (MEM) is also known under its French, Danish and Esperantist titles which are, respectively, *Mouvement espérantiste pour la paix mondiale*, *Esperantistisk Verdensfredsbevaegelse* and *Mondpaca Esperatista Movada*. Its headquarters is at 54 rue des Hineux, B–4400, Herstal, Belgium.

Origins

After Esperanto, the language initiated by a Pole, Dr. Ludovic Lazarus Zamenhof, was launched as an auxiliary international language in 1887, Esperantists fell into two groups: those who saw its use as technical and pragmatic and those who sought to use it as a medium for political propaganda. In the early years of the Soviet Union, its use was at first strongly encouraged and then, under Stalin, as strongly discouraged. Towards the end of Stalin's life however it was again in favour not only with the Soviet, but also with other Communist régimes, including China.

An Esperanto 'international peace movement' with WPC connections was first mentioned at the WPC's Congress of the Peoples for Peace in Vienna in December 1952. At that Congress, the Esperantist Friends of Peace decided to set up an international organisation, and an International Gathering of Esperantist Friends of Peace was duly held in Austria, in July 1953, under the sponsorship of the Austrian Esperanto Peace Committee. MEM claims to have been founded on 6 December 1953 at St Polten, Austria (according to a Danish report dating from December 1955, it was set up by the Soviet Union with Hungarian and Czechoslovak support).

According to an article in the British communist newspaper, *Morning Star*, 27 August 1973:

> it is quite inconceivable that the practical experience of the first successful, planned, inter-language will not provide valuable material for the next stage—the inter-language of the Socialist nations of the world, when Zamenhof's dream will be realised, even if in a way he could not foresee.
>
> New left-wing Esperantists are needed in Britain, especially young people to match the new generations in the Socialist countries . . .

Declared Aims

The MEM aims to unite Esperantists for world peace, irrespective of nationality, race, religion, or politics; practise the use of Esperanto for the purpose of promoting world peace and international understanding; work for the establishment of Esperanto as one of the official languages of the world peace movement; promote and organise contacts and exchanges.

Organisation and Membership

The MEM holds General Conferences every three years at which its President, Board and International Committee are elected. There are also eight specialised commissions and a staff of about 80. It has members in 34 countries, namely Argentina, Brazil,

Canada, Cuba, USA, Japan, Kampuchea, Mongolia, Syria, Vietnam, Australia, New Zealand, Austria, Belgium, Bulgaria, Czechoslovakia, Denmark, Finland, France, German Democratic Republic, German Federal Republic, Hungary, Iceland, Italy, Netherlands, Norway, Poland, Romania, Spain, Sweden, USSR, Yugoslavia, Zaire.

Office Holders
The President is Dr. I. PETHES (Hungary); the Secretary-General Clement THOLLET (Belgium).

Publications and Information
The MEM publishes *Paco*, monthly, and *La Pacaktivulo*, quarterly, both in Esperanto.

Finance
The MEM claims to be financed by members' dues and subscriptions for publications.

Relations with Other Bodies
(1) Other International Front Organisations The MEM has very close relations with the WPC. Its President, Secretary-General and another leading official are represented on that body. During the WPC's World Congress of Peace Forces in Moscow, in October 1973 the two organisations signed a joint agreement. *Paco* regularly features articles on WPC activities and WPC publications occasionally contain articles on the MEM. MEM officials are also members of their respective national peace committees.

It is also of interest that Esperanto is one of the languages in use at the World Youth Festivals organised by two International Front Organisations, the World Federation of Democratic Youth (WFDY)* and the International Union of Students (IUS)*.

(2) Non-communist Organisations The MEM is often confused with the politically neutral Universal Esperanto Association/ Universala Esperanto Asociao (UEA), which was founded in Switzerland in 1908 and has its headquarters in Rotterdam. The MEM claims to have close relations with the UEA. The UEA is parent organisation to between 50 and 100 small international Esperantist organisations ranging from such themes as boy scouts, philatelists, railwaymen, musicians, vegetarians and naturists. The MEM has sent delegates to UEA's annual

congresses. For example, in September 1959, the British communist newspaper the *Daily Worker* reported that MEM had been represented at the 44th World Congress of Esperantists held in Poland during 1959 under the auspices of the non-communist UEA, sometimes known as the World Union of Esperantists. This was the first international Esperanto Congress to be held in a communist state. According to the *Daily Worker* report, the Congress was notable because it brought together the two main trends in the Esperanto movement (the non-communist Universal Esperanto Association and the World Peace Esperanto Movement MEM 'which functioned mainly in the Socialist countries'). A resolution adopted at the Congress expressed the determination to 'win Esperantists for the defence of peace' and called upon all Esperantists to take an . . . active part in 'the World Peace Movement'.

Congresses
The MEM holds triennial congresses; the latest was held in Augsburg, Federal Republic of Germany, in 1985.

4. International Committee of Children's and Adolescents' Movements

The International Committee of Children's and Adolescents' Movements, commonly known by its French initials, CIMEA, is also known under its French, Spanish and Russian titles which are, respectively, *Comité international des mouvements d'enfants et d'adolescents*, *Comite Internacional de Movimientos Infantiles y de Adolescentes* and *Mezhdunarodny Komitet Detskikh i Yunosheskikh Organizatsii*. Its headquarters is at 1389 Budapest, POB 147, Hungary.

Origins
CIMEA was founded on 15 February 1958 in Budapest as a specialised autonomous organisation associated with the World Federation of Democratic Youth (WFDY)* which is also based in Budapest. The decision to set up the body had been taken at the WFDY's 4th Assembly in Kiev in August 1957 and that Assembly's resolution pointed out that 'the education of children in the spirit of humanity, love of their country and people, friendship between the peoples, as well as the activity of children's organisations throughout the world could be of great

significance for the development of the movement for the defence of peace'.

The CIMEA's founding organisations are children's and adolescents' groups in Argentina, Cyprus, Finland, France, GDR, Hungary, Indonesia, Poland, USSR and North Vietnam. Since then its membership has increased, particularly in the developing world, and it now has 71 affiliates in 65 countries.

Declared Aims

According to the *Yearbook of International Organisations* 1986–87, CIMEA aims to 'promote education of children and adolescents in the spirit of peace, friendship and mutual under-standing, on the basis of the United Nations Charter of Children's Rights, work for humane and harmonious education of children and adolescents, oppose any activities which could demoralize the child, particularly unwholesome literature and films.'

General perspective

The significance of CIMEA lies in the fact that the children and adolescents who are the object of its activities have no effective say in its administration or policies. The organisation is in the hands of, and under the direction of, adults. This is not surprising considering that the ages of the children and adolescents range from six to 15. But in this respect CIMEA differs from the other organisations considered in this book in that there is no pretence that it is being run by those whom it is supposed to benefit. It is difficult to fault its declared aims. But it has to be remembered that the way in which they are to be interpreted to the young and impressionable membership of CIMEA's affiliates is deter-mined by the adults who run the organisation. The political and ideological observations of these people are therefore of particular significance. This underlines the importance of the financial, organisational and operational links between CIMEA and the principal Soviet controlled organisations and their subsidiaries. These are described below. The opportunities for indoctrination are readily available and fully exploited.

Organisation and Membership

CIMEA is controlled by an Assembly which meets every four years, within the framework of the WFDY Assembly, a Pres-idium which meets once or twice a year (as required), and by its Secretariat.

CIMEA has three categories of membership—affiliated members, observer members and corresponding members.

Office Holders
The main officers are President: Jean-Baptiste DZANGUÉ (Congo); the principal Vice-President is Victor YEVSENKOV (USSR), and the Secretary-General is Sandor MOLNARI (Hungary).

Publications and Information
CIMEA publishes *CIMEA Information*, quarterly, in English, French and Spanish and *CIMEA Magazine*, annually in the same languages.

Finance
CIMEA claims to be financed by its member organisations' dues, by donations and by a WFDY grant.

Relations with Other Bodies
(1) United Nations CIMEA claims that it has important links with the UN and its specialised agencies, particularly with UNESCO and UNICEF. The UN International Year of the Child (1979) 'considerably contributed to broadening and deepening the cooperation of CIMEA and the UN system'. It is now hoping to obtain Consultative Status with ECOSOC and UNESCO and closer relations with UN/DPI [Development of Public Information].

(2) Other international front organisations Apart from its organisational ties with WFDY, CIMEA has close links with WFDY's two other specialised bodies, the International Bureau for Tourism and Exchanges of Youth (BITEJ) and the International Voluntary Service for Solidarity and Friendship of Youth (SIVSAJ), and also with the WPC, WIDF, IUS, FISE, IADL, IOJ and WFTU. (all *)

(3) Non-communist Organisations CIMEA claims to cooperate with a large number of established international children's organisations, such as the International Falcon Movement/Socialist Educational International (IFM/SEI), the World Organisation of the Scout Movement, International Young Nature Friends, the Children's International Summer Villages and others. CIMEA considers that the recently renewed activities of the Framework

for All European Youth and Student Cooperation [see under IUS] will allow it to work for the further broadening and strengthening of the Children's and Adolescents' International Cooperation (CAIC).

Congresses
CIMEA holds congresses every four years, within the framework of successive WFDY Assemblies. These have so far met as follows:

Warsaw	(August 1962)
Sofia	(June 1966)
Budapest	(October 1970)
Varna (Bulgaria)	(November 1974)
East Berlin	(February 1978)
Prague	(June 1982)
Budapest	(November 1986)

Other Activities
CIMEA's plan of work for 1987 'is based on and considered the first stage in the implementation of the general principles and political tasks' determined by the Programme of Action for 1987–90, which was adopted at the 7th CIMEA Assembly in Budapest, November 1986, under the title 'children are building up peace together'. In addition to activities for 'safeguarding peace', CIMEA also works for the implementation and defence of children's rights, for the 'just cause of the peoples, youth and children struggling against imperialism, colonialism and neo-colonialism, fascism, racism, Zionism and all kinds of discrimination, for peace, national independence, democracy and social progress', and for the strengthening of cooperation with children's and adolescents' movements with 'different tendencies'. It considers its active participation in the preparation and organisation of the World Youth Festivals, particularly in the children's programme (the thirteenth Festival will be held in Pyongyang in 1989) as one of its primary tasks.

5. International Liaison Forum of Peace Forces

The International Liaison Forum of Peace Forces (ILF) is also known under its French and Russian titles which are, respectively, *Forum international de liaison des forces de la paix* and

Mezhdunarodny Forum po Svyazyam Mirolyubivkh Sil. Its head-quarters is at Prospekt Mira 36, Moscow, USSR.

Origins
The ILF is in one sense the prime example of a 'front for a front', in this instance for the World Peace Council. It was founded in 1973 at the WPC's World Congress of Peace Forces in Moscow; originally it was the Congress' Continuing Committee and was an attempt by the Soviet Peace Committee* and the WPC to maintain permanent links with, and thereby further exploit for propagandist purposes, some of the non-communist individuals and organisations which had been involved in the Congress preparations and proceedings. It especially aims at promoting Soviet policies within the UN network. The new body's original title was the Continuing Liaison Committee of the World Congress of Peace Forces and it adopted its present name in 1977. As Vladimir Kornilov of the Soviet Peace Committee wrote in *New Times* (Moscow, October 1984), the forum:

> brings together prestigious representatives of political parties, members of parliaments and other elective bodies, public organisations and anti-war movements, trade unions, scientific and religious quarters, women's and youth organisations, professional groups and non-governmental organisations of different political orientations.

What Kornilov did not spell out, however, is that the Forum works among these organisations precisely because it is calculated by its sponsors that many of them would not respond to direct appeals from the parent WPC itself. It is significant that the ILF's Moscow address is also that of the Soviet Peace Committee, the largest national affiliate of the WPC.

Organisation and Membership
The ILF Committee includes 'representatives of national and international organisations working towards peace' in sixteen countries, apart from the Soviet Union itself, namely Austria, Australia, Belgium, Canada, Chile, Colombia, Denmark, Egypt, Finland, Guinea-Bissau, India, Ireland, Italy, Poland, the United Kingdom and the USA.

Senior officials of the International Peace Bureau (IPB), the World Association of World Federalists (WAWF) and the Women's International League for Peace and Freedom (WILPF)* have provided ILF Vice-Presidents. (At present only the WAWF and the WILPF are so represented; the IPB has a 'permanent participant in officers' meetings'.)

The Soviet Union, exceptionally, has its own national 'Committee of Peace Forces'.

Office Holders
The ILF President is Romesh CHANDRA (who is also the Indian Communist president of the WPC itself) and the Secretary-General is Oleg KHARKHARDIN (a secretary of the WPC). The Vice-presidents include Mrs Edith BALLANTYNE (Canada) who was co-president of the WPC's Prague Peace Assembly in 1983; Apolinar Diaz CALLEGAS (Colombia); Hermod LANNUNG (Denmark), who was chairman of the WPC's Copenhagen Peace Congress in 1986. The Secretariat includes Beryl HUFFINLEY (Great Britian), a British communist trade unionist.

Publications and Information
The ILF has published a number of *ad hoc* publications, mostly records of meetings which it has convened, notably the record of the Dialogue on Security and Disarmament in Europe (Stockholm, March 1984), the record of the International Dialogue on the United Nations and the Peace Forces: Ways to Strengthen Cooperation (Geneva, September 1984), the record of the International Dialogue for the Prevention of an Arms Race in Outer Space (Geneva, June 1985) and the proceedings of the Four Vienna Dialogues held in January 1982, November 1983, January 1985 and March 1987.

Finance
The ILF does not publish accounts but its close connection with the WPC and, in particular, the Soviet Peace Committee makes it clear that it is almost entirely, if not entirely, financed from Soviet funds.

Other Campaigns
In 1975 the ILF, then still called the Continuing Liaison Committee and acting as surrogate for the WPC, promoted an International Conference for a Just and Peaceful Solution to the Middle East Problem, an International Conference of Forces for Peace and Security in Asia and a World Conference for Solidarity with Chile. In 1976 it staged a World Conference of Parliamentarians and an International Conference for Solidarity with

Cyprus (these were the forerunners of several related conferences on Cyprus in 1977 and 1978). Also in 1976 it, in cooperation with the WPC, attempted to stage an International Forum on Disarmament in York but, because the British Government had refused certain visas, that event was in the end purely national in character: the international forum itself was subsequently held in Helsinki six months later. But the ILF's main activity is holding the successive Vienna Dialogues: the latest to be held, in April 1987, was rather smaller than its immediate predecessors and was attended by some 200 delegates from 56 countries, who met in the Austrian capital to debate the theme 'For a World without Wars'.

6. Trade Union Internationals

The Trade Union Internationals (TUIs) which function as offshoots of the WFTU* and which were formerly known as Trade Departments, are intended to represent workers throughout the world, organised in their particular trades and crafts. There are now eleven TUIs, including the most senior the FISE*, formed in 1946. They were mostly set up in and after 1949 to rival the newly organised International Trade Secretariats (ITSs) set up by the non-communist International Confederation of Free Trade Unions (ICFTU) in Brussels. The TUIs claimed a combined membership of over 240 million (including the FISE's 20 million) the bulk of which is included in, rather than additional to, the corporate WFTU membership.

The TUIs strive to appear independent. Each has its own Secretariat and officials, holds its own meetings and publishes its own bulletins. In December 1966, they were given their individual constitutions in the hope that they would be enabled thereby to join other international bodies, particularly the Special Agencies of the United Nations, as separate organisations. In practice, their activities and finances continue to be as closely controlled by the special TUI Department at WFTU headquarters as before, and their ultimate dependence on the Soviet Union is widely known in genuine trade union circles.

The main tasks of the TUIs are to recruit individual unions which do not already belong to the WFTU and to attract the support of non-communist unions for campaigns on current issues, particularly those of immediate concern to the WFTU and the AUCCTU* in Moscow.

One of the eleven existing TUIs is of very recent origin, namely the Energy Workers TUI. This has been formed to replace the relevant section of the earlier Miners' and Energy Workers' TUI which was dissolved in September 1985, when the International Mineworkers' Organisation* was formed. A profile of FISE appears in Part A; brief profiles of the other 12 TUIs are given below.

(i) *Agricultural, Forestry and Plantation Workers' TUI*

Headquarters: Opletalova 57, 11000 Prague 1, Czechoslovakia.

Origins
The TUI was founded in 1949 at a constituent conference in Warsaw. It is the largest TUI, with a corporate membership of 60 million representing 98 national trade union organisations in 61 countries. A total of 110 organisations from 71 countries, 'representing 73 million workers', were present at its ninth International Conference in Warsaw in October 1983. It has set up agricultural, plantation, forestry and peasants' commissions.

Office Holders
The TUI's President is Andreas KYRIAKOU (Cyprus); the General Secretary is André HEMMERLE; Secretaries are Hussein HADDAR and Bernardo ZUNIGA (Costa Rica).

Publications and Information
The TUI publishes an Information Bulletin in English, French, Russian and Spanish as well as various booklets and publications encompassing its documents.

Relations with Other Bodies
The TUI has had special consultative status with the FAO (Food and Agriculture Organisation of the UN) since 1972 and claims to take an active part in the work of the ILO and UNESCO, as well as of the FAO.

Conferences
The TUI holds its International Conferences at intervals of approximately four years. These have been held in Warsaw (November 1949); Vienna (October 1953); Bucharest (October 1958); Sofia (November 1962); East Berlin (November 1966); Nicosia (October 1970); Moscow (May 1975); Warsaw (May

1979); and Warsaw (October 1983). The next will be held in Prague in March 1988.

(ii) *Building, Wood and Building Materials Industries' TUI*

Headquarters: 00101 Helsinki, PB 10281, Finland.

Origins
The TUI was founded in Milan in 1949. It claims to embrace 73 organisations from 57 countries, totalling 17 million members. Representatives from 86 organisations from 64 countries participated in its ninth International Conference in Sofia in October 1983. It has subsidiary commissions and working groups on construction, wood, building materials, work safety and health, youth, women, engineers and architects and technicians.

Office Holders
The TUI's President is Lothar LINDNER (GDR); the General Secretary is Mauri PERA (Finland) and the Secretary is Yevgeny RESHETNIKOV (USSR).

Publications and Information
The TUI publishes a quarterly Information Bulletin and at more frequent intervals a news bulletin in English, French, German and Russian.

Relations with Other Bodies
The TUI plays an active part inside the ILO and maintains regular contact with the UN Centre for Habitat and UNIDO (UN Industrial Development Organisation). It also has close relations with the Latin American Federation of Building and Woodworkers Unions (FLEMACON) and with the Arab Federation of Building, Wood and Building Materials' Industry.

Conferences
The TUI holds international conferences at intervals of approximately four years. These have been held in Milan (July 1949); East Berlin (March 1955); Budapest (October 1959); Budapest (September 1963); East Berlin (May 1967); Moscow (June 1971); Prague (October 1975); Warsaw (September 1979); and Sofia (October 1983). The next will be held in East Berlin in May 1988.

(iii) *Chemical, Oil and Allied Workers' TUI*

Headquarters: Benczur ut. 45, 1415 Budapest, Hungary.

Origins
Founded in 1950, the TUI claims the support of about 100 organisations from 50 countries, representing 13 million members. The ninth International Conference in Prague in May 1983 was attended by representatives from 93 organisations from 59 countries. It has subsidiary commissions on chemicals, petroleum, paper, glass and ceramics and rubber.

Office Holders
The TUI's President is Ferenc DAJKA (Hungary); the General Secretary is Alain COVET (France) and the Secretaries are Pal GERGELY (Hungary) and Yevgeni MOKHOV (USSR).

Publications and Information
The TUI regularly publishes an Information Bulletin in English, French, German, Russian and Spanish.

Relations with Other Bodies
The TUI cooperates with the Arab Oil Federation and the African Federation of Trade Unions in Oil and Allied Industries.

Conferences
The TUI holds its international conferences at approximately four yearly intervals. There have been ten so far, namely Budapest (March 1950); Bucharest (September 1954); Leipzig, GDR (May 1959); Moscow (May 1963); Budapest (May 1967); Leuna, GDR (May 1971); Tarnow, Poland (May 1975); Sofia (May 1979); Prague (May 1983); and Moscow (October 1987).

(iv) *Commercial, Office and Bank Workers' TUI*

Headquarters: Opletalova 57, 110 Prague 1, Czechoslovakia.

Origins
Founded in 1959, the TUI comprises 70 member organisations from 61 countries representing more than 23 million workers. The seventh International Conference in East Berlin in September 1984 was attended by 26 non-affiliates. The TUI has a standing committee responsible for the problems of working women.

Office Holders
The TUI's President is Janos VAS (Hungary); the General Secretary is Ilie FRUNZA (Romania) and the Secretaries are Anatoli MOROZOV (USSR) and Alvaro VILLAMARIN (Colombia).

Publications and Information
The TUI produces a quarterly Information Bulletin and a monthly newsletter, the latter in English, French, German, Russian and Spanish.

Conferences
The TUI has held international conferences at intervals of approximately four years, as follows: Prague (June 1959); Warsaw (May 1964); Bucharest (June 1968); Cairo (September 1972); Sofia (October 1976); Budapest (July 1980); and East Berlin (September 1984). The next is being held in Moscow in September 1988.

(v) *Energy Workers' TUI*

Headquarters: Ulica Kopernika 34–40, 00–924 Warsaw, Poland.

Origins
The Energy Workers' TUI, which adopted its present truncated title in 1986, is the remnant of the Miners' TUI, founded in Florence in June 1949 which was later extended to include energy workers as the Miners' and Energy Workers' TUI. The latter dissolved itself on 20 September 1985 and the miners' section now forms part of the International Mineworkers' Organisation (IMO*), which was founded immediately after the dissolution of the joint TUI (Alain Simon (France), who had been the TUI's General Secretary now holds the same position in the IMO).

As the new IMO, which had taken over many of the miners' functions of the dissolved TUI, was not intended to embrace energy workers, such workers who had formerly belonged to it held a preparatory meeting in Warsaw on 12 November 1985 with the object of launching a new Energy Workers' TUI. When the new TUI's inaugural or 'constituent' conference was held in Czechoslovakia, 5–6 June 1986, sixty delegates from 28 countries attended. It now has 17 affiliates from 17 countries and claims a total corporate membership of some six and a half million. It has already established commissions on security and hygiene, transnational corporations and 'peace and disarmament', as well as an auditors' commission.

Office Holders
The TUI's President is François DUTEIL (France); its General Secretary is Mieczyslaw JUREK (Poland) and its Secretaries are Bohumir BOBAK (Czechoslovakia), Valery CHESTAKOV (USSR) and Vladimir TCHOUGOUNOV (country unknown).

Publications and Information
The TUI publishes a bulletin for energy workers at regular intervals.

Conferences
The inaugural conference was held in Podbanske, Czechoslovakia in June 1986.

(vi) *Food, Tobacco, Hotel and Allied Industries' TUI*

Headquarters: 4, Ul. 6 September, Sofia, Bulgaria.

Origins
Founded in 1949, the TUI comprises 94 organisations from 54 countries representing over 20 million workers. Representatives of 110 organisations from 78 countries participated in its seventh International Conference in Moscow in September 1983. There are also several subsidiary commissions. They are concerned with the sugar industry, meats and fats, milk and milk products, bread and confectionery, tobacco, hotels and restaurants.

Office Holders
The TUI's President is Freddy HUCK; the General Secretary is Luis MARTELL (Cuba) and the Secretaries are Ibrahim DAHAR (Lebanon) and Serge FLOUTIER.

Publications and Information
The TUI publishes a bulletin every two months in English, French, Russian and Spanish.

Relations with Other Bodies
The TUI (which has a joint committee with the Transport TUI on the problems of workers in the fishing industry) has consultative status with the FAO.

Conferences
The TUI has held international conferences at intervals of approximately four years, as follows: Sofia (November 1949); Sofia (September 1955); Budapest (August 1960); Prague (September 1965); East Berlin (November–December 1969); Budapest (May 1974); Warsaw (November 1979); Moscow (September 1983); and Prague (November 1987).

(vii) *Metal and Engineering Industries' TUI*

Headquarters: P.O. Box 158, K–9 Moscow, USSR.

Origins
The TUI was established in 1949. It has 60 affiliates in 43 countries, representing over 22 million workers. Representatives of 113 organisations from 70 countries attended its ninth International Conference in Moscow in September 1982. It has five industrial commissions—iron and steel, automobiles, shipbuilding, electrotechnical, mechanical and engineering, and, in addition, a Standing group on 'peace and disarmament'.

Office Holders
The President is Reinhard SOMMER (GDR); the General Secretary is Daniel BAILLY (France) and the Secretaries are Valentin GOSHCHINSKY (USSR), Aristobulo MARCIALES (Colombia) and Rouska MAVROVA.

Relations with Other Bodies
The General Secretary is also the president of the WFTU's special commission of transnational corporations.

Publications
The TUI publishes a monthly review *Metal Workers Unions in Action* in English, French, German, Russian and Spanish and a bulletin every two months.

Conferences
The TUI has held international conferences at intervals of approximately four years, as follows: Turin, Italy (June 1949); Vienna (June 1954); Prague (September 1958); East Berlin (October 1962); Sofia (October 1966); Budapest (November 1970); Vichy, France (December 1974); Warsaw (September 1987).

(viii) *Public and Allied Employees' TUI*

Headquarters: Französische Strasse 47, 108 Berlin, GDR.

Origins
The TUI was founded at a conference in Berlin in 1949 as the International Union of Trade Unions of Postal, Telephone and Telegraph Workers. Its field of activities was broadened in 1955 to include workers in public administration, health, finance and public services. It has now 104 affiliates in 44 countries, claiming to represent about 29 million workers. Representatives of 140 organisations from 69 countries attended its seventh international conference in Prague in October 1982.

It has five subsidiary industrial commissions (on public workers, public services, bank employees, communication workers, and health workers).

Office Holders
The President is Alain POUCHOL (France); the General Secretary is Jochen MEINEL (GDR) and the Secretary is Frank BOULIN.

Publications and Information
The TUI regularly publishes an information bulletin and a review, *Public Service*.

Conferences
The TUI has held international conferences at approximately four year intervals as follows: Vienna (April 1955); Leipzig, GDR (August 1959); Prague (April 1964); Budapest (April 1968); Moscow (September 1972); Warsaw (October 1977); and Prague (October 1982).

(ix) *Textile, Clothing, Leather and Fur Workers' TUI*

Headquarters: Opletalova 57, Prague, Czechoslovakia.

Origins
This TUI evolved from a merger in 1958 between the International Union of Textile and Clothing Trade Unions with the International Union of Fur and Leather Workers, both of which had been founded in 1949.

The TUI has 75 affiliates in 58 countries with a total corporate membership of about 12 million. Its eighth International Conference in East Berlin in 1982 was attended by representatives of 83 organisations, 32 of them not formally affiliated to it, from 59 countries. It has set up textile clothing and fur leather commissions, as well as a working group on 'peace and disarmament'.

Office Holders
The TUI's President is Gilberto MORALES (Colombia); its General Secretary is Jan HÜBNER (Czechoslovakia); its Deputy General Secretary Antoine HERRERO (France) and its Secretaries are Anatoli KOLMAKOV (USSR) and Jean-Marie KOUTCHINSKI (France).

Publications and Information
The TUI regularly publishes two information Bulletins—*Courier* and *News*.

Conferences
The TUI has held international conferences at intervals of approximately four years as follows: Sofia (July 1958); Bucharest (May 1962); East Berlin (May 1966); Prague (October 1970); Budapest (September 1978); East Berlin (September 1982); and Sofia (May 1987).

(x) *Transport Workers' TUI*

Headquarters: Vaci ut. 73, 1139 Budapest, Hungary.

Origins
The TUI was founded in 1949 and it currently includes port and fishery, as well as transport, workers in its ranks. It has 145 affiliates in 72 countries, representing a corporate total of 18 million workers. Its International Conference in Damascus in 1981 was also attended by the representatives of 57 non-affiliated organisations in a further 45 countries. It has established five subsidiary commissions (maritime, ports, railroads, motor transport, and civil aviation).

Office Holders
The TUI's President is Georges LANOUE (France); its General Secretary is Kulangara MATHEW (India) and its Secretaries are Alexander BOGUSHEVSKY (USSR) and Gyula CZENKI (Hungary).

Publications

The TUI publishes a quarterly, *Transport Workers of the World*, as well as a monthly information bulletin in English, French, Russian and Spanish.

Conferences

The TUI has held international conferences at intervals of approximately four years, as follows: Prague (March 1953); Bucharest (May 1957); Budapest (May 1961); Sofia (May 1965); East Berlin (May 1969); Warsaw (June 1973); Moscow (September 1977); Damascus (October 1981); and Prague (October 1985).

SECTION III

Soviet-influenced Organisations

INTRODUCTION

The descriptions given in Section II of Soviet-controlled international front organisations have shown two things; first, how the fifteen principal organisations were established (or, in several instances, taken over) by Moscow's agents for the exclusive purpose of promoting Soviet policies in their respective fields of interest; and, secondly, how these organisations have proliferated round the world, spawning subsidiaries of varying degrees of permanency as the opportunity or need arose.

This section describes different types of bodies, which are, for convenience, described as the 'Soviet-influenced organisations'. They are not international front organisations in the sense that they are directly controlled by Moscow. They are specialist or professional peace groups, organisations which have been created by individuals in different professions who, either through conviction or from a misplaced sense of balance, present Soviet policies in the most favourable possible light; and, following the same thought process, put the most unfavourable interpretation on Western, especially American, policies. As such they are encouraged, and often manipulated, by 'equivalent' Soviet professional organisations in Moscow. Unlike the traditional 'fronts', their leading members are not, or are not necessarily, communists. They may not even be in any true sense 'fellow travellers', to use a term which has dropped out of common use in recent years; while some may be communists, either openly or covertly, the majority are almost certainly not. Yet their activities and their sympathies are supportive of the Soviet propaganda line, and they are welcomed by the 'official' Soviet organisations as supplementing their efforts.

Many of the leading officials of these newer Soviet-influenced organisations also hold office in, or are members of, the WPC or other Soviet-controlled international organisations. This provides a 'transmission belt' (in Lenin's phrase) for Soviet influence and ensures that, in general, the activities of the Soviet-influenced organisations do not deviate from official policy and accurately reflect the current preoccupations of Soviet propaganda.

With two major exceptions—the WILPF and AALAPSO—this category is of recent origin, with new entrants still emerging. The organisations have been launched, for the most part, as a result of proposals made at the World Peace Council's World Parliament of the Peoples for Peace (Sofia, Bulgaria, September 1980). They do not, unlike the traditional international front organisations, tend to conform to a common model. Some (e.g. the Generals for Peace and Disarmament) are self-appointed international liaison committees. Others (e.g. the Working Presidium of the World Conference for Saving the Sacred Gift of Life from Nuclear Catastrophe) are based in Moscow and controlled by compliant officials there and at the headquarters of the CPC and WPC. And other new international groups, supplementing the older 'fronts' active in the same areas, have recently emerged for lawyers, journalists and scientists. Representatives of these newer groups—Generals for Peace and Disarmament, International Physicians and International Scientists—played leading parts in the Soviet organised International Peace Forum in Moscow in February 1987 which was addressed by General Secretary Gorbachev. Increasingly, these newer organisations give the impression of being almost as much 'disguised instruments of Soviet foreign policy' as the traditional international front organisations.

Although most of the 14 organisations described in this section are of fairly recent creation, the technique of involving professional people in activities in support of Soviet policies is not new. It has evolved from the Comintern's policy in the 1920s and 1930s of employing every ruse available to capture the sympathies of prominent artists, scientists, intellectuals, lawyers and non-communist (but left-wing) politicians for the building of a socialist society in the Soviet Union. The evolution of this policy is described in Section I.

The underlying doctrine was clearly restated by the late D.N. PRITT, the British lawyer and Member of Parliament who was expelled from the Labour Party for his Communist activities in 1948, in these words:

In the western capitalist world, where the main work for peace must be done, we should seek cooperation wherever it can be found . . . Doctors, lawyers, civil servants, artists, musicians, writers, university and school teachers, ministers of the churches, scientists and many others are so placed in the life of the community as to exert an influence out of proportion to their numbers . . . We must win as an ally every individual who has a vested interest in preserving peace, however 'unpolitical' he or she may be . . . . (*World Trade Union Movement*, journal of the WFTU, 5 November 1950)

Pritt's call, issued at the height of the Cold War, was to prove the genesis, with apparent spontaneity, of a host of professional peace organisations in the United Kingdom, most, although not all, of which are now defunct. They included Architects for Peace, Artists for Peace, the Authors' World Peace Appeal, the Medical Association for the Prevention of War, the Musicians' Organisation for Peace, Science for Peace and Teachers for Peace. These British bodies were at the time loosely associated with a Liaison Committee of the Peace Organisations of the Professions, which existed from about 1955 to 1960. Most of them had similarly communist-inspired counterparts in other western countries. Many of these were included in the Labour Party's proscribed lists between 1933 and 1972 (see Appendices B and C).

As Pritt's definition shows, there is endless scope for Soviet penetration of professional and special interest groups. Some of the organisations described below are newcomers which are only just beginning to establish themselves. Two which have recently emerged in the international field are:

(1) *Performing Artists for Nuclear Disarmament (PAND) International.*

First launched by three American performers in 1982, PAND was joined by groups in several West European countries and invited a delegation from the Soviet Union to attend a meeting in Hamburg in September 1983 to discuss future plans. A further meeting was held in Moscow in March 1984 when 'International' was added to the title. By then there were branches in 21 countries. PAND co-operates with the WPC as well as with UNESCO and other non-communist organisations.

(2) *International Architects Designers Planners for the Prevention of Nuclear War (IADPPNW).*

IADPPNW was established in Brighton, England, in July 1987 during the Congress of the International Union of Architects. Its joint Chairmen are Tician PAPACHRISTOU, President of the US Architects Designers and Planners for Social Responsibility, and Yuri PLATONOV, President of the USSR Union of Architects. Delegates from professional bodies in 29 countries elected an Executive Committee consisting of the Co-Chairmen and representatives from Argentina, India, Kenya, Morocco, New Zealand, Poland, Sweden and the United Kingdom. The headquarters will probably be in Stockholm.

Another recently established organisation, International Pensioners for Peace, whose headquarters is in the United Kingdom, has exchanged visits with Soviet pensioners and, in 1985, produced a booklet 'The Russian Threat' which was described in the *Morning Star* (15 October 1985) as having 'exploded the myth of the Soviet threat in a very simple and comprehensive manner.'

PROFILES

1. Afro–Asian Latin American Peoples' Solidarity Organisation

The Afro–Asian/Latin American Peoples' Solidarity Organisation (AALAPSO) is also known under its French and, most commonly, its Spanish title and initials which are, respectively, *Organisation de solidarité des peuples d'Afrique, d'Asie et d'Amérique Latine* and *Organización de Solidaridad de los Pueblos de Africa, Asia y America Latina* (OSPAAAL). Its headquarters is at Calle C No. 668 e/27 y 29 Vedado, Havana, Cuba.

Origins
When the council of the newly-formed Afro-Asian Peoples' Solidarity Organisation (AAPSO) met in Bandung in 1961 it was agreed that Latin American bodies should be incorporated into the organisation. The process of extending AAPSO to the Americas was, however, a slow one and the first Tricontinental Conference was not held until January 1966 in Havana. It was originally intended that this new Tricontinental name would replace that of AAPSO but that the new body would still be situated in Cairo where the AAPSO's headquarters already were (and still are): but both the Chinese, who had not yet left the movement, and the Cubans were strongly opposed. Eventually the Cubans set up AALAPSO as a separate organisation in Havana and it remains effectively under their control as surrogates for the Soviet Union.

Its first Secretary-General, Osmani Cienfuegos, was a high-ranking Cuban communist.

Declared Aims
According to the *Yearbook of International Organisations* (1986–87), AALAPSO aims

> to support the struggle of the peoples of Africa, Asia and Latin America against imperialism, colonialism and neo-colonialism, and defend their right to govern themselves according to the socio-economic system of their choice without external interference; promote solidarity of the peoples of these three continents with respect to independence, sovereignty and liberation; combat racism and all forms of discrimination; promote peaceful coexistence and development, resisting the increase in armaments (particularly nuclear arms); foster the new international economic order.

Organisation and Membership
AALAPSO has an Executive Secretariat composed of represen-tatives from countries located in all three continents—Angola, Chile, Cuba, Guinea, North Korea, Syria and Vietnam, as well as the US Territory of Puerto Rico. At the foundation conference in 1966 there had been participants from 28 countries in Africa, 27 in Asia and 27 in Latin America. Friendly comments on AALAPSO's twentieth anniversary referred to a 'rise of its membership base' (IOJ Newsletter, 13/86), but a description in the *Yearbook of International Organisations* 1986–87, based on AALAPSO's response to a questionnaire, gave no details.

Office Holders
Executive Secretary General: Dr. Rene ANILLO Capote (Cuba) (a former Cuban Ambassador to the Soviet Union); Department Chiefs: Evelia GALICH Menendez, Eduardo RODRIGUEZ Cordero (Cuba); Committee: Rafael COURAIGE (Cuba), Dr. Miguel D'ESTEFANO Pisani (Cuba), Cristina GONZALEZ, Juan PARDO, Dr. Ruben De LOS ANGELES Gavalda (Cuba), Lisa YOUNG, Miriam ALMANZA Rodriguez (Cuba), NGUYEN Xuan Phong.

Relations with Other Bodies
AALAPSO is represented on the WPC Presidential Committee by its Secretary-General.

AALAPSO also has close working links with other Soviet controlled international front organisations and participates from time to time in the regular liaison meetings. (The last such meeting which the AALAPSO is known to have attended was in Helsinki in April 1985).

Activities
As an organisation, AALAPSO is relatively quiescent; its main activity is the publication of *Tricontinental* six times a year in English, French and Spanish, and to issue statements. On 13 April 1987, for example, it issued a statement 'on the fifth anniversary of the British aggression against the Malvinas [Falklands] and Great Britain's imperialist war against Argentine sovereignty', in which it reaffirms support for Argentina's sovereign right over the Malvinas islands in the South Atlantic and reiterates its denunciation of the colonialist policy of the Margaret Thatcher government: 'The Malvinas have been illegally occupied by Great Britain for 154 years, and the unilateral measure establishing an extensive fishing exclusion zone around the islands is an affront to and attack on Argentine sovereignty.'

2. Ecoforum for Peace

The Ecoforum for Peace was established at an International Conference on the Protection of the Environment and the Defence of World Peace which was held in Varna, Bulgaria in August 1986. It was attended by 88 natural and social scientists from 32 countries and by delegates from 12 international organisations including UNESCO, the UN Environment Programme (UNEP), the International Union for the Conservation of Native and Natural Resources, the World Future Studies Federation, the Pugwash movement and the Life Institute. The participants elected a governing board consisting of representatives from Bulgaria, France, Great Britain, Japan, the Netherlands, the USA and the USSR; the board's secretary is Veyelin NEYKOV (Bulgaria), who is editor of the Bulgarian magazine *Nature* and who addressed the Moscow Peace Forum, February 1987. The movement currently comprises representatives from 37 countries and has its headquarters in Bulgaria.

In its declaration, the Ecoforum identified the 'three goals of the new movement' as

(1) to rally the efforts of the global scientific community and all committed towards assuring the co-development or co-evolution of humankind and nature as a necessary condition for life and social progress;

(2) to encourage the world ecological and related communities in their efforts to mobilize the peoples and oblige the governments of all nations to achieve and safeguard peace in the world and to promote appropriate development on a sound ecological basis;

(3) to mobilise our fellow researchers throughout the world to help create the trust among nations necessary to achieve these aims.

According to a Soviet source, the Ecoforum for Peace 'proceeds from the assumption that the joint strategy of tackling global problems must be permeated with humanism and the ideals of social progress and international cooperation. It is called upon to stimulate the whole of mankind in its efforts to solve the problems of peace and disarmament. The movement's ideas are expressed in the Appeal for the Survival of Humankind and Life on the Planet, addressed to the peoples and governments of the world. An important feature of the new united anti-war and ecological movement that distinguishes it from other movements is that it transcends various specialized sciences and social groups, includes ecology in the context of current world socio-political problems and makes each scientist and each individual aware of his responsibility for life on earth'. (Ivan Frolov, Corresponding Member, USSR Academy of Sciences, writing in the *New Times*, Moscow, No. 12, 30 March 1987.)

3. Generals for Peace and Disarmament

One of the more interesting of the new generation of Soviet-influenced organisations, Generals for Peace and Disarmament, was formed in 1981. Alone among the organisations described in this and the preceding section, it is not, by definition, a mass movement: it is a group of 15 retired West European and North American generals, admirals and other senior officers. At its third meeting in Vienna, 15–18 May 1984, eight comparable Warsaw Pact generals were present for the first time; the meeting endorsed the Soviet Union's position on intermediate-range nuclear forces and other defence issues. Those contacts with like-minded groups in Warsaw Pact countries culminated, in December 1986, in the formation of the USSR Retired Generals and Admirals for Peace and Disarmament* group, with which the western group is now associated. Similar groups have also recently been set up in Bulgaria, Czechoslovakia, Hungary and Poland.

Origins
The western group originally came to notice in 1981, when eight retired NATO officers jointly contributed to a book, *Generals for Peace*, published in Cologne in German. It consisted of interviews between the West German Professor Gerhard KADE and General Wolf von BAUDISSIN (FRG), Marshal Francisco da COSTA Gomes (Portugal), Brigadier Michael HARBOTTLE (UK), General George KOUMANAKOS (Greece), Admiral John Marshal LEE (USA), General-Major Michiel Hermann von MEYENFELDT (Netherlands), General Nino PASTI (Italy) and Admiral Antoine SANGUINETTI (France). They aimed to analyse the 'threat to peace' which, they claimed, was posed by NATO's current policies. Their formal existence was first recorded when an interview with General Pasti appeared in the Communist newspaper *Morning Star*, London, 23 July 1981.

The new group had its genesis in the participation by several retired officers, including da Costa Gomes, Pasti and Sanguinetti, in a 'round table' held during the WPC's World Parliament of the Peoples for Peace in Sofia in September 1980. Five members of the group subsequently signed an appeal (published in *Blätter für deutsche und internationale Politik*, Cologne, June 1981) to the 35 nations that adhere to the 1975 Helsinki Final Act of the Conference on Security and Cooperation in Europe (CSCE), calling for renewed arms control negotiations and criticising the decision to deploy the new Pershing II and cruise missiles in Western Europe. The signatories were General Gert BASTIAN (FRG), da Costa Gomes, Koumanakos, von Meyenfeldt and Pasti. Subsequently, in November 1981, on the eve of a NATO Council meeting in Brussels, Bastian, Koumanakos, von Meyenfeldt, Pasti and Sanguinetti issued a 'Memorandum to the Foreign and Defence Ministers of the North Atlantic Alliance and to NATO Commanders and Staff Officers' at a press conference in The Hague. They demanded an end to 'the arms race' and to 'nuclear confrontation'. The Memorandum was also supported by da Costa Gomes and by General Johan CHRISTIE (Norway). The continuing build-up of SS-20 deployments by the Soviet Union was completely ignored in these declarations and in subsequent publications by the group.

The group was at first run from West Berlin by Professor Kade. In March 1983 new headquarters were established in London at the premises of the London Centre for International Peace building, the British counterpart to the Center for Defense Information in Washington, run by Admiral Gene LA ROCQUE, which, in 1982, co-ordinated the plans for a joint meeting of retired officers from West and East, to coincide with the Second UN Special Session on Disarmament (New York, June–July 1982). Brigadier Michael Harbottle, the director of the London Centre, then became the administrator of Generals for Peace and Disarmament in place of Kade (his wife, Eirwen, is its secretary). Von Meyenfeldt, from whose address in Ittervoort, Netherlands, the group had issued its first circular letter in 1982, remains its chairman.

WPC connections
At least five members of the groups are prominent in the WPC: da Costa Gomes (a Vice-President); Koumanakos (since June 1983 a member of the Presidential Committee); Pasti, Sanguinetti and Michalis TOMBOPOULOS (Greece), all ordinary WPC members. Kade's close involvement with the group reinforced its links with the WPC at the outset; he is a WPC member and a leading member of its offshoot, the International Institute for Peace (IIP)*, which is based in Vienna.

Activities
After the group's first meeting, arranged in Vienna in February 1982 by the IIP, Christie, Harbottle, Koumanakos and Lee gave a Press conference to discuss the document which they proposed to submit to the Second UN Special Session on Disarmament in New York, 7 June–9 July 1982. The document, subsequently launched as a memorandum at a Press conference in Bonn on 4 June 1982, called for an immediate moratorium on the deployment of nuclear weapons in East and West as a first step towards disarmament talks. The signatories were Bastian, Christie, da Costa Gomes, Harbottle, Koumanakos, Lee, von Meyenfeldt, General Antonios PAPASPYROU (Greece), General Militiades PAPATHANASSIOU (Greece), Pasti, Sanguinetti, Tombopoulos and General Günter VOLLMER (FRG).

Subsequently, da Costa Gomes, Koumanakos, Papathanassiou, Pasti and Tombopoulos attended the (WPC) World Assembly for Peace and Life, Against Nuclear War, in Prague, 21–26 June 1983. At Prague, as at Sofia in 1980, 'round tables' of special interest groups were held in connection with the Assembly and one of these consisted of retired officers. On that occasion Koumanakos and Pasti, with Professor (Colonel) Daniil PROEKTOR (USSR), shared responsibility for the 'military doctrine panel'.

Harbottle, Pasti and Tombopoulos attended a meeting of civilian and military experts, held at the IIP headquarters in Vienna in 1983, at which the Austrian, Dr. Georg FUCHS, who is President of the IIP and a WPC member, and Nikolai POLYANOV (USSR), the IIP's Scientific Director and also a WPC member, were present, as was a representative of the Soviet-edited *World Marxist Review* (published in Prague) and Dr. Daniel ELLSBERG (USA), Dr. Carl JACOBSEN (USA), Lt-Gen. Mikhail KIRYAN (USSR), Dr. Josef MRAZEK (Czechoslovakia), Dr. Walter SCHÜTZE (France) and Dr. Joachim WERNICHE (West Berlin).

Early in 1983 Bastian, Christie, da Costa Gomes, Harbottle, Koumanakos, Lee, von Meyenfeldt, Papaspyrou, Papathanassiou, Pasti, Sanguinetti, Tombopoulos and Vollmer contributed to a booklet, *Ten Questions Answered*. Published in English in London (and subsequently translated into Flemish and German), it was said to reflect the views of those concerned 'on the matter of the new missiles which are, or are planned to be, deployed in Europe'. It contained many of the inaccuracies and dubious arguments which were current in Soviet propaganda. The same people, except Lee, were contributors to *Generals Against Rearmament*, published in German in Hamburg in 1983 and subsequently published in English, in which they criticised the new US 'first strike weapons'. On 16 November Bastian, Christie, da Costa Gomes, Harbottle, Koumanakos, von Meyenfeldt, Papathanassiou, Pasti, Sanguinetti and Tombopoulos jointly signed a document which they sent to the Canadian parliament in Ottawa, among other recipients, demanding 'an end to the deployment of US missiles in Europe' and calling for 'effective negotiations for nuclear disarmament'.

Some members of the Generals' group—notably Bastian and Pasti—have produced pamphlets which have been published by the WPC Information Centre in Helsinki.

Warsaw Pact participation
After 1982 the group made a number of approaches to organisations in the Soviet Union and other Warsaw Pact countries in the hope of beginning a dialogue with a comparable officers' group. During a visit to Moscow in January 1984, Harbottle met representatives of the Soviet Peace Committee*, the Institute of

the USA and Canada* (headed by Georgy ARBATOV, a WPC member and member of the Scientific Council of the IIP), the Committee for European Security and Cooperation* and the Soviet War Veterans' Association*, and was successful in arranging Warsaw Pact participation in the third Generals for Peace and Disarmament meeting. As a result the third meeting in Vienna in May 1984 became the first between representatives of the western group and Warsaw Pact officers.

Described by its participants as 'unprecedented', this gathering adopted a final statement which expressed interest in the continuation of 'this new and useful form of cooperation' and also pressed for 'regular consultations between European States at all possible levels'. Those present included Christie, Harbottle, Koumanakos, von Meyenfeldt, Pasti and General Joao RANGEL da Lima (Portugal), described as the 'NATO members', and Colonel-General Alexander N. PONOMAREV (USSR), Major-General Rair A. SIMONYAN (USSR), Major-General Marian NASZKOWSKI (Poland), Lt.-General Peter ILIEV (Bulgaria), Colonel-General Samuel KODAJ (Czechoslovakia), General Ion TUTOVEANO (Romania), Major-General Tibor SAARDY (Hungary) and Major-General Kurt LOHBERGER (GDR), on behalf of the Warsaw Pact. (Naszkowski, a former Polish Deputy Minister for Foreign Affairs, is a WPC member.) According to Soviet sources, Vladislav Kornilov, secretary of the Soviet Peace Committee, was also present.

General Ponomarev (a serving officer in the Soviet Army, who had jointly chaired it with von Meyenfeldt) reported that

> in its reciprocal statement . . . the Soviet delegation set out the attitude of our country and our public towards the nuclear arms race, pointed to the danger to the cause of peace in Europe and throughout the world which arises as a result of the deployment of American medium-range nuclear missiles in Europe, and adduced convincing evidence showing that the threat to the peoples of Europe and other areas of the planet of perishing in the conflagration of thermonuclear war arises from the most reactionary circles of American imperialism and of those who think like them in certain NATO countries . . . .

The Western participants 'showed understanding of the position of principle of the USSR' concerning the situation in which a resumption of the Geneva talks would be possible, i.e. if the USA and NATO 'take steps to restore the situation existing before the deployment of new American missiles in Western Europe was begun' (*Za Rubezhom*, Soviet weekly, No. 22, 31

May 1984). Ponomarev also reported that there had been detailed discussion of the initiatives tabled by the Soviet Union at the Stockholm (CDE) Conference, President Chernenko's call for agreement on 'nuclear norms', Soviet proposals on banning chemical warfare, prevention of an 'arms race in outer space' and a possible Warsaw Pact/NATO 'Treaty on the Non-use of Force'. Ponomarev remarked that it was 'characteristic that views of the participants from both East and West either coincided, or were very close to each other' on all these Soviet items. Simonyan and Kornilov, both members of the Soviet Peace Committee commented: 'the aims of the group [Generals for Peace and Disarmament]—an end to the arms race and a return to detente—are identical to those of the Soviet peace movement and the ideas of the anti-war movements of all honest-minded people in the world . . .' (*New Times*, Soviet international weekly, No. 24, June 1984).

Kornilov was an important participant. As secretary of the Soviet Peace Committee he takes a special interest in WPC activities. He is also a director of Estate Kongressorganisation, the Soviet company registered in Liechtenstein which owns the Vienna headquarters from which the WPC operated until 1957 and from which its subsidiary, the International Institute for Peace, still operates. He thus has close links with the Institute, which has played a key role in the development of Generals for Peace and Disarmament.

Speaking in the British House of Lords on 30 October 1984, the then Minister of State at the Foreign and Commonwealth Office (Lady Young) said that the British Government was aware of the links between the Generals' group and the WPC and made it clear that the generals, whatever appointments they may have held in the past, 'in no sense represent the [North Atlantic] Alliance or their countries'.

US Counterpart

In the US, Harbottle's two organisations, the London Centre for International Peacebuilding, and, more immediately, the Generals' group itself, have a counterpart in Admiral La Rocque's Center for Defense Information, which is based in Washington. Admiral La Rocque, although not formally a member of the Generals' group, has often been openly associated with it. As Harbottle himself recently wrote, the Center which is

. . . staffed largely by former members of the armed forces, works for the same basic objectives as the Generals. In April this year [1987], they were hosts to members of the Soviet group at a seminar [in Washington] not dissimilar to those held [by the Generals] in Vienna. (London *Daily News*, 17 July 1987).

The 1987 seminar to which Harbottle refers comprised a US group of nine retired Admirals and Generals, led by Admiral La Rocque, and including Admiral Lee, at that time also a member of the Generals for Peace and Disarmament; and a Soviet group of seven, led by Lieutenant-General Mikhail MILSTEIN, a senior member of the Institute for US and Canada and including one serving official, Major-General Boris SURIKOV nominated by the Soviet Ministry of Defence.

Membership of the Group
As will be seen from the above, membership of the group has varied since its inception in 1981. The following is a list of currently known members taken from Circular letter No. 3, January 1986:

General-Major Gert BASTIAN (West Germany),
    former senior officer in the Bundeswehr
General Johan CHRISTIE (Norway),
    former senior officer in NATO Allied Command Europe
Marshall Francisco da COSTA GOMES (Portugal),
    former Portuguese President 1974–76
Brigadier Michael HARBOTTLE (Britain),
    former Chief of Staff of the UN Peace Keeping Force in
    Cyprus
Major-General Leonard JOHNSON (Canada),
    former Commandant of the Canadian National Defence
    College
General Georgios KOUMANAKOS (Greece),
    former senior officer in NATO's Southern Command
General Joao RANGEL da Lima (Portugal)
Air Commodore Alistair MACKIE (Britain),
    formerly on the staff of the Chief of Air Staff
General Michiel von MEYENFELDT (Netherlands),
    formerly Governor of the Royal Military Academy, Breda
General Antonios PAPASPYROU (Greece),
    former senior officer
Admiral Miltiades PAPATHANASSIOU (Greece),
    retired naval officer
General Nino PASTI (Italy), former senior NATO officer

Admiral Antoine SANGUINETTI (France),
   former deputy chief of staff of the French Navy
Brigadier-General Michalis TOMBOPOULOS (Greece),
   former senior NATO officer
General-Major Günter VOLLMER (West Germany),
   formerly Commander, Military District, Hanover

4. International Health Workers for Peace (IHWP)

In June 1987 delegates, representing health workers' trade
unions, public health associations and professional societies from
51 countries and all continents, attended a World Conference
of Health Workers on Social Well-Being, Health and Peace in
Moscow. This conference set up an International Federation of
Medical Workers' Organisations Working for Peace and Health,
subsequently re-named the International Health Workers for
Peace (IHWP). Significantly, the conference was held in the
same place and at the same time as the seventh Congress of
the International Physicians for the Prevention of Nuclear War
(IPPNW)*; it was organised by an *ad hoc* International
Committee drawn from medical trade unions, public health
associations and professional organisations and claimed to be
open to 'all medical workers through their collective organisations'. The conference agreed that the 'arms race was the great
enemy of humankind' and called for (1) a total ban on nuclear
testing, (2) the reduction and then elimination of nuclear
weapons and (3) a total ban on chemical and bacteriological
weapons.

A programme of action was also agreed upon, namely

1 October is to be marked as Health Workers for Peace Day. It will be a
focal point for mobilisation and action in all countries, including meetings,
demonstrations, or other activities appropriate to the situation in each
country.

There is to be wide distribution and collection of signatures for the Appeal
from Hiroshimna and Nagasaki for a Total Ban and Elimination of Nuclear
Weapons.

There will be increased cooperation with the World Health Organisation and
other agencies of the United Nations as well as religious groups and voluntary
organisations devoted to peace, disarmament, health, social well-being and
economic development.

International coordination and joint action by all health workers' organisations, is to be extended and strengthened.

British trade unions 'represented' at the conference included the Medical Practitioners' Union (MPU), the Association of Scientific, Technical and Managerial Staffs (ASTMS), the Confederation of Health Service Employees (COHSE) and the National Union of Public Employees (NUPE): a member of the Health Visitors' Association attended in a personal capacity. A senior MPU official, Chris Butler, describing the new organisation in the British Communist newspaper, *Morning Star*, said that the new organisation saw itself, not as a rival to the IPPNW, but as complementing it.

5. International Mineworkers' Organisation

The International Mineworkers' Organisation (IMO), based in Paris, was founded in September 1985, partly to replace the Miners' and Energy Workers' Trade Union International which had functioned as a subsidiary of the Soviet-controlled World Federation of Trade Unions (WFTU).

The Miners' and Energy Workers' TUI, based in Warsaw, had claimed a membership of nine and a half million; it had a Polish President (Jan KONIECZNY) and a French communist General Secretary (Alain SIMON), although for the last year of its existence, its acting President was Gunther WOLF (GDR) who is now a Vice-President of the Energy Workers' TUI. When the Miners' and Energy Workers' TUI was dissolved on 20 September 1985, the IMO, significantly, came into being the following day with Arthur SCARGILL, Marxist President of the British National Union of Mineworkers (NUM), as its founder and President, Mikhail SREBNY (USSR) and Barry SWAN (Australia) as Vice-Presidents, and the dissolved TUI's former general secretary, Alain SIMON, as its own secretary. Within a few weeks of its foundation, IMO representatives were being listed among 'guests and observers' at the WFTU's 37th General Council meeting in Moscow (30 September–4 October 1985). IMO's headquarters are in the offices of the Confédération Général du Travail (the French communist trade union organisation) in Paris; there is a branch office at the NUM headquarters in Sheffield.

Origins
The first steps towards setting up the IMO had been taken at an international miners' meeting in Paris on 23–24 April 1983. The

initiative came from Arthur Scargill and Augustin Dufresne, General Secretary of the French Fédération National des Travailleurs du Sous Sol (FNTSS), a branch of the CGT, which is the WFTU's major affiliate in the West. A meeting of the Miners' and Energy Workers' TUI in Larnaca, Cyprus, in March 1983 welcomed the Paris meeting as an opportunity to end trade union divisions through the formation of a new united international miners' body.

The Paris meeting was attended by representatives of 25 unions from 23 countries (there were two from both Britain and Chile), drew up guidelines and a constitution for the proposed miners' international and issued a Miners' Charter. It elected a preparatory committee composed of representatives from Britain, France, Australia, the USSR, the German Democratic Republic (GDR), Algeria, Bolivia, Chile and Zambia. As co-sponsors of the meeting, the British were invited to chair the committee, the French providing a Secretary. Interested miners' organisations were asked to join the new body by January 1984, by which time it was hoped that membership of other international miners' bodies would cease, as the new one, it was claimed, would be 'non-aligned'. Another preparatory meeting, held in Sheffield on 28–29 January 1984, was attended by miners' representatives from France, the USSR, the GDR, Poland and Chile.

The founding congress for the new body, originally to have been held in Britain in September 1984, was postponed because of the British miners' strike. There were suggestions that the project might be abandoned because of lack of interest on the part of many non-communist miners' organisations and disagreement behind the scenes about the likely extent of Soviet control. Nevertheless, the Miners' and Energy Workers' TUI's Ninth Conference, in October 1984, again supported the initiative for a new international body, to include all miners' and energy workers' trade union organisations 'regardless of their current affiliations'. When the British miners' strike ended in March 1985, Scargill went to Prague and Moscow to discuss arrangements for the postponed founding congress. In May he had talks with Sandor GASPAR, head of the Hungarian trade unions and President of WFTU: the result was the decision to convene the congress.

Foundation meeting

The founding congress, held in Paris on 21–22 September 1985, was attended by trade unionists from 32 countries[a], at least nine of them communist. Professor Vic Allen of Leeds University, described in *The Scotsman*, 7 September 1985, as 'the communist chronicler of militancy in the British coalfield', was also present. The IMO has a 16-member Executive Board, on which the four principal officers serve together with the chairmen of the six permanent committees and regional representatives from Europe, Asia, the Middle East, Africa and the Americas. Peter HEATHFIELD, General Secretary of the British NUM, was elected head of the General Policy Committee, Augustin DUFRESNE, head of the Organisation Committee and Juan ANTINAO (Chile), head of the committee dealing with multinational organisations.

The organisers claimed that in addition to the 3.8 million workers nominally represented by the 32 unions attending the Paris Congress, miners from another ten countries, including China, had expressed interest. Some of these unions were WFTU or ICFTU affiliates; others belonged to no international organisation.

The Soviet trade union newspaper *Trud* said on 24 September 1985 that the IMO aimed to 'defend miners' socio-economic interests and develop their international solidarity and their struggle for peace and disarmament'; its Charter 'enshrines demands directed against the rapacious activity of multinational corporations and speaks of the importance of the struggle for peace, disarmament and conversion of the arms industry to peaceful purposes'. In a special resolution, the founding Congress had 'expressed deep concern at America's dangerous plans to militarise space'; speakers had also 'supported the USSR's peace initiatives'.

Subsequent developments

After the founding congress, Arthur Scargill said that the IMO intended to recruit members from among those working in power stations and the oil industry in addition to miners. In practice IMO membership is largely confined to miners, despite reports

---

[a] Countries represented at the founding Congress were: Afghanistan, Australia, Benin, Britain, Bulgaria, Chile, Cyprus, Colombia, Congo, Cuba, Czechoslovakia, Ethiopia, France, Ghana, East Germany, Guinea, Hungary, India, Iraq, Morocco, Philippines, Poland, Portugal, Romania, Señegal, South Africa, Spain, Syria, Togo, USSR, Vietnam, Zambia.

that it had applied for observer status on the International Labour Organisation's Petroleum Committee. Moreover, a new TUI for energy workers only*, came into being early in 1986 after a preparatory meeting in Warsaw, where it is now based, carrying on some of the functions of the old Miners' and Energy Workers' TUI.

The IMO held its first regular meeting in Budapest from 18–19 March 1986 with Scargill in the chair (who again had talks with Sandor Gaspar, the WFTU president). IMO's first annual conference, in London on 22–23 November 1986, was attended by miners and energy workers from 36 countries. It called on affiliated bodies to seek improvements in miners' conditions 'in the widest possible unity', passed an emergency resolution in support of South African miners and decided to lobby European Community countries in favour of sanctions against coal imports from South Africa. Subsequently in an interview with Moscow Radio, Arthur Scargill said that participants in the IMO conference had urged the governments of Western countries, above all the USA, to 'respond positively to the Soviet peace proposals'.

ICFTU Comment

According to the non-communist International Confederation of Free Trade Unions (ICFTU), the IMO is

> nothing but the continuation of the WFTU-incorporated trade department or TUI for miners, with the inclusion of the British NUM. The difference is a new name and address. . . . By setting up the International Mineworkers' Organisation a further attempt is being made to undermine the international free trade union movement. However, the organisers of the manoeuvre have not been able to weaken the ICFTU-associated Miners' International Federation, nor have they succeeded in convincing major democratic miners' organisations that have no international affiliation to join. (ICFTU circular, 4 October 1985)

The ICFTU circular pointed out that it was no accident that the TUI's former affiliates had joined the IMO *en masse* after the TUI's 'dissolution' on 20 September, alongside communist-controlled unions without previous international affiliation, such as those in Spain and Portugal. The ICFTU also noted that the IMO's structure was identical with that of the dissolved TUI, one of its Secretaries, Valery CHESTAKOV (USSR), being a former TUI Secretary, and the IMO's Vice-President Srebny (USSR) being a former TUI Vice-President.

The Miners' International Federation stated, in a document

issued on 2 October 1985, that the IMO's foundation would in no way help miners' unity, nor could it claim to be independent when its members included not only the Soviet miners' union but Poland's official miners' trade union, set up after the suppression of the independent trade union Solidarity. As most of the organisations joining the IMO were 'strictly dependent on the main lines of a party's policy, on a State administration and on their government's economic plans', they could not be independent internationally when they were 'obediently following the international policy of their respective governments'. On 23 July 1985, the West German miners' union IGBE accused Scargill and his allies of preparing to 'smash the free and democratic Miners' International Federation'.

Force Ouvrière, the moderate French trade union organisation, urged President Mitterrand to expel the new WFTU-linked organisation from Paris. They recalled that the WFTU's original headquarters were in Paris, from 1945 until 1951, when the organisation was expelled by the French Government for subversive activities; it then settled in Vienna, whence it was expelled in 1956 for 'endangering Austrian neutrality', finally moving to Prague. When in 1984 the WFTU made known a wish to return to the French capital, the legal provision enabling the government to expel it in 1951 having been revoked, the proposal was resisted by the French authorities. IMO has so far remained in Paris, but on sufferance.

6. International Physicians for the Prevention of Nuclear War

Probably the most successful, so far, of the new wave of Soviet-influenced professional organisations is the International Physicians for the Prevention of Nuclear War (IPPNW), where—most notably—the appropriate Soviet national affiliate functions as the major element in the new organisation. Since the IPPNW was established in 1980, the Committee of Soviet Physicians' for the Prevention of Nuclear War* has played a leading role in its affairs. IPPNW's international headquarters is in the US in Boston, Massachussetts.

Origins

IPPNW claims as its 'co-founders' two eminent cardiologists: Academician Yevgeni CHAZOV (Soviet Union) and Dr.

Bernard LOWN, Professor of Cardiology at the Harvard School of Public Health in Cambridge, Massachusetts. It is still jointly controlled by Dr. Lown and by the Soviet Academician Mikhail KUZIN, who succeeded Dr. Chazov after he resigned from active participation in IPPNW on his appointment in 1987 as Soviet Minister of Health.

Dr. Lown, originally Boruchas Lakas and born in Lithuania in 1922, emigrated to the US in 1935. He was active in the Association of Interns and Medical Students there and attended the inaugural congress of the Soviet-controlled International Union of Students (IUS) in Prague in 1946. According to the Swiss newspaper *Aargauer Tagblatt*, 29 May 1986, he has been a 'practising Marxist' for over 40 years. He had corresponded with Dr. Chazov before meeting him at an 'extraordinary meeting of six Soviet and American physicians' in Geneva in December 1980 when the new group was launched. Again, according to Dr. Chazov's former interpreter, now a defector in the west, the original idea for its foundation came from Brezhnev and his Politburo colleagues (*Morgenbladet*, Oslo, 25 November 1985). Its stated aims are to encourage doctors internationally to unite in helping to educate the public about the medical and social consequences of nuclear war—which its sponsors claimed would be 'the last epidemic'—and thereby to put 'pressure on governments' to take appropriate counter measures.

Membership
The IPPNW, not an organisation of individual members, is described as a 'league of national affiliates' whose formation it has encouraged. It currently claims the support of over 200,000 physicians in about 50 countries. The US affiliate, Physicians for Social Responsibility, which had been founded by Dr. Lown nearly 20 years earlier, was revived in 1979 with the help of Dr. Helen CALDICOTT, an Australian 'peace activist' then living in the USA. The IPPNW affiliates in the USSR and in other communist countries were initiated by their respective Academies of Medical Sciences, in other words, with the official support of the State-approved professional organisations. Of the non-communist countries Finland is probably the only one in which membership of the IPPNW is by professional organisation rather than merely by voluntary groups of individual supporters. The largest national affiliate is that of the Soviet Union, comprising some 60,000 Soviet physicians, which thus effectively dominates the IPPNW's structure.

Congresses

The IPPNW has so far held seven international Congresses, in Airlie, Virginia, USA, in 1981; Cambridge, England, 1982; Amsterdam, 1983; Helsinki, 1984; Budapest, 1985; Cologne, 1986; and Moscow, 1987. Attendance has risen from about 100 at the first Congress to 800 at Budapest, over 3000 in Cologne. Attendance in Moscow in 1987 (2000 from 55 countries) was marginally down.

The congress organisers have on each occasion solicited messages from various western heads of State. President Reagan sent one to the Cologne congress which was addressed by David Lange, Prime Minister of New Zealand. Predictably, the IPPNW has received extensive favourable coverage in the Soviet media. For the most part, IPPNW proceedings have tended to echo familiar Soviet propaganda themes and its activities have been commended by the WPC. In 1984, for instance, the WPC's Executive Secretary instructed the Council's member organisations to ensure that their countries' physicians participated in the IPPNW Congress held that year. The WPC officially supported the IPPNW's activities in its 1984, 1985, 1986 and 1987 'Programmes of Action'. Georgy Arbatov, Director of the USA and Canada Institute of the USSR Academy of Sciences and a member of the CPSU Central Committee, and General Mikhail MILSTEIN, a former military intelligence officer who is on the Institute's staff, both played leading roles at early IPPNW congresses.

IPPNW's international headquarters in Boston has a permanent staff of ten. There are also regional European offices in London and Moscow. Between 1983 and 1984 the London office was also the address of, among other organisations, the Generals for Peace and Disarmament* and the Medical Association for the Prevention of War (MAPW), an organisation originally founded in 1951 and proscribed in 1952 by the British Labour Party as a Communist front organisation. The MAPW is now one of the IPPNW's two British affiliates, the other being the Medical Campaign against Nuclear Weapons, founded in 1980 at the suggestion of Dr. Caldicott.

Themes and objectives

While the IPPNW undoubtedly enjoys the support of many respectable physicians, it is clearly more than merely a bridge-building organisation between East and West. Despite its purported evenhandedness in addressing appeals to both US and

Soviet leaders, the IPPNW in practice supports proposals which accord with the current preoccupations of Soviet peace propaganda—e.g. nuclear freeze, 'no first use' of nuclear weapons, opposition to the 'militarisation of space' and support for other Soviet 'peace initiatives'. IPPNW's three main arguments are that no nuclear war could be limited, that civil defence measures are both expensive and pointlessly encourage an illusory hope of survival, and that money spent on nuclear weapons should be directed to such areas as medicine, education and employment and to the relief of poverty and hunger internationally. Its public opposition to Western defence policies is not matched by balancing concern for the nature or purpose of Soviet defence policies, the existing Soviet nuclear stockpiles or the Soviet Government's own military research into the use of outer space. This was evident in the report on the IPPNW Fifth Congress (held in Budapest), published by the Soviet-controlled World Federation of Trade Unions (WFTU):

> The Congress received various messages, one of which came from Mikhail Gorbachev, General Secretary of the CPSU, stressing that the USSR was pursuing the same goals as the physicians: ridding mankind of the danger posed by the unbridled arms race on earth and in space and striving to safeguard peace. Soviet and US Co-Presidents Yevgeni Chazov and Bernard Lown presented the Congress with a joint message appealing for a nuclear freeze, and the reduction and elimination of nuclear arsenals. They also called on the nuclear powers to renounce first use of nuclear arsenals. . . .
> (*Flashes from the Trade Unions*, WFTU publication, Prague, No. 29, 19 July 1985)

In the newer specialist organisations, however, the Soviet collaborators cannot always take every trick. There seems to have been a split among the organisers of the Cologne Congress, for instance, about the appropriateness of even debating the Soviet nuclear disaster at Chernobyl. In the end there was some discussion, but the issue was generally glossed over; the leadership subsequently issued a notably bland statement. Significantly, a key speaker at this Congress was Professor Vadim Zagladin, the first deputy head of the CPSU Central Committee's International Department, the organisation in Moscow which directs all international front organisations.

In his address to the International Peace Forum in Moscow in February 1987, at which he was one of the principal speakers, Dr. Lown's total endorsement of Soviet 'peace policies' was balanced only by his total criticism of the United States. When the Norwegian Nobel Committee awarded the 1985 Nobel Peace Prize to the IPPNW's joint founders, the announcement was welcomed by the Soviet participants despite 'previous coolness in the Soviet Union towards the Nobel awards' (*The Times*, London, 12 October 1985). Questions were asked in the British House of Lords on 10 December 1985, the day on which the Nobel Peace Prize award was announced. Baroness Young, then an FCO Minister of State, replied that, in the British Government's view, 'the achievements of the IPPNW . . . has been markedly one-sided, as the group has lent uncritical support to Soviet propaganda themes. The group is not in our judgment a genuine bridge-building organisation . . . It is significant that the World Peace Council has given prominent support to the IPPNW in its current programme of action. I also understand that the programme of the World Peace Council's sub-committee for scientists and doctors urges its members to co-operate with IPPNW and that the organisation receives considerable publicity in World Peace Council publications' (*Hansard*, House of Lords, London, 10 December 1985).

7. International Scientists for Peace

The latest of the new international professional groups to be launched from Moscow is the new group loosely known as 'Scientists for Peace'. This movement was originally foreshadowed, in common with many others, by a meeting of scientists held during the WPC's World Assembly for Peace and Life, against Nuclear War, in Prague in June 1983, when it was proposed that a World Congress of Scientists against War and Armaments should be held, at the same time as number of national committees of Scientists for Peace were launched.

Such an International Scientists' Peace Congress was eventually held in Hamburg from 14–16 November 1986. The WFTU publication *Flashes* (No. 48, 5 December 1986) no doubt accurately described it as the 'First International Congress of Scientists for Peace'. Also subtitled, 'Ways out of the Arms Race'; the congress was attended by some 3,700 delegates, including about 400 participants from outside the Federal Republic, and it adopted the 'Hamburg Proposals for Disarmament' which included a call for a ban on nuclear weapon tests and 'the prohibition of space weapons'. The initial signatories to it included six Britons (at least one of whom, Prof. Dorothy HODGKIN, has had many international front connexions in the past) and a larger group of American signatories which included Dr. Bernard Lown (of IPPNW) and Dr. Linus PAULING who, like Prof. Hodgkin, also has many connexions with the older international fronts.

The preparations for the Congress had been undertaken by an *ad hoc* international organising committee and international advisory committee. But the principal host organisation was the West German scientists' organisation, Responsibility for Peace, acting in conjunction with the Hamburg Peace Forum.

National groups which form part of this new movement and which existed before this Congress include, in Britain, Scientists Against Nuclear Arms (SANA), which was set up on 21 March 1981 at a meeting chaired by Dr. Hodgkin. Similar groups also exist in Argentina, Canada, Finland, France, the German Democratic Republic, Iceland, Italy, New Zealand, Norway, Sweden and the US (where it is known as the Union of Concerned Scientists). The most significant of these bodies is, however, that in the Soviet Union, which is called the Committee of Soviet Scientists for Peace and Against the Nuclear Threat.* Its Second All Union Conference of Scientists on the Problem of Peace and against the Threat of Nuclear War was held in Moscow in May 1986 and attended by 159 scientists from 47 countries.

8. International Trade Union Committee for Peace and Disarmament

The International Trade Union Committee for Peace and Disarmament (the 'Dublin Committee'), also known under its French title of *Comité syndical international pour la paix et le désarmement*, is another organisation of a new type which reflects Soviet propaganda in a specialist field. In a Parliamentary answer, 15 February 1984, Mr. David Waddington, a Home Office Minister, said that the Dublin Committee 'was formed by the World Federation of Trade Unions, an international Communist front organisation'. Its headquarters is at PO Box 514, 11121 Prague 1, Czechoslovakia.

Origins and Purpose
At the WFTU's ninth World Trade Union Congress in Prague in April 1978, it was decided to hold at some future date a World Conference on the Socio-economic Aspects of Disarmament. One year later, in April 1979, the WPC* and the WFTU* signed

in Helsinki, where the WPC's headquarters are situated, an agreement which provided for mutual support of each other's initiatives on peace and disarmament. Subsequently, a WFTU working group on the socio-economic consequences of disarmament was set up and met, for the first time, in Prague on 31 May 1979. As the WFTU as such preferred not to be seen as the prime mover in this project, it was decided that the working group should be used to make contact with trade union organisations throughout the world of varying affiliations and to persuade them to join an *ad hoc* preparatory committee for an international conference on this theme. Owing to lack of interest, still less support, from non-communists, little progress was at first made.

During the WPC's World Parliament of the Peoples for Peace in Sofia in September 1980, however, a 'round-table' meeting of trade unionists issued a call for just such a conference to be held. The next major step was the delayed establishment of a preparatory committee at a meeting in Prague in September 1981. (There had been earlier informal preparatory meetings in London, Lisbon, Geneva and Paris.) A well-known Scottish communist trade union leader, the late James MILNE, was elected as its President.

The long delayed World Conference on the Socio-economic Aspects of Disarmament was finally held in Paris in December 1981. According to WFTU sources, it was attended by 215 delegates representing 115 trade union organisations in 62 countries 'in all continents'. The WPC, IOJ*, WIDF* and WFDY* were also represented and so, disingenuously, was the WFTU. The Conference adopted a statement urging trade unionists everywhere to 'struggle against the arms race'.

In May 1982, the international preparatory committee was transformed into a permanent committee at a meeting in Dublin with the title, International Trade Union Committee for Peace and Disarmament; in practice, it has been usually known as the Dublin Committee, as much to disguise its communist origin as for the sake of brevity. It has, however, been based in Prague, where the WFTU has its headquarters, from the start and another British trade unionist, Brian PRICE, was made Secretary. Price, long resident in Prague where he combines that job with the post of head of the WFTU's West European Department, is now also Secretary of the WFTU's Commission for Engineers, Managerial Staffs and Technicians. In practice the Dublin Committee appears to have taken over the WFTU's campaigning in the 'peace and disarmament' field and, while patently heavily dependent on WFTU, operates as a separate organisation. Its role, as described by Brian Price, in an interview which appeared in the Committee's bulletin in January 1983,

> has been to provide a common forum for the trade unions of many different countries and orientations to come together not only to discuss the arms race, nuclear war and the threat to world peace but to join in common actions at national, regional and international ievel.

As an example, Price quoted:

> the response of the trade unions, in conjunction with the broader peace movement, in mounting massive demonstrations and campaigning against the placement of cruise and Pershing-2 missiles in Europe.
> The trade union leaders and the rank-and-file membership were heavily involved in the organisation and coordination of these activities, irrespective of political or social standpoints. I believe that this is a classic example of how unity of purpose and unity of action can produce the essential ingredients that are so necessary in the development of the peace movement.

As regards future activities, Price added:

> Our major task is to continue building on the experience gained by the Committee. There is no doubt that the phenomenal growth of the peace movement in recent times and, particularly, the massive trade union involvement, which is quite unique, has created a very healthy atmosphere in which the Committee can broaden its role and activities. We should also be capable of supporting and participating in peace activities sponsored by other progressive forces. Our criteria for participation are clear and simple; we will continue to support all those peace initiatives that give the working class movement the opportunity to get involved in common actions of unity.

The subject matter of its regular meetings (see below) reflects these statements. But the agenda are dictated by the current communist propaganda themes, e.g. the NATO Double-Track decision, the US nuclear freeze, Nuclear-Free Zones in the Indian Ocean and Mediterranean.

The Committee publishes an occasional unnumbered *Bulletin* in English, French, Russian and Spanish and also pamphlets such as *Workers and the Arms Race*.

Organisation and Membership
In 1985 the Committee claimed the support of 2,850 members. The Committee is composed of 'representatives' from Algeria, Australia, Bulgaria, Canada, Cuba, Czechoslovakia, Denmark,

France, Federal Republic of Germany, GDR, Hungary, India, Ireland, Japan, Soviet Union, UK and USA. The President of the Committee is now Campbell CHRISTIE, Chairman of the Scottish TUC, who replaced the late James MILNE in both posts; the Secretary is Brian PRICE: other leading members of the Committee include Ray STEVENSON (Canada), Pat TOBIN (USA), D. NEVIN (Ireland), Ernie BOATSWAIN (Australia) and Jim SLATER (UK). The Committee has no affiliates as such but it has strong connexions with the UK through its two most senior officials. It gives as one of its addresses the address in Glasgow of its President.

The Committee has set up a study group on the prevention of the militarisation of space, a working group on 'disarmament and conversion' and a special working group to prepare a detailed report on 'the social impact of the arms race'.

Relations with Other Bodies

(1) United Nations Brian Price said at the end of 1984 that 'particularly satisfying is the fact that both the UN and UNESCO regard us as an NGO [Non-Governmental Organisation] which considerably enhances our committee stature'.

The Committee claims to be a member of the NGO Special Committee on Disarmament.

The Committee held sessions at the headquarters of the International Labour Organisation (ILO) in Geneva in June 1985, 1986 and 1987.

(2) Other International Front Organisations The Committee has close links with the World Peace Council and held a meeting of its own during the WPC's World Assembly for Peace and Life, Against Nuclear War, Prague, June 1983; it was also represented at the trade union 'round-table' which was a feature of the WPC's World Congress Devoted to UN International Year of Peace in Copenhagen, October 1986. Price was also one of those in charge of the Peace and Disarmament Commission at the WFTU's Eleventh Congress, East Berlin, September 1986.

Meetings

Since it was established in Dublin in May 1982, the Committee has met in Copenhagen (November 1982), Vienna (May 1983), Sofia (October 1983), Glasgow (February 1984), Larnaca (Cyprus), (October 1984), Toronto, Canada (November 1984), New Delhi (February 1985), Moscow (April 1985), Geneva (June

1985), Helsinki (October 1985), Geneva (June 1986), Sofia (May 1987), Geneva (June 1987). The Committee also held a Seminar on Arms Conversion (London, November 1983) and sponsored the Second World Conference on the Socio-economic Aspects of Disarmament in Dublin in May 1986.

9. Journalists for Peace

Journalists and the media have always been a major target of Soviet propaganda and, when suitably influenced, are a key factor in transmitting Soviet views. Among the new groups which had their inspiration in the margins of the WPC's World Parliament of the Peoples for Peace in Sofia in September 1980 was 'Journalists for Peace'. During the Parliament itself, meetings of professional groups were held, including journalists, and after a very short interval several national Journalists for Peace groups began to emerge. The first, in 1981, was Journalists Against Nuclear Extermination (JANE), established in Great Britain, with Norma TURNER as its secretary, followed not long after by similar groups in Finland, Denmark, Sweden, Norway, the FRG, Portugal, the Soviet Union, Czechoslovakia, Hungary and West Berlin.

The Journalists for Peace movement does not yet have a formal central structure. It is instead still a loose grouping of 'peace organisations and movements of journalists for peace', representatives of which meet periodically within a common framework. There are reported to have been at least six such liaison meetings so far namely, during the WPC's World Assembly for Peace and Life, Against Nuclear War, Prague, June 1983; at the First Congress of West European Journalists for Peace, Helsinki, October 1983; at a Forum of Journalists for Peace in Paris in November 1983 (within the framework of a meeting of the IOJ* Presidium); at the Second Congress of West European Journalists for Peace in West Berlin in May 1985; during the WPC's World Congress Devoted to International Year of Peace in Copenhagen, October 1986; and during the IOJ's Tenth Congress, Sofia, October 1986.

Although the movement has so far been confined to Europe, it was suggested at the latest liaison meeting that the time has come to enlarge it to cover the world.

10. Lawyers Against Nuclear War

The International Organisation of Lawyers against Nuclear Weapons under the chairmanship of Stig GUSTAFSSON, a Swedish trade union lawyer, was established in autumn 1987 in New York, according to *Neues Deutschland*, the East German party newspaper (20 November 1987). Certain national lawyers' organisations with a pro-Soviet bias had taken the initiative in forming such a group and at an international lawyers' conference in New York, 30–31 August 1987, agreed to establish a preparatory committee to set up the anti-war group. Its inaugural conference was held in Stockholm in April 1988.

A meeting of lawyers sympathetic to the Soviet policies was held as one of the 'special interest' groups at the WPC's World Assembly for Peace and Life, Against Nuclear War, in Prague in June 1983. Previously an international peace conference with strong WPC connections was held in Vienna in February 1983 and its members urged that an international lawyers' conference should be held to discuss the legal aspects of a ban on nuclear weapons. In addition the IADL*, at its 12th Congress in Athens in October 1984, appealed to lawyers to put their profession into the service of peace.

Among those who have responded are the Lawyers' Committee on Nuclear Policy and the Lawyers' Committee on Nuclear Disarmament, both American organisations, and, for some years, there have been regular exchanges of delegations between US and Soviet lawyers which, it is hoped, would lead to the holding of an international lawyers' conference on peace and disarmament. (Similar contacts, be it noted, between US and Soviet doctors led to the IPPNW's formation.)

In the United Kingdom, an organisation called Lawyers for Nuclear Disarmament was formed in 1982 at a meeting which was covered by only three journalists: Mikhail BOGDANOV, the *Socialist Industry* (Moscow) correspondent in London, plus one from Bulgaria and one from the British Communist *Morning Star* (*New Times* No. 4, 1985). Two members of this organisation attended a meeting of the International Peace Bureau (IPB) in Geneva in September 1984 on 'the legal status of weapons of societal destruction'. According to their report this meeting was 'regarded very much as a preparatory event for the Nuclear Warfare Tribunal' which, after discussions at a further meeting in Luxembourg, was held in London in January 1985. Other organisations which supported the Tribunal included the National

Peace Council, the Society of Friends, the Ecology Party, the United Nations Association, the National Union of Public Employees and CND. It was also sponsored by the Haldane Society of Socialist Lawyers, Journalists Against Nuclear Extermination (JANE), Medical Campaign Against Nuclear Weapons, Scientists Against Nuclear Arms (SANA), Scottish Lawyers for Nuclear Disarmament and Architects for Peace. Of the sponsoring groups of the 1985 Tribunal, the Haldane Society is the British affiliate of IADL; the founders of SANA, including Prof. Dorothy HODGKIN and Prof. Michael PENTZ, have had close connections with the World Federation of Scientific Workers*; JANE, founded in 1981, has close links through its secretary, Ms. Norma Turner, with the International Organisation of Journalists, and the Medical Campaign Against Nuclear Weapons is affiliated to the IPPNW.

Of the Tribunal's self-appointed 'judges and witnesses', many were acknowledged pacifists or unilateral nuclear disarmers. Others had identifiable connections with international front organisations, such as Gert Bastian (FGR), a founder member of the Generals for Peace and Disarmament*, Michael Harbottle (UK), current administrator of the same organisation, Dan SMITH (UK) a former assistant general secretary of the All-Britain Peace Liaison Group when it was the WPC's British affiliate, Dr. Peter STANIA (Austria) a leading member of the International Institute for Peace*, and Tair TAIROV (USSR) who was at that time a full-time member of the WPC Secretariat (who was in the event denied a visa to attend the Tribunal). The advertised North American participants included Daniel ARBESS (Lawyers Committee on Nuclear Policy) and David WRIGHT QC (Canadian Lawyers for Social Responsibility).

The Chairman of the Tribunal was the late Sean MacBride, holder of both the Nobel and Lenin Peace Prizes and a former Vice-President of the International Liaison Forum of Peace Forces* and at that time President of the International Peace Bureau (IPB). It was clear from a very early stage, that a Tribunal so constituted could only conclude as it did, that NATO's current strategy was illegal. The IPB is still pursuing the theoretical question of the illegality of nuclear weapons and it is now preparing to launch a major international petition on this issue.

Evidence that the international lawyers for peace movement is a major concern of Soviet propagandists was apparent when the IADL held an international lawyers' conference for peace in

Prague, 13–14 June 1987. In the same month it was announced that the US Lawyers Committee on the Nuclear Policy had 'agreed to co-sponsor an international conference of lawyers and legal scholars on the theme of nuclear weapons and international law', and this was eventually held in New York in August 1987.

> Invitations to the conference will be extended to lawyers' organisations around the world. The programme for the conference includes the following panels: Conceptions of Security in the Nuclear Age; The Use of Nuclear Weapons under International Law; The Arms Control Dimension, including Star Wars; Nuclear Deterrence under International Law; and Toward a Legal Regime for Nuclear Weapons. A session of the Conference will be devoted to the formation of an international lawyers' organisation dedicated to the prevention of nuclear war, which is intended to educate public opinion on the legal consequences of prevailing nuclear weapons policies to and advocate non-violent methods of resolving disputes between nations. In addition, the Conference will issue a closing statement representing a broad consensus of participants on the legal status of nuclear weapons. (*Disarmament Newsletter* (UN) June 1987)

In the event the New York conference, held 'at the initiative of the US Lawyers Committee on Nuclear Policy and the Soviet Lawyers' Association', was addressed, among others by Alexander SUKHAREV, the Soviet Minister of Justice and Chairman of the Soviet Lawyers' Association, and by Paul WARNKE, former director of the US Arms Control and Disarmament Agency (Tass in English, 1 September 1987). The conference ended by preparing for the establishment of 'an international organisation of Lawyers against Nuclear War'.

11. Psychologists for Peace

Psychologists for Peace (or International Psychologists in the Struggle for Peace against Nuclear War) was founded in 1985 on the initiative of the general assembly of the International Union of Psychological Sciences (IUPsyS), an organisation which has its headquarters in Hamburg and which was established in July 1951 in Stockholm at the Thirteenth International Congress of Psychology (which in turn had its origins in the first such international congress held in Paris in 1889).

According to the Soviet magazine *20th Century and Peace* No. 11, 1985, the main task of Psychologists in the Struggle for Peace, against the Threat of Nuclear War 'is to coordinate research in the psychologically verifiable concept of world peace and discussion of the results obtained at representative symposiums, conferences and congresses and information of the broad public about scientific conclusions'.

Yekaterina SHOROKHOVA, a member of this new group and the Vice-Director of the Institute of Psychology of the USSR Academy of Sciences, said in an interview:

> Science on war was developing in parallel with the evolution of human civilisation while the science of peace was born by the demand of time. And it became clear—if the latter was not created and its ideas failed to seize everyone—earth is doomed. Philologists, physicists, philosophers, physicians and scientists of different trends all make their contribution to the development of the interdisciplinary science on peace. The International Union of Psychological Science has actively entered this process.

Subsequently, in 1986, the first 'European Psychologists for Peace' congress was held in Helsinki, early August. It was organised by Finnish psychologists and was attended by some 200 scientists from over 20 countries. The initiative for the congress appeared to have come from the group of psychologists against nuclear war associated with IUPsyS and, coordinated by Prof. Adolf KOSSAKOWSKI (GDR), chairman of the GDR Psychology Society, and also the chairman of Psychologists for Peace. This group is mainly controlled by psychologists' organisations in the Soviet Bloc, particularly by the GDR Psychology Society.

12. Teachers for Peace

It was participants in a meeting of the educationalists' group at WPC's World Assembly for Peace and Life, Against Nuclear War in Prague in June 1983 who stressed the importance of their members' role in 'the struggle against nuclear war'. They urged that peace education should be integrated in all subjects. This foreshadowed the emergence in 1985 of the Teachers for Peace movement, a campaign launched by the World Federation of Teachers' Unions (FISE)* and co-ordinated by its Secretariat in East Berlin with the aim of 'promoting peace and disarmament initiatives' among its affiliated and friendly organisations.

Subsequently, national Teachers for Peace groups in Denmark, Norway and the Federal Republic of Germany organised a joint meeting in Cologne in April 1985 which was attended by 33 delegates from a total of 18 such national groups, teachers' peace movements and teachers' unions, as well as FISE representatives. At the meeting, it was decided to hold an 'international conference on peace education' in August 1986.

That conference was duly held in Copenhagen, under the title of the Conference for Educators on Work and Education for Peace, Disarmament and International Understanding. Attended by over 200 delegates from 16 (most European) countries, it had been organised by an *ad hoc* International Preparatory Committee which had included FISE representatives and was chaired by John Baltzersen, a Danish teacher. A second conference in this series is to be held in Bonn in May 1988.

There are now national Teachers for Peace organisations in Denmark, the Federal Republic of Germany, Hungary, Norway, Sweden, UK and USA. Chris SEWELL, who is on the executive of the British Teachers for Peace group was among those who represented that organisation at the Copenhagen conference. The comparable US group is called the Parents and Teachers for Social Responsibility.

13. Women's International League for Peace and Freedom

The Women's International League for Peace and Freedom (WILPF) is one of the best known, and certainly the oldest, of the specialist international organisations which may be classified as Soviet-influenced organisations but which are not Soviet international front organisations. In practice it has close working links with the Women's International Democratic Federation (WIDF)* in East Berlin, as also with the WPC itself.

The WILPF, is also known by its French, Spanish and German titles as the *Ligue internationale de femmes pour la paix et la liberté* (LIFPL), the *Liga Internacional de Mujeres pro Paz y Libertad* (LIMPL) and the *Internationale Frauenliga für Frieden und Freiheit* (IFFF) respectively. It is largely dominated by its British Section (at 29 Great James Street, WC1) and also has a contact office in Paris (at 24 Quai Louis Blériot, F 75016). It was founded in 1915 by a group of Quaker, pacifist and socialist women, led by Jane ADDAMS, who met at the International Women's Congress held in the Hague in that year and decided to try to bring the First World War to an end. Originally known as the International Women's Committee for a Durable Peace, it adopted its present title in 1919. It aims to bring together 'women of different political and philosophical tendencies . . . to study, make known and help abolish the political, social, economic and psychological causes of war and to work for a constructive peace'.

Jane Addams was awarded the Nobel Peace prize in 1931 and the WILPF claims to be financed, at least in part, by a 40 per cent share in two invested Nobel Peace Prizes, as well as by regular contributions from its national sections, of which there are currently 21, notably in the UK, US, Sweden and Canada (none exists in a communist country).

WILPF has extensive UN connections, including consultative status with ECOSOC, UNESCO, ILO, FAO, UNCTAD and UNICEF. It publishes a quarterly bulletin, *Pax et Libertas*.

In recent years a number of WILPF officials have had Communist 'front' connections. The present international secretary-general, elected by the international executive committee, Mrs. Edith BALLANTYNE, a Canadian of Czechoslovak origin, acted as co-chairman of the WPC's Prague Peace Assembly in 1983 and is a Vice-President of the International Liaison Forum of Peace Forces*. Also in 1983, Edith Ballantyne and Carol PENDELL (USA), the League's President, were both members of the organising Committee for the Vienna Conference on Proposals to Avert the Dangers of War from Europe, held 6–9 February 1983, on the initiative of Canon Raymond GOOR (Belgium), at that time a WPC Presidential Committee observer and Chairman of the International Committee for European Security and Cooperation*. In 1975 Kay CAMP, who represented the WILPF at the UN in New York, chaired a commission of the WIDF's World Congress of Women held in East Berlin. Marguerite THIBERT, the League's representative at the ILO in Geneva, was in 1967 a member of the presidium of the Liaison Bureau whose task was to make contact with other women's organisations and to secure support for the Women's International Democratic Federation (WIDF). From all this it is apparent that the WILPF's links with the older Soviet international front organisations extend over many years.

In 1983, WILPF launched a major world-wide campaign to mobilise people, especially women, in opposition to the 'arms race and plans for installing US Cruise and Pershing missiles, and to work for disarmament in both West and East'. Activities in Brussels, organised jointly by the WILPF and the National Council of Belgian Women, started on 7 March with the arrival of a 'Peace Plane' carrying over 100 American women, joined the following day by women from Canada, Finland, Denmark, Federal Republic of Germany, Sweden, France, New Zealand and Britain. This was called the 'Star Campaign'. On March 8, there was also a major Star Rally and peace march through the centre of Brussels, and visits by various women's peace delegations to embassies of the nuclear powers, as well as the presentation to 'senior officials in NATO of the one million signatures of women throughout the world who have joined Star'. This campaign, although wholly supportive of Soviet objectives, is not in itself evidence of Soviet influence. Besides the connections noted above, however, what is significant is that it was not balanced by any parallel criticisms of Soviet policies and actions and the WILPF remained silent on the continuing Soviet deployment of SS-20's.

14. Working Presidium of the World Conference for Saving the Sacred Gift of Life from Nuclear Catastrophe

Another specialist organisation with international appeal at the disposal of Soviet propaganda is the 'Working Presidium of the World Conference for Saving the Sacred Gift of Life from Nuclear Catastrophe', also known by its Russian title, *Rabochii Prezidium Vsemirnoi Konferentsii dlya spaseniya svyaschennovo dara zhizni ot yadernovo katastrofa*. It shares its headquarters with the Moscow Patriarchates, External Church Relations Department, 18/2 Ulitsa Ryleyeva, Moscow G-2 121002, Soviet Union.

Origins
In July 1948 the then head of the Russian Orthodox Church, the Patriarch ALEXEI of Moscow and All Russia, together with other participants in the Conference of Heads and Representatives of the Autocephalous Orthodox Churches in connexion with the celebration of the 500th anniversary of the Autocephaly of the Russian Orthodox Church, issued an appeal to all Christians, 'all people yearning for peace', calling on them to 'become an armour against all encroachments and actions aimed at violating peace, and to disable any intention and any plan of a war conflagration'. During the subsequent 30 years Russian Orthodox Church leaders have devoted their efforts to 'peace' with the support of (and under strict oversight by) the Soviet Govern-

ment's Committee for Religious Affairs. Most significantly, in October 1973, the initiative for holding a World Conference of Religious Leaders for Peace came from the Patriarch PIMEN on behalf of the Russian Orthodox Church, at a special meeting of churchmen in the monastery of Zagorsk which took place immediately after the World Peace Council's World Congress of Peace Forces had been held in Moscow. The preparations for the Conference were in the hands of the Christian Peace Conference (CPC)* and the Conference itself was held in Moscow in June 1977: it assembled 'representatives' of the Christian, Muslim, Hindu, Jewish, Buddhist, Sikh and Shintoist religions from 107 countries, adopted two appeals, an 'Appeal to the Religious Leaders and Believers of all Religions throughout the World' and an 'Appeal to the Government of All States of the World', both of which stressed the need for 'religious cooperation in the struggle for peace'.

Subsequent Developments

Subsequently the Patriarch Pimen attended the WPC's World Parliament of the Peoples for Peace in Sofia in September 1980, in the margins of which there was a special meeting of religious leaders. In July of the following year he first proposed the holding of what was to become the World Conference of Religious Workers for Saving the Sacred Gift of Life from Nuclear Catastrophe, held in Moscow in May 1982, a gathering ostensibly organised by an *ad hoc* International Preparatory Committee, which had been chaired by the Metropolitan FILARET of Minsk and Belorussia and which included a number of CPC leaders and WPC members.

That Conference was attended by almost 600 'representatives' of Christian churches, Buddhism, Hinduism, Islam, Judaism, Sikhism, Shintoism and Zoroastrianism from about 100 countries. They included the American evangelist, Billy Graham, and a number of British delegates, as well as observers from the Church of England, and issued an Appeal to Religious Leaders, an Appeal to all Governments and an Appeal to the UN General Assembly Second Special Session.

According to a report of this Moscow Conference in *The Times*, London, 18 May 1982,

The international credibility of the Russian Orthodox church was saved last week by 27 American clergymen who battled until the early hours of the morning to prevent a world religious conference issuing a statement that would be seen in the West as an instrument of Soviet propaganda.

For a week the Americans, senior church leaders who defied pressure from the Reagan Administration to stop them taking part in the conference on nuclear disarmament, virtually single-handedly fought off attempts by some of the 450 delegates to blame the United States alone for world tensions, and insisted that the Russians change the wording of the final document to acknowledge Washington's proclaimed desire to seek reductions in nuclear arms.

Ironically the Russian Orthodox church, hosts of the biggest religious conference ever held in the Soviet Union, appeared delighted by the American stance, and privately hinted they were glad the Soviet Government approved draft had been altered.

A Dutch leader of the Western peace movement walked out of the meeting because he was not allowed to deliver in public sessions a speech mentioning the peace movement in East Germany, the Polish Solidarity trade union and the Charter-77 dissident movement in Czechoslovakia.

Dr. Billy Graham, the American evangelist, felt obliged to go out of his way not to offend his hosts by speaking out against religious repression during this visit, and the importance of his presence here was emphasised by the special treatment accorded him and the eagerness with which Tass, the official news agency reported his remarks that there were more churches open and more religious freedom than he expected.

A continuing committee or 'working presidium' emerged as a permanent legacy of the Conference. After its first meeting in Moscow in March 1983 it met, for a while, frequently. A series of, in practice, annual religious gatherings in Moscow of this stamp have ensued as a result of the presidium's activities, the latest having been held early in 1987. Presidium meetings were held in Moscow in January 1984, and February 1985; and a round-table conference on 'Space without Weapons' was also organised by the Working Presidium, also in Moscow, in April 1984.

SECTION IV

National Organisations

INTRODUCTION

Principal among national organisations engaged in the business of promoting support for Soviet policies have been, since the early years after the Revolution, the local communist parties. The strict discipline imposed on them as a condition of membership of the Third International (the Comintern) of which they were technically 'sections' ensured, at least until the Comintern was dissolved in 1943 and in practice during the remainder of Stalin's reign, that they all—with the sole exception of the Yugoslav party from 1949 onwards—slavishly followed the Soviet line. The CPSU has not been able, since at least the 1960s, to impose its discipline through the Central Committee's International Department with the same tight rein. Apart from the Chinese and Albanian defections, there have been disagreements with Moscow especially among the West European parties who nominally look to the CPSU for leadership and guidance. Differences with the Soviet Union in the early 1970s over the meaning of détente for East-West relations led to the assertion by some West European communist parties of greater independence and their rejection of the concept of 'proletarian internationalism', i.e. Soviet hegemony. This said, however, the Soviet Government can still assume support from most of these parties for the broad lines of its foreign policy.

National Communist parties are, however, of little value as instruments for the dissemination of Soviet propaganda in the West. They are overt political parties whose affiliations and sympathies cannot be concealed. For wider propaganda purposes more subtle means are needed. Since the Second World War organisations of three kinds have evolved from earlier organisations or have been created afresh. These are, first the national affiliates of the World Peace Council and of some other Soviet-controlled international front organisations. The WPC*, for example, claims the existence of such affiliates in 143 countries. In the United Kingdom and the United States these are, respectively, the British Peace Assembly and the United States Peace Council. Among other affiliates of Soviet-controlled organisations in the United Kingdom are the Haldane Society of Socialist Lawyers (see IADL*) and the National Assembly of Women (Women's International Democratic Federation*).

The second group comprises the 'friendship' societies. These are affiliated to the Union of Soviet Societies for Friendship and Cultural Relations (SSOD)*. In the United Kingdom they include the Society for Cultural Relations with the USSR (which, in fact, dates from 1924), the Scotland-USSR Friendship Association, and the British Soviet Friendship Society and its Welsh and Northern Irish affiliates. The ostensible role of these organisations is to promote cultural relations with the Soviet Union and visits to the Soviet Union are organised for a variety of 'cultural' purposes. Though no special attempt is made to hide their orientation, which is blatantly pro-Soviet, they provide a useful basis for disseminating a 'popular' image of the Soviet Union and, it is suspected, for providing a ready pool of the well-disposed on which Soviet intelligence talent scouts may on occasion draw. The final group consists of the 'peace' organisations which were mentioned in the introduction to Section III. D.N. Pritt's article in the WFTU Journal in 1950 aptly described the doctrine. These organisations foreshadowed the international Soviet-influenced organisations based on professional or other special interests. Some of these early post-war national organisations still exist; for example, the Medical Association for the Prevention of War. Others have been revived in the context of the 'Peace Movement'. Few, if any, of these 'peace' organisations is wholly communist-controlled. But in all of them members of the Communist Party hold positions of influence. The leading British 'peace' organisation, CND, has never been a communist organisation and is not a member of this group. Members of the CPGB held senior office in the CND in the 1970s but since 1981 no member of the CPGB has been elected to national office, although communists have served as elected members of the Executive Committee. A recently established British organisation, Mothers for Peace, is a newcomer whose precise orientation is still not clear.

Counterparts of the British organisations mentioned above exist in most countries of the West, and national affiliates of the

Soviet-controlled international organisations have been established in many other countries outside the Soviet *bloc*. The number of these organisations, in all groups, throughout all countries of the non-communist world, is so large that it would be impossible to describe or even list them all.

PROFILES

(Examples only)

1. British–Soviet Friendship Society

The forerunner of the British–Soviet Friendship Society (BSFS), the Friends of Soviet Russia Committee, was founded in Moscow in 1927 by British communist visitors to the Soviet Union, as part of an international chain of national Soviet Friendship Societies which still exists. It should be noted that this communist-controlled organisation has no connection with the Great Britain–USSR Association, whose headquarters is at 14 Grosvenor Place, London SW1, and which is independent of any communist influence and has the support of all the main political parties.

Since 1927, the organisation has changed its name five times, and has been proscribed by the Labour Party as a communist front organisation under each of its titles. In 1932, the Committee was reconstituted as the Friends of the International Association of Friends of the Soviet Union, an agency of the Comintern, in Moscow. At the height of the 'Popular Front' campaign in 1938 it became the Russia Today Society. In 1941, after the German attack on Russia, the society re-emerged as the main component of the National Council for British-Soviet Unity, and, as such, was proscribed by the Labour Party in 1943. It is interesting that at the time the Soviet Embassy in London (which ostensibly had no formal connexion with the organisation) offered to close it down if that would suit the British authorities at a time when official Anglo–Soviet cooperation was paramount. In 1946 the title was altered to British–Soviet Society (later British–Soviet Friendship Society), under which guise it was proscribed by the Labour Party again in 1948; it so remained until the Labour Party ceased to publish a list of proscribed organisations after 1973.

Affiliations

The BSFS was for many years affiliated to the British Peace Committee, another organisation proscribed by the Labour Party from 1950 to 1973 and which was, until 1980, the British affiliate of the World Peace Council (WPC)*. More recently the BSFS has worked closely with the WPC's current British affiliate, the British Peace Assembly (BPA)*. Historically, it also maintains close links with the Society for Cultural Relations with the USSR (SCR), the doyen of British communist front organisations, founded at the instigation of the Comintern in 1924, and another longstanding communist front, the Scottish–USSR Society for Friendship and Cooperation. It is also linked to the USSR–Great Britain Society in Moscow, an offshoot of SSOD.

Principal Office-holders

President: Andrew ROTHSTEIN; Chairman: William WILSON; General Secretary: Pam MEISTER.

Membership

The BSFS has two classes of members, individual and affiliated (i.e. mostly through trade unions). The individual membership stood at some 12,000 in 1954, but fell heavily after the Hungarian revolution in 1956. By 1968, it had only about 1,500 members but claimed it had 'not lost any members since the Russian invasion of Czechoslovakia' (*Sheffield Morning Telegraph*, 3 September 1968): but a resolution expressing unease 'at the continuing decline' was passed at the Conference held in September 1970 (*British–Soviet Friendship*, November, 1970). Subsequently membership somewhat revived and is currently about 3,000.

Organisation

In its heyday, the BSFS maintained a widespread network of local branches, similar in composition to those of the CPGB. In 1950, there were 123 local branches, 63 being in the Greater London area. By February 1986 the number of branches had fallen to 57. For many years the society had its headquarters at 36 Spencer Street, London, EC1, a building owned by its subsidiary, British–Soviet Friendship Houses Ltd., (a body which was also proscribed by the Labour Party until 1973); its address is now 36 St John's Square, EC1.

Activities

The BSFS has always attached great importance to the regular exchange of visiting delegations between this country and Russia, while ensuring that parties it sponsored were under communist influence. Indeed, it owes its origin to such a visit. Its first secretary was William PAUL, editor of a now defunct communist paper, the *Sunday Worker*: in 1929 two of its leading members— part of its original 'front'—resigned because the secretary 'had been appointed without consultation with the national committee and . . . is issuing circulars without authority and identifying the organisation with the Communist Party'. The accuracy of that analysis was confirmed a decade later by a British police report of June 1941 (now declassified) which recorded that the Russia Today Society, as the BSFS was then called:

> has always been under the complete direction of the Communist Party . . . Albert S. Inkpin, the Secretary, was General Secretary of the Communist Party of Great Britain from 1923 to 1929, but was superseded owing to scandalous behaviour to women Communists, and serious defalcations in his accounts. He obtained his present post as the result of the direct intervention of the Comintern, which insisted on his being given a position in a Communist organisation. . . .

The BSFS' celebration of the anniversary of the Bolshevik Revolution each November used to take the form of a 'British– Soviet Friendship Month', planned on a national basis and with the visit of a large Soviet 'cultural delegation' as its main event. Since the Hungarian revolution in 1956, when the event for that year was cancelled, these annual celebrations have often been curtailed for both financial and politicial reasons. In November 1957, a 'British–Soviet Friendship Month' was held on a very small scale: since 1958, a small number of local events, featuring Soviet guests, has been organised instead. In 1970, the Society celebrated Lenin's centenary with a 'two-day cultural festival'.

The BSFS' links with the Soviet Embassy are particularly close, and the Soviet Ambassador in London regularly attends its events and 'members of the staff of the Soviet Embassy have kindly offered to visit branches and affiliated bodies of the Society to give talks . . .' (*British–Soviet Friendship*, July 1971). In February 1986, the BSFS were co-organisers of a party to celebrate the 44th anniversary of *Soviet Weekly*, the weekly news- paper using material from the *Novosti* and *Tass* press agencies which is produced by the Soviet Embassy's Information Section. It is probable that, as a result of the current 'Eurocommunist' bias of the CPGB, the BSFS's dependence on support from the Soviet Embassy is even greater than in the past.

Publications
The BSFS publishes a monthly illustrated magazine, *British–Soviet Friendship*.

2. British Peace Assembly

The forerunner of the British Peace Assembly, the British Peace Committee, (BPC) was founded in 1948 after the postwar Soviet 'peace campaign' had been launched at the 'World Congress of Intellectuals' in Wroclaw, Poland in the summer of that year.

The British Peace Committee was originally called the British Cultural Committee for Peace and its founder and first chairman was the late J.G. CROWTHER, then general secretary of the WFSW*. In 1949 it became the British Peace Committee, and by late 1950, had emerged as the British affiliate of the WPC* (as is the British Peace Assembly today), when it was proscribed by the Labour Party as a Communist front organisation. In November 1950 the Prime Minister, then Clement ATTLEE, denounced the BPC as '. . . an offshoot of the WPC, an instrument of the Politburo: more than ninety per cent of the members of its permanent committee are known to be Communists or fellow travellers' (*The Times*, 1 November 1950). In the 1950s it was the BPC which inspired the network of British artistic and professional 'peace organisations'—Artists for Peace, etc.—most of which are now defunct (the Medical Association for the Prevention of War being an exception). In the 1960s the BPC and the presidential committee of the WPC, then under the direction of the late Prof. J.D. BERNAL, were based in the same building at 94 Charlotte Street, London, W1. At that time many other British front organisations were affiliated to the BPC, the British Soviet Friendship Society*, for instance, among them. Later in the 1960s the BPC became unreliable from the WPC's standpoint, as a result of personal rivalries inside the secretariat and a new body, the All-Britain Peace Liaison Group, was founded to supplant it (for some years the two organisations existed side by side). Eventually, in 1980, the Group renamed itself the British Peace Assembly (BPA) at 'a weekend meeting in London of representatives of trade unions and peace organisations' (*Morning Star*, 29 April 1950).

Principal Office-holders
President: James LAMOND MP; Chairman: Jim LAYZELL;
General Secretary: Rosemary BECHLER; Acting Treasurer:
Frank SWIFT.

Affiliations
The BPA is the WPC's British affiliate. A number of British
organisations and trade unions, which were formerly affiliated to
the BPC, are now in turn BPA affiliates.

Activities
The BPA is probably closer in spirit to the minority and neo-
Stalinist New Communist Party than to the older and now 'Eurocommunist' CPGB. The BPA arranges peace delegations to and
from the Soviet Union and occasionally organises conferences
and seminars: in general it is not at present very active.

Publication
The BPA publishes a monthly *Newsletter*, *Facts the Media Ignore*,
which is edited by the veteran WPC official, Gordon Schaffer.
The issue for July–August 1987 highlighted the BPA's support
for the Soviet disinformation theme that the AIDS virus 'was
man-made, probably at Fort Detrick' in Maryland, US (the
'evidence' was available from the BPA at a cost of £1.50, post
free) and, moreover, it did so at some length in an article which
recalled how 'the leading French scientist, Professor Joliot-Curie,
affirmed in 1952 that the 'use by the Americans of germ warfare
in Korea and China was one of the most sinister chapters in
human history . . . ' This reference to the discredited Soviet
'germ-warfare campaign' at the time of the Korean War, which
had been 'proved' by a bogus 'international scientific commission'
appointed by the WPC in 1952, was itself evidence of Soviet
propagandists' cynical use of even so minor a 'front organisation'
as the BPA when it seemed to serve their purpose. The BPA
should have been suitably embarrassed when, shortly after, the
Moscow newspaper *Izvestiya* on 30 October 1987, officially
published the open denial by senior Soviet scientists of the possibility that the AIDS virus could have been man-made, in the US
or anywhere else.

3. Labour Research Department

The origins of the Labour Research Department (LRD) differ from those of the British–Soviet Friendship Society or the British Peace Assembly in that, although it has been continuously under communist control since 1922, and to that extent antedates even the Society for Cultural Relations with the USSR, the oldest organisation founded in this country as a Communist front organisation, it was not in fact founded by communists or with a communist purpose.

LRD originated in a Committee of Enquiry into the Control of Industry which was established in 1912 under the aegis of the executive committee of the Fabian Society, then under Beatrice Webb's chairmanship. By 1913 it had become established as the Fabian Research Department. In 1914, however, the new full-time secretary was Robin Page ARNOT, then aged 23, who, in 1920 was to be one of the founder members of the British Communist Party. Although other eminent Socialists (e.g. the Webbs, G.B. Shaw and G.D.H. Cole) were at first closely involved in its work, it was Arnot's appointment which ensured that within seven years the new body, by then renamed LRD, would be under tight communist direction. The self-perpetuating communist caucus which then gained control directs LRD to this day. The Labour Party and the Fabian Society soon severed all connexion with it.

At a Comintern 'information conference' held in Moscow in April 1925, a British communist trade union leader, Tom BELL, asserted that: 'in Great Britain, we already have a kind of information department, the Labour Research Department . . . This department is not a [Communist] Party concern, but it is under the control of the Party . . . '.

Eight years later, in 1933, the National Council of Labour formally warned its supporters in the Labour Party and the trade union and cooperative movements that LRD was a communist front organisation. In April 1942, both the Labour Party and the Trade Union Congress proscribed LRD as a communist front organisation: as was stated at the time,

the LRD has never been associated with the official Labour movement, though it is often confused with the research departments of the TUC and the Labour Party . . . Members and supporters of the Communist Party have secured substantial control over the activities of the LRD, frequently to the detriment of the [Labour] movement. . . . (*Daily Herald*, 18 April 1942)

The LRD continues to exist under firm communist control. But since it is careful to express its political views less stridently than formerly, it has been able to pass itself off in the eyes of most of the media as an 'independent body' concerned with trade union affairs. Its headquarters is at 78 Blackfriars Road, London SE1.

Office Holder
Secretary: Lionel FULTON.

Publication
LRD publishes a monthly magazine, *Labour Research*.

4. National Assembly of Women.

The National Assembly of Women (NAW) is an example of a domestic British front organisation which, after a long period of relative inactivity, has recently experienced a revival. It was founded in March 1952 by a smaller communist body, the International Women's Day Committee, on which the then secretary of the CPGB Women's Committee, Mrs. Tamara RUST, played a major part. The new NAW soon established itself as the British affiliate of the WIDF* in East Berlin.

By 1956, the NAW claimed over 470 branches and a total of 59,000 members. As Harry POLLITT, then the CPGB's general secretary, had told the CP Congress in 1952, 'we welcome the splendid signs of the awakening movement among women, and the new signs of the strength and initiative which is developing from the work of the National Assembly of Women . . . ' (*World News and Views*, 19 April 1952). By 1960 another veteran Communist official, J.R. Campbell, was describing NAW as an organisation inside which 'Communist Party members united with other progressive women in a radiant struggle for peace'. It was not surprising that the Labour Party proscribed the NAW as a communist front organisation after 1954. In the previous year the NAW had attracted considerable notoriety when its first chairman, Mrs.. Monica FELTON, had toured the prisoner-of-war camps in North Korea, at the invitation of the Chinese and North Korean military authorities, at a time when at home in Britain NAW officials had subjected captured British servicemen's families to moral blackmail in attempts to win their support for the Soviet 'peace movement'. One Yorkshire mother was persistently visited by NAW emissaries. 'They asked me', she said later, 'to go to a meeting in London last March [in 1953]. I told them I couldn't afford to go, but then they said they would pay my fare. I had never been to London so I thought it was a good chance . . . When I got there it all seemed to be communist and anti-British talk and I wasn't happy about it. Then we had a procession to the House of Commons and I had to carry a banner reading "Bring Back our Lads from Korea". I felt rather ashamed and tried to hide it down my side . . . ' (*Yorkshire Post*, 14 August 1953).

In the 1970s the NAW was relatively dormant. It is now once again very active. It was striking that a high proportion of the British delegates to the WPC's Copenhagen Peace Congress in October 1986 were NAW members, and in May 1987 the NAW was able to organise a large British delegation to the Ninth World Congress of Women, organised in Moscow by the WIDF, which included—rather surprisingly—one or two distinguished British ladies not normally associated with Soviet propagandist activities.

Principal Office-holders
President: Joan MAYNARD; Chairwoman: Betty TEBBS; General Secretary: Elsie WATSON; Treasurer: Ann MUNSEY.

5. National Council of American–Soviet Friendship

Among the most important Soviet front groups in the US is the National Council of American–Soviet Friendship (NCASF), the American equivalent of the BSFS*. According to the US State Department, the organisation is 'largely financed and controlled by the Soviet Union, [it] attempts to obscure ties with the USSR to avoid having to register with the US Government under the Foreign Agents Registration Act and to maintain a facade of independence'.

The NCASF was originally formed in 1943 at the instigation of the CPUSA, at much the same time as the National Council for British–Soviet Unity, a forerunner of the BSFS, was formed in London. The NCASF, to quote a US State Department publication of August 1987, currently consists of approximately 25 active chapters and 'Soviet direction of NCASF is channelled through (SSOD), under the authority of the International Department. Soviet representatives of SSOD, who are in regular contact with NCASF officials, direct some NCASF activities in support of Soviet active measures campaigns. Certain KGB agents are assigned to maintain contact with key NCASF officials'.

Another function of the NCASF, according to the US State Department, is to provide a 'conduit to promote active measures campaigns . . . Additionally, NCASF-sponsored "goodwill tours" enable KGB personnel to travel to various American cities where they previously had limited access or to travel in areas closed to Soviet diplomats in the US'. The example cited is the Mississippi Peace Cruise in 1986, modelled on seven previous Soviet 'peace cruises' down the Volga (in which there had been some American participation). The Soviet Peace Committee* selected the Soviet participants in the Mississippi cruise and, as the State Department concludes, 'the fact that the cruise was conceived in the Kremlin, staged with Soviet support and involved Soviet front-group activity—all the while purporting to be a genuine grass roots "people's movement"—marks it as an active measure' (*Soviet Influence Activities: A Report on Active Measures and Propaganda 1986–87*, published by the US State Department, August 1987, page 80).

6. United States Peace Council

The US Peace Council (USPC), founded in November 1979, is another and more recent Soviet front. It attempts to influence Americans' views on defence and is the US affiliate of the WPC. According to the US State Department, it is 'largely financed and controlled by the Soviet Union and . . . [it] attempts to obscure ties with the USSR . . . '.

Key positions in the USPC have always been held by trusted CPUSA members. Robert PRINCE of the USPC is the United States representative on the WPC Secretariat in Helsinki; he replaced Karen TALBOT, who has returned to the US to become the WPC representative at the United Nations and is now on the USPC's Executive Board. According to the US State Department, the USPC has 'consistently worked to promote the causes of the WPC and has regularly supported the policies of the Soviet Union. Because the USPC increasingly suffers from being exposed as a Soviet front, it has become less open about its Soviet affiliations. Early USPC letterhead openly listed affiliation to the WPC; a 1985 letterhead no longer does'.

Activities

One of the functions of the USPC is to influence other US peace groups. For example, leaders of the USPC are reported to have been

> instrumental in forming the Religious Circles Committee, an effort initiated by the Soviet Peace Committee to involve US religious organisations in activities of the USPC. By establishing contact with churches and other religious organisations, the USPC is attempting to tap the very large body of US citizens genuinely concerned about the arms race and the potential for nuclear war.

The US State Department has also recorded that the Soviet Union

> continues to devote manpower and resources in overt and covert attempts to influence the arms control and disarmament movement in the United States. The KGB has covertly requested its contacts in the peace and nuclear disarmament movements to continue to report on meetings, participate in upcoming conferences, and obtain information on individuals who are active within the movement. Several KGB officers currently assigned to the United States have been in regular contact with the leaders of such Soviet-controlled organisations as the CPUSA, USPC, and NCASF.

The CPUSA has always been one of the most pro-Soviet communist parties in the world and again according to the US State Department, 'has received substantial financial support from the Soviet Union. Although relatively small and politically weak, the CPUSA continues systematically to promote Soviet views on arms control proposals and the peace movement through its overt publications and party operations. The CPUSA also operates a small network of its own front organisations in the United States'. The US State Department concludes that, on Moscow's instructions, the various national front organisartions in the US have in recent years mounted 'campaigns against the neutron bomb, NATO theatre nuclear force modernisation, US defence policies, and more recently the Strategic Defence Initiative (SDI). The CPUSA has sponsored and participated in demonstrations and rallies, formed coalitions with other peace organisations, and sponsored seminars and workshops to promote Soviet policies and goals within the US peace movement'. (*Soviet Influence Activities: A Report on Active Measures and Propaganda 1986–87*, published by the US State Department, August 1987, page 81).

SECTION V

Soviet Matrix Organisations

INTRODUCTION

At the apex of the structure described in the preceding Section is the International Department of the CPSU's Central Committee, which operates within policies laid down by the Politburo and is headed by a Central Committee Secretary. The channel through which the International Department directs the Soviet-controlled international front organisations and 'guides' the Soviet-influenced organisations is provided by what may be called the Soviet matrix organisations and, to some extent, by their counterparts in the East European communist countries. The Russians refer to these as 'Public Organisations' (Obshchestvennye Organizatsii) although they are, of course, wholly Party-controlled.

As regards the international front organisations, control is assured by three means. First, influence in each organisation is exerted by leading members of the corresponding Soviet matrix organisation, which always plays a dominant, if sometimes disguised, role in all major events and programmes and generally has one or more of its officials posted at the international organisation's headquarters. Secondly, each organisation depends on annual subventions from the Soviet Peace Fund* or some comparable Soviet body, even though great care is taken in practice to conceal the details of these financial transactions. Thirdly, the Soviet authorities are thus able to ensure that all the key office-holders and members of committees having executive responsibility are communists, or at least reliable fellow-travellers. Although the control may be less standardised and may not be so absolute in the case of the Soviet-influenced organisations, for reasons discussed in Section III, yet the nature of these organisations and their connection with the corresponding Soviet matrix organisations ensures that, in practice, there is little deviation from the propaganda lines laid down by Moscow. The inspiration for the formation of the IPPNW*, for example, came from the officials who comprise the

Soviet Physicians' Committee for the Prevention of Nuclear War*
which was set up at about the same time. From the start it has
had American and Soviet Co-Chairmen. The Generals for Peace
and Disarmament*, on the other hand, originally had no Soviet
counterpart, being entirely a 'western' organisation (with several
of its members occupying prominent positions in the WPC, over
which the Soviet Peace Committee exercises effective control). The
function of the newly founded corresponding Soviet organisation,
USSR Retired Generals and Admirals for Peace (founded in 1986),
is evidently to provide a Soviet interlocutor for western groups.

The Soviet Peace Committee* also seeks to equate itself with
national peace movements in the West. Because it is the only
officially recognised Soviet body with which delegations from the
western peace movements can converse, it has some success in
this role, however sceptical many (but not all) western visitors
may be about its standing.

Apart from providing subventions to various Soviet-controlled
organisations and for specific activities, (see Appendix D), the
Soviet Peace Fund is primarily used as the vehicle for various
forms of financial support for Soviet 'peace' and propaganda
activities. These include contributions to Congresses organised
by the international fronts; 'sponsorship' i.e. payment of air
fares and expenses of members of western 'peace' movements
attending such congresses; meeting the costs of travel and accom-
modation for Western delegations invited to visit Moscow. The
Soviet Peace Fund even made a major financial contribution to
the British National Union of Mineworkers during the 1984
strike, through a special Aid Fund for British Miners. Despite
repeated Soviet assertions that the Soviet Peace fund is financed
by the voluntary contributions of some 80 million of ordinary
Soviet citizens who wish to demonstrate their support for 'peace',
it is, in fact, under the direct control of the International Department and such 'contributions' as it receives are mostly obligatory
levies or taxes levied at the work place.

PROFILES OF PRINCIPAL ORGANISATIONS

1. Soviet Peace Committee (SPC)

Russian title: *SOVETSKY KOMITET ZASHCHITY MIRA*
(also known as the Soviet Committee for the Defence of Peace)
Address: Moscow 129010, 36 Prospekt Mira 36.

Origins and Structure

The SPC was established in 1949 at the First All-Union Peace Conference in Moscow. It claims to be the 'co-ordinating body of a multi-million strong peace movement in the Soviet Union'. It claimed credit, for example, for organising in 1976 the signature of the New Stockholm Appeal for Stopping the Arms Race by 180 million Soviet citizens, nearly the entire adult population of the Soviet Union. It is certainly the leading Soviet matrix organisation, and the main link between the International Department and the principal organisations in the propaganda network. The Committee itself numbers about 450 people elected by All-Union Peace Conferences, held every five years.

The Committee has a number of Departments responsible for subjects and areas such as International Relations, International Organisations, Information, Africa and the Middle East and Northern Europe; and with commissions dealing with Disarmament, Developing Countries, Cultural Relations, Contacts with the Media, Contacts with Scientists, Contacts with foreign religions, Youth, Economic Affairs and Ecology. There are also about 120 local Peace Committees, one for each Republic and at regional and city level throughout the Soviet Union.

Officials

Chairman: Genrikh A. BOROVIK; First Deputies: Yevgeni M. PRIMAKOV, Vladimir N. OREL; Secretaries: Vladimir I. FEDOSOV, Grigory M. LOKSHIN, Vladislav V. KORNILOV, Igor P. FILIN, Leonid S. SEREBRYANNIK.

Among other leading personalities, Metropolitan FILARET of Minsk and Byelorussia is chairman of the Commission for contacts with foreign religious groups, and Lieutenant-General M.A. MILSTEIN, a member of both the Institute of the USA and Canada* and Soviet Retired Generals and Admirals for Peace and Disarmament*, and a former officer in the Soviet Military Intelligence (GRU), is Deputy Chairman of the Commission for Disarmament.

Borovik replaced the veteran G.A. ZHUKOV as Chairman in March 1987. He is a former *Novosti* journalist who has long been closely associated with the KGB and is a Vice-President of the WPC*. Primakov is director of IMEMO*. Orel, another recent appointment and full-time SPC official is responsible for the day-to-day direction of the SPC, since the Chairman and other Deputies all have other full-time positions.

Publication
A monthly magazine, *20th Century and Peace*, in Russian, French, German, English and Spanish.

International Affiliations
The SPC is the Soviet affiliate of the WPC, in which it is the main instrument of Soviet influence. Soviet influence is exercised through three principal Soviet staff members at the WPC's headquarters, Oleg Sergeyevich KHARKHARDIN (Orel's predecessor in the SPC and now a WPC Secretary), Alexei Valeriyevich TRESKIN and Dzhangir Validovich ATAMALI. The SPC has the status of Associate National Non-governmental Organisation (NGO) with the UN Department of Public Information and is also a member of the Geneva NGO's Special Committee on Disarmament.

Activities
In 1986–87 the SPC underwent major changes of personnel and of style. At an Extraordinary Joint Plenum of the SPC and the Soviet Peace Fund* in December 1986 to assess the impact of the UN International Year of Peace, the then Chairman, Zhukov, said that the SPC had to acquire a more 'diversified character' to deal with the 'anti-war movement' and that the time had come for serious restructuring to enable the SPC to engage in activities beyond the scope of the WPC, which was being increasingly 'ignored' by the main Western peace movements; in future the SPC would rely more on its own commissions to 'promote direct contact' with such groups as 'scientists, physicians, sportsmen, cultural personalities and retired military leaders'. Under his successor, Borovik, these changes have been inaugurated. Speaking to *Tass* on 17 June 1987, Borovik said 'our purpose is to turn the SPC into a centre of popular diplomacy in the USSR', through links with 'various informal anti-war associations and groups' such as a 'Movement of Soviet Rock Musicians for Peace' and another called 'Ecology and Peace'. The SPC has also increased bilateral contacts in NATO countries, especially the United States, and, by sending a delegation to the Sixth European Nuclear Disarmament Convention in Coventry in 1987, continued the trend towards closer relations which had been damaged in 1982 as a result of a heavy-handed attempt by Zhukov to impose Soviet control on END and other European Peace Movements.

With the object of publicising the SPC's new popular image,

Borovik and other leading officials joined with the Soviet Peace Fund in a Soviet television phone-in programme on 11 September 1987 entitled 'People's Diplomacy'. People's Diplomacy was defined as 'the development of ties between ordinary people, the humanisation of international relations and the establishment of new political thinking at the level of the masses'. Rather surprisingly, it was claimed that the recent Soviet moratorium on nuclear tests was the result of a SPC initiative, following a suggestion by 'US peace activists'. Metropolitan Filaret spoke enthusiastically of Mother Theresa's visit to the Soviet Union at the instigation of the SPC and claimed to have numerous contacts with foreign religious bodies, especially with the Roman Catholic Church through Pax Christi. Other questions about the SPC's activities were answered somewhat defensively on standard lines. All the indications are that the SPC is to be given a more prominent role in future Soviet propaganda activities.

2. Soviet Peace Fund (SPF)

Russian title: *SOVETSKY FOND MIRA*
Address: Moscow 119034, Kropotinskaya Ulitsa 10

The SPF was founded in 1961 for the purpose of financing the Soviet 'peace' propaganda programme. It acts as a financial clearing-house administered by the Soviet Peace Committee* and some other Soviet 'public organisations', i.e. the matrix organisations. It is the channel for financial support of the main International Front Organisations (see Section II and Appendix C). Financial transactions are carried out through the agency of the State Bank (Gosbank), whose Chairman, Viktor DEMENTSEV, is a Deputy Chairman of the SPC.

The SPF is organised nationally, like the SPC, with local groups throughout the fifteen Republics. Soviet citizens make 'Donations' to the Fund either direct to its Moscow headquarters or through Gosbank. The most common method of collecting money is for factories, collective farms and other plants to work a 'shift for peace', which means that all wages due for that shift are donated to the Fund. Such donations are, in practice, tantamount to levies imposed by the State. Soviet officials working abroad are required to pay a proportion of their earnings to the SPF. According to Metropolitan Filaret (speaking in the TV phone-in programme on 11 September 1987) the Russian

Orthodox Church donates 30 million roubles annually to the Fund.

On the same programme, the SPF's Deputy Chairman, Svetlana SAVITSKAYA, the Soviet woman cosmonaut, explained how the SPF spends its resources. She said 'the Peace Fund is the material supply base of the Soviet Peace Movement. The resources of the fund finance the activities of the 16 mass public organisations, such as the Committee for the Defence of Peace (SPC), the Committee for Solidarity with Asian and African countries*, the War Veterans' Committee*, the Committee of Soviet Women* and a whole number of others. The most important international congresses, meetings and forums are held with the fund's resources'. She gave as examples the Moscow forum held in February 1987 For a Nuclear-Free World for the Survival of Humanity, the Ninth World Congress of Women organised by WIDF* in Moscow in June 1987 and the Seventh Congress of the International Physicians for the Prevention of Nuclear War, which was held in Moscow in May 1987. Savitskaya added that aid is also given to 'victims of aggression, war and natural disaster', giving as examples children in Afghanistan and Nicaragua, refugees from the Republic of South Africa and people in drought-affected areas of India and Ethiopia. She claimed that 100 million Soviet citizens contributed to the SPF, which boasted 4 million 'volunteer grass roots activists'.

Although Soviet spokeswomen try to maintain the non-governmental character of the SPF and its role as an organ of the people, the Fund's Chairman, former World Chess champion Anatoly KARPOV admitted, in an interview reported in *Sovetskaya Rossiya* on 26 April 1986, that the Fund operates under CPSU control in accordance with decisions of the 27th Party Congress.

Other leading officials of the SPF are: First Deputies: Vasily YEMELYANOV, Vladimir P. MASLIN; Secretaries: Dmitry MAMLEYEV, Tomas GRIGORIEV.

3. All-Union Central Council of Trade Unions (AUCCTU)

Russian title: *VSESOYUZNY TSENTRALNY SOVET PROFSOYUZOV (VTsSPS)*
Address: Moscow 117179, Leninsky Prospekt 42.

Origins

Trade Unions were in existence in Russia in Tsarist times. Since the Revolution the AUCCTU has been established as the single body for the co-ordination and direction of individual trade unions representing different branches of industry. All its activities are subject to strict Party direction; those in the international field are under the control of the CPSU Central Committee's International Department.

Officials

Chairman: Stepan A. SHALAYEV; Secretary (responsible for International Relations): Gennady I. YANAYEV; Head of International Department: Boris A. AVERYANOV.

International Connections

The AUCCTU is the Soviet affiliate of the World Federation of Trade Unions*, in which it plays the leading role. The close co-ordination between the two organisations is shown by the careers of the two Soviet officials who have dominated international communist trade union affairs for two decades, Boris Averyanov and Vsevolod MOZHAEV. Averyanov was head of the AUCCTU's International Department from 1961 until 1975, when he was succeeded by Mozhaev on moving to Prague as a WFTU Secretary. In 1986 the two swapped jobs, Averyanov returning to his previous appointment and Mozhaev going to Prague. The AUCCTU also maintains bilateral links with 160 Central Trade Union Organisations throughout the world.

Individual Trade Unions have also for many years maintained extensive links with their foreign counterparts, both bilaterally and through the Trade Union Internationals (TUIs)*. Many of the larger industrial Unions, such as the Mine Workers (now a member of the recently formed International Mineworkers' Organisation*) and the Automobile Workers have their own International Departments.

Activities

The aims of the Soviet Trade Unions international activities were frankly described by G. Ya Tarle in the journal *Voprosi Istorii* (Questions of History), No. 2, 1980:

> Soviet Trade unions take an active part in all major international actions of left wing forces, render every possible support to class manifestations of the proletariat of capitalist countries and to national liberation movements. The

support of Soviet trade unions for the strike battle of workers of capitalist countries takes first and foremost political forms, likewise counter-action against economic measures aimed at strike-breaking.

During 1987 the AUCCTU attempted to broaden its activities by holding an unusual number of international meetings in Moscow. These have included an International Trade Union Conference Devoted to the 70th Anniversary of the October Revolution (in May), an International Trade Union Youth Forum (in July) and a meeting with West European and WFTU participation on the 'Day of Trade Union Action for Peace' (1 September).

Publication
The AUCCTU publishes a daily newspaper, *Trud*.

4. Association of Soviet Lawyers

Russian title: *ASSOTSIATSIYA SOVETSKIKH YURISTOV*
Address: Moscow, Ulitsa Kalinina 14.

Officials
Chairman: Alexander Y. SUKHAREV; Deputy Chairmen: Igor I. KARPETS, Igor P. BLISCHENKO, Vadim K. SOBAKIN.

International Affiliations
The Association of Soviet Lawyers is the Soviet affiliate of the International Association of Democratic Lawyers (IADL)* and the main channel for Soviet influence over that organisation. The Soviet official currrently stationed at IADL headquarters in Brussels (as an IADL Secretary) is M.V. MAZOV. Vadim Sobakin is also a member of the CPSU Central Committee International Department Consultants' Group.

Activities
In addition to its activities in the IADL context, the Association, in 1987, played a key role in preparations for the establishment of the new international organisation of Lawyers against Nuclear War. The Association's chairman, Alexander Sukharev, attended a conference jointly convened with the US Lawyers' Committee on Nuclear Policy in New York, 30–31 August 1987, at which the new international organisation was formed.

5. Committee of Soviet Physicians for the Prevention of Nuclear War (PPNW)

Russian title: *KOMITET SOVETSKIKH VRACHEI ZA PREDOTVRASHCHENIYE YADERNOI VOINY*. Established 1981.
Address: c/o USSR Academy of Medical Sciences, Moscow 109801, Ulitsa Solyanka 14.

Officials
Chairman: Academician M. KUZIN; Deputy Chairman: Academician N. BOCHKOV, Academician Leonid A. ILYIN; Executive Secretary: Alexei I. DMITRIEV; Secretaries: Andrei M. VAVILOV, Alexander N. SHCHERBAKOV, Vladimir B. TULINOV.

International Affiliations and Activities
The Soviet PPNW was set up, nominally under the auspices of the Presidium of the USSR Academy of Medical Sciences, as the Soviet component of the International Physicians for the Prevention of Nuclear War (IPPNW)* at a meeting in Moscow in July 1981. The latter's original Co-Chairman, Academician Yevgeni Chazov, was also the Chairman of Soviet PPNW until February 1987, when he was appointed Soviet Minister of Health. The Soviet Committee plays a leading role inside IPPNW and houses in Moscow one of its two European regional offices (the other is in London) and it was host to the Seventh IPPNW Congress held in Moscow in May 1987. It also played an important role, along with the Soviet Scientists' Committee for Peace, in organising the International Peace Forum in Moscow in February 1987. A number of the key officials involved in the running of the Soviet PPNW are not themselves doctors but are either former members of the various foreign affairs institutes, former Soviet Ministry of Foreign Affairs officials, or propaganda experts. Alexei Dmitriev, for example, the PPNW's Executive Secretary, describes himself as an 'historian'; Vladimir Tulinov, who was closely involved with the Fourth IPPNW Congress in Helsinki in June 1984, is a career diplomat, who in the 1980s has served in posts in the USA and Canada Institute* and the former Central Committee's International Information Department; Andrei Vavilov is also a career diplomat with extensive experience of arms control matters.

6. Committee of Soviet Scientists for the Defence of Peace and Against the Nuclear Threat

Russian title: *KOMITET SOVETSKIKH UCHENYKH V ZASHCHITU MIRA PROTIV YADERNOI UGROZY*. Established on 19 May 1983 at an All-Union Conference of Scientists in Moscow.

Officials
Chairman: Yevgeni VELIKHOV; Deputies: Roald SAGDEYEV, Andrei KOKOSHIN; Executive Secretary: Ye F. LOSHCHENKOVA.

International Affiliations and Activities
The Soviet Scientists' Committee was set up specifically to forge links with foreign scientists and enlist their support for the Soviet line on nuclear disarmament issues (the desirability of a new international scientists' forum to further these aims had been emphasised by Brezhnev at the 26th CPSU Congress in 1981). The Soviet Scientists' Committee played a prominent part in the 'First International Scientists' Peace Congress' in Hamburg in November 1986. The Committee has established contact with the Federation of American Scientists, the Commission on International Disarmament and Arms Control of the National Academy of Sciences of the USA and with various organisations in Western Europe. It has also been involved in a number of television and radio discussion programmes with US scientists. The Committee, moreover, (in particular its Chairman Academician Yevgeni Velikhov) was a prime mover with the Soviet Peace Committee* of the Moscow Peace Forum in February 1987: a scientists round-table, including many of those who had attended the Hamburg Congress, was held during the Forum.

One of the Committee's most important recent tasks has been to spearhead the Soviet propaganda campaign against the United States Strategic Defence Initiative (SDI). Velikhov and Roald Sagdeyev, himself a space scientist, have been extremely active in this field. Velikhov also associates with the Italian physicist, Antonio Zichichi, in the World Laboratory which has headquarters at Erice, Sicily. A Soviet branch was opened during the Moscow Peace Forum in February 1987, during which Soviet and US scientists discussed linking the project Health via Space, proposed by Dr. Lown of the IPPNW*, with the World Laboratory.

7. Committee of Youth Organisations of the USSR (CYO)

Russian title: *KOMITET MOLODEZHNYKH ORGANIZ-ATSIY SSSR* (KMO). Established in 1956.
Address: Moscow 101000, Ulitsa Bogdana Khmelnitskogo 7/8.

Officials
Chairman: Sergei N. CHELNOKOV; Deputies: Vsevolod G. NAKHODKIN (Also Vice-President of WFDY), Sergei V. ZHURAVLEV, Viktor I. KAMYSHANOV (member of WDFY Bureau), Nikolai N. MUKHIN.

International Affiliations
The Committee of Youth Organisations exists solely as a propaganda and foreign relations organisation to maintain ties with youth movements abroad mainly on behalf of its largest member, the Soviet Komsomol (Young Communist League). The Komsomol was responsible for the arrangements for the 12th World Festival of Youth and Students in Moscow in 1985. The CYO is the Soviet affiliate of the World Federation of Democratic Youth (WFDY)* and plays the major role in controlling that organisation.

8. Institute of the USA and Canada (IUSAC)

Russian title: *INSTITUT SOYEDINENNYKH SHTATOV AMERIKI I KANADY* (ISShAK).
Address: Moscow 121069, Khlebnyy Pereulok 2/3. Established in 1967 as Institute of the USA: Canada was added to title in 1974.

Officials
Director: Georgi Arkadyevich ARBATOV; Deputies: Radomir G. BOGDANOV, Andrey A. KOKOSHIN, Vitaly V. ZHURKIN, Georgi Y. SKOROV; Heads of Department: Genrikh A. TROFIMENKO (US Foreign Policy), Yuri A. ZAMOSHKIN (Social and Ideological Problems), Mikhail A.

MILSTEIN (Military-Political), Leon A. BAGRAMOV (Canada).

Activities
The IUSAC, nominally part of the Economics Department of the USSR Academy of Sciences, in practice operates under the direct control of the International Department of the Soviet Communist Party (CPSU). It has a staff of about 350, of whom about half are professional researchers and scientific workers. According to (Miss) G. ORIONOVA, who claims to be a former employee of the Institute, in a letter to the *Daily Telegraph* on 27 November 1980 'several key people'—she gives the number as 'less than a quarter'—work for the KGB, including Bogdanov. The Institute provides expert information and analysis on US affairs, and East–West relations in general, to the CPSU Central Committee Departments and Secretariat, as well as to the Ministry of Foreign Affairs and the KGB, but is not a policy-making body. Its reports form only one of a number of contributions to the process by which the Central Committee Secretariat decides policy. The Institute's Director, Georgi Arbatov, is well-known internationally, but his influence is believed to have declined recently.

Apart from its research functions, the Institute performs an important public relations and propaganda role. It is the channel for many non-executive bilateral exchanges between the Soviet Union and the United States, and its officials, who are virtually all Party or Komsomol members, are skilled operators. The Institute's activities extend well beyond the USA and Canada; its staff members are frequent visitors to western Europe and most other parts of the world. In particular, Arbatov and Milstein were involved with the Palme Commission on Disarmament Issues in Europe and in setting up the IPPNW*: Milstein is also involved with Generals for Peace and Disarmament* and is a prominent member of the Soviet Peace Committee*.

9. Institute for World Economy and International Relations (IMEMO)

Russian title: *INSTITUT MIROVOY EKONOMIKI I MEZH-DUNARDODNYKH OTNOSHENIY*. Established in 1956 as the successor to the Institute of World Economy and World

Politics, which had been formed in the 1920s under the USSR Academy of Sciences.
Address: Moscow 117418, Profsoyuznaya Stranyy 23.

Officials
Director: Yevgeni M. PRIMAKOV; Deputies: Oleg N. BYKOV, Igor Y. GURYEV, Ivan D. IVANOV, Ivan KORO-LYEV, Alexander K. KISLOV, Vladlen A. MARTYNOV.

Activities
IMEMO, although nominally under the Economics Department of the USSR Academy of Sciences, operates in practice under the control and guidance of the Central Committee's International Department. It has a staff of about 1,000, of whom some 700 are research workers and, although covering issues world-wide, it specialises particularly in the affairs of Western Europe and in East–West disarmament issues (there are similar Institutes covering the other principal geographic regions). IMEMO also produces world economic, political and social forecasts for Central Committee departments, the Ministry of Foreign Affairs and the KGB. It is not, however, a policy-making body and its reports form only one of many contributions to the decisions taken by the Central Committee Secretariat. As with the other institutes, IMEMO, in addition to its research functions, plays an important public relations and propaganda role. Its officials frequently travel abroad as members of Soviet delegations, visiting Western political parties, academics and peace groups. IMEMO's Director, Yevgeni Primakov, is a First Deputy Chairman of the Soviet Peace Committee*.

Publication
IMEMO publishes a monthly journal, *Mirovaya Ekonomika i Mezhdunarodnye Otnosheniya*; in June 1987, Primakov also launched a new annual review, *Disarmament and Security*, to be produced by his Institute in conjunction with *Novosti* in Russian and English.

10. Soviet Afro-Asian Solidarity Committee (SAASC)

Russian title: *SOVETSKY KOMITET SOLIDARNOSTI STRAN AZII I AFRIKI*. Established in 1956.
Address: Moscow 119034, Kropotkinskaya Ulitsa 10.

Officials
Chairman: Mikhail S. KAPITSA; First Deputy: Vladimir G. TOLSTIKOV; Secretary: Samandar KALANDAROV.

International Affiliations
The SAASC is the Soviet affiliate of, and the principal means of Soviet control over, the Afro-Asian Peoples' Solidarity Organisation (AAPSO)*. The SAASC generally has a full time official on the AAPSO Secretariat in Cairo (currently Mirpasha ZEINALOV).

Activities
The SAASC often acts as host in Moscow to visitors from the PLO, ANC, SWAPO and other similar organisations. Like other Soviet 'public organisations', the SAASC has recently sought to expand its contacts in countries outside the normal Soviet sphere of influence, for example, Kenya: in September 1987 a SAASC delegation visited Nairobi.

Publication
The SAASC publishes a bi-monthly journal *Asia and Africa Today* in Russian, English, French, Portuguese, Arabic and Dari.

11. Soviet Committee for European Security and Cooperation (SCESC)

Russian title: *SOVETSKY KOMITET ZA YEVROPEYSKUYU BEZOPASNOST I SOTRUDNICHESTVO*. Established 1971.
Address: Moscow 121019, Kropotkinskaya Ulitsa 3.

Officials
Chairman: Lev N. TOLKUNOV, Deputy Chairman: Yevgeni K. SILIN, Secretary: Yevgeni M. YURIEV.

International Affiliations
The SCESC was set up as the Soviet affiliate of the International
Committee for European Security and Co-operation (ICESC)*.

Activities
The SCESC was founded by a conference of a number of the
other Soviet 'public organisations', including the Soviet Peace
Committee*, the Soviet Women's Committee* and SSOD*.
These bodies re-convened for a meeting in Moscow on 5 June
1985 to approve a Statute for the SCESC and to appoint new
Committee members: the Committee now numbers 194, with a
Bureau of 25.

Yevgeni Silin is the most important and active of the five
Deputy Chairmen. He pays frequent visits to the ICESC headquarters in Brussels and, in 1987, the SCESC played an active
part in encouraging Soviet and CMEA contacts with the European Community and the European Parliament.

Publication
The SCESC produces an irregular *Information Bulletin*,
published by the Novosti news agency.

12. Soviet Committee for Solidarity with Latin American Peoples (SCSLAP)

Russian title: *SOVETSKY KOMITET SOLIDARNOSTI
NARODOV LATINSKOI AMERIKI*. Established 1984.
Address: Moscow 119034, Kroptkinskaya Ulitsa 10.

Officials
Chairman: Alexander Borisovich CHAKOVSKY.

International Affiliations and Activities
The SCSLAP was founded in Moscow on 6 February 1984,
evidently to provide a Soviet counterpart for the Afro-Asian
Latin American People's Solidarity Organisation*. Speaking to
the Soviet news agency TASS, 15 February 1984, Chakovsky
said that the Committee would work to promote the international
movement of solidarity with the peoples of Cuba, Nicaragua,
El Salvador, Guatemala, Honduras, Haiti, Paraguay, Chile and
'other countries struggling against dictatorial regimes'. It would
also promote the Soviet Union's 'domestic and peace-loving

foreign policy' and disseminate 'truthful information about real socialism'.

Chakovsky, who is chief editor of the Soviet Writers' Union weekly *Literaturnaya Gazeta* (Literary Gazette), visited Havana as the Committee's Chairman in September 1984.

13. Soviet Committee of War Veterans (SCWV)

Russian title: *SOVETSKY KOMITET VETERANOV VOYNY*.
Established in 1956.
Address: Moscow 121019 Gogolevski Bulvar 4.

Officials
Chairman: Col Gen (Retired) Alexei S. ZHELTOV; Executive Secretary: Col (Retired) Alexei P. MARESYEV.

International Affiliations
The SCWV is the Soviet affiliate of the International Federation of Resistance Fighters (FIR)*. Alexei Maresyev is a Vice-President of FIR. The Committee also maintains an extensive network of ties with over 100 national veterans' organisations and resistance movements in other countries.

Activities
The SCWV has recently broadened its activities in co-operation with foreign groups, specifically those in the USA and the United Kingdom (according to Maresyev at a press conference in Moscow, 27 April 1987).

The Committee sent a delegation to the USA in April–May 1986 and there have also recently been exchanges with British and Canadian groups. Moreover, at a meeting of socialist countries' veterans' organisations in Moscow in August 1986, Zheltov referred to the situation of the veterans' movement in the countries of Asia and Africa, saying that the Soviet Committee was looking for ways to engage them in the anti-war movement.

In December 1986 a new organisation was formed in Moscow, called the All-Union organisation of War and Labour Veterans, but the Central Committee Secretary responsible for Communist Party organisational matters, Georgy RAZUMOVSKY, speaking at the constituent conference, said that the existing Soviet Committee would survive as a constituent of the new organisation (*Tass*, 17 December 1986).

14. Soviet Women's Committee (SWC)

Russian title: *KOMITET SOVETSKIKH ZHENSHCHIN* (KSZh)
Address: Moscow 103009, Ulitsa Nemirovicha-Danchenko 6

Officials
Chairman: Zoya PUKHOVA; First Deputy: Alevtina V. FEDULOVA; Head of International Department: Adelina A. IVANOVA.

For many years the leading figure in the Soviet Women's Committee was the first woman in space, Valentina TERESH-KOVA. In January 1987 she was succeeded as Chairman by Zoya Pukhova, the director of a Textile Mill, but in a move which illustrates the interchangeability of officials in these Soviet 'public organisations', Mrs. Tereshkova was subsequently appointed chairman of the Union of Soviet Friendship Societies (SSOD)*.

International Affiliations
The Soviet Women's Committee is the Soviet affiliate of the Women's International Democratic Federation (WIDF)*. The Committee's chairman has usually served as a WIDF vice-president and there is a Soviet Secretary at the WIDF headquarters (Valeria KALMYK).

Activities
In 1987 the SWC played host to the WIDF's Ninth World Congress of Women. With the aim of widening the audiences for its propaganda the SWC used the occasion to invite to Moscow, in its own name, prominent non-Communist women from the UK and other Western countries, some of whom accepted invitations.

Publication
The SWC publishes the glossy magazine *Soviet Woman* in Russian, English and 12 other languages.

15. Union of Soviet Societies for Friendship and Cultural Relations with Foreign Countries (SSOD)

Russian title: *SOYUZ SOVETSKIKH OBSHCHESTV DRUZHBY I KULTURNOY SVYAZI S ZARUBEZHNYMI*

STRANAMI. Established in 1958 in succession to the All-Union Society for Cultural Relations with Abroad, known as VUKS. Address: Moscow 103009, Prospekt Kalinina 14

Officials
Chairman: Valentina V. TERESHKOVA; First Deputy: Yuri SMIRNOV; General Secretary: Anatoly N. MASKO.

International Affiliations and Activities
SSOD is an umbrella organisation uniting some 80 individual societies for friendship with foreign countries and regions. It claims contact with more than nine thousand organisations in 141 countries. SSOD is also responsible for co-ordinating Soviet town twinning links, joining at least 140 Soviet towns and cities with over 320 cities in non-Communist countries. Through SSOD, the Soviet Union participates in such organisations as the World Federation of Twinned Towns, the European Cultural Society and the World Esperantist Movement for Peace (MEM)*.

In an article in the CPSU Central Committee journal *Politicheskoye Samoobrazovanie* (Political Self-Education), No. 3, 1979, it was stated that SSOD:

> conducts all its work in close contact and co-operation with Soviet departments and organisations including union ministries, the USSR Academy of Sciences, the AUCCTU, the Komsomol etc. The many-sided activity of Soviet friendship societies is a kind of 'peoples diplomacy' . . . fulfilling the role of public aides of the party and state in resolving important international problems, the Soviet friendship societies simultaneously also fulfil the noble functions of strengthening the socialist commonwealth, the development of social progress and the establishment of peace on the planet.

Publication
SSOD publishes a monthly journal *Culture and Life* in Russian, English, French, German and Spanish.

16. Soviet Retired Generals and Admirals for Peace and Disarmament

Russian title: *SOVETSKIY GENERALY I ADMIRALY V OTSTAVKE ZA MIR I RAZORUZHENIYE.* Established in Moscow, 25 Decmeber 1986.
Address: c/o Soviet Peace Committee, Moscow 129010, Prospekt mira 36.

Officials
'Co-ordinator' (1987) Maj-Gen V. MAKAREVSKY; Members:
Lt-Gen M.A. MILSTEIN, A.K. GORLEVSKY, Maj-Gen Y.A.
NOZHIN, Lt-Gen A.M. SHEVCHENKO, B.D. YASIN.

In addition, the following are also believed to belong to the
group: Rear Adm A.R. ASTAFAYEV, V.J. PETRENKO, A.
PONOMAREV, R. SIMONYAN, B. SURIKOV.

International Affiliations and Activities
This group was set up to complement the western group
'Generals for Peace and Disarmament'* which had been formed
in 1981 and which had already held *ad hoc* meetings with retired
Warsaw Pact military officers in Vienna.

Unusually, the chairmanship of the Soviet group is to rotate
annually. The 'Co-ordinator' for 1987 was Maj-Gen Vadim
Makarevsky, a former deputy head of the Kuibishev Military
Engineering Academy who retired in the 1970s and a member
of the Soviet Peace Committee's Disarmament Commission.

The new group held a meeting with 'Generals for Peace and
Disarmament' in Vienna on 4–7 May 1987. In April 1987 a
delegation from the Soviet group, led by General Mikhail
Milstein (see also under SPC*) visited the United States. The
delegation visited the US Centre for Defence Information (CDI):
a return visit to the Soviet Union was planned for 1988.

17. USSR Students' Council

Russian title: *STUDENCHESKY SOVET SSSR*

Officials
Chairman: Sergei V. ZHURAVLEV; Secretary: Vladimir A.
PLAKSIN.

International Affiliations
The Soviet Students' Council is a member of Committee of
Youth Organisations (KMO) and its Chairman is also a deputy
chairman of KMO. In its own right the Students' Council is also
the Soviet affiliate of, and the principal means of Soviet control
over, the International Union of Students (IUS)*. The present
Soviet representative in the IUS Secretariat is Andrei
MOROZOV.

18. USSR Union of Journalists

Russian title: *SOYUZ ZHURNALISTOV SSSR*. Established 1959.
Address: Moscow 121019, Suvorovsky Bulvar 8

Officials
Chairman: Viktor G. AFANASIEV; First Deputies: Sergei A. LOSEV, Ivan A. ZUBKOV; Head of External Relations Department: Y.A. YERSHOV.

International Affiliations
The Union of Journalists is the Soviet affiliate of the International Organisation of Journalists (IOJ)*. Soviet control of the IOJ is thought to be exercised mainly through I.A. Zubkov and Y.A. Yershov: there is also usually a Soviet official holding the post of an IOJ Secretary at its Prague headquarters (currently Vladimir Lvovich Artemov).

Activities
The Union of Journalists is a 'creative voluntary public organisation' (as opposed to a trade union) embracing 'professionals of the mass media information agencies'; its membership is around 75,000. As well as taking a full part in IOJ activities, senior Soviet journalists and editors undertake numerous bilateral foreign exchanges with Western countries. In 1986 the Union established the Moscow International Institute of Journalism to journalists from the developing countries: it is modelled on existing IOJ training schools in Czechoslovakia, the GDR and Hungary.

Publications
The Union of Journalists publishes two magazines, the monthly *Zhurnalist* (Journalist) and the weekly *Za Rubezhom* (Abroad).

APPENDIX A: DIAGRAM OF THE SOVIET PROPAGANDA NETWORK

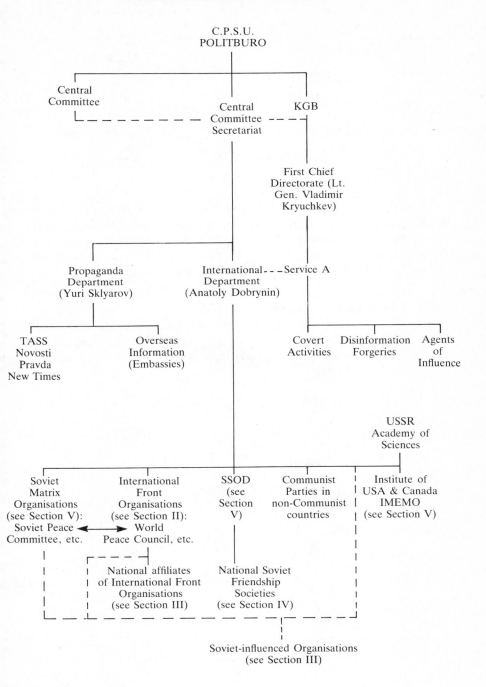

Appendix B: British Labour Party Proscribed List 1933–34

The text of the decision of the National Executive Committee of the British Labour Party, adopted by the Labour Party Conference in 1933, is given below. One further organisation, the Relief Committee for the Victims of German Fascism, which was proscribed in 1934, has been added.

The National Executive Committee of the Labour Party has decided that the organisations mentioned below are Political Parties or Organisations ancillary or subsidiary to the Communist Party, and has declared them ineligible for affiliation to the Labour Party.

The League Against Imperialism.
The Left Wing Movement.
The Minority Movement.
The Workers' International Relief.
The National Unemployed Workers' Movement.
The Friends of the Soviet Union.
The International Labour Defence.
The National Charter Campaign Committee.
The Anti-War Movement.
The European Workers' Anti-Fascist Congress: British Delegation Committee.
Relief Committee for the Victims of German Fascism (German Relief Committee).

Members of these Organisations are accordingly ineligible as:

(a) Individual Members of the Party.
(b) Delegates to the Party, locally or nationally.

(c) Candidates of the Party for Parliamentary or Local Government Elections.

The Rules governing Constituency and Local Labour Parties provide that:

A Party may not enter into affiliation with or give support financially or otherwise to any Political Party or Organisation ancillary or subsidiary thereto declared by the Annual Party Conference of the Labour Party or by the National Executive Committee in pursuance of Conference decisions to be ineligible for membership of the Party.

APPENDIX C: BRITISH LABOUR PARTY PROSCRIBED LIST 1972–73

The British Labour Party published its last annual list of proscribed organisations in 1972. The text, taken from Appendix II to the report of the Party's 71st Annual Conference in Blackpool in October 1972, is given below. Thereafter annual publication was discontinued. All the organisations on this list were included because of their Communist orientation with the exceptions of the Union Movement, which was neo-fascist, and the last four organisations named, three of which were Trotskyist. The Labour Research Department*, although it was (and still is) a Communist organisation, had been included on the proscribed list until 1970, as had been the Medical Association for the Prevention of War until 1968.

Proscribed Organisations

The Annual Party Conference has had to declare certain organisations ineligible for affiliation to the Labour Party, and members of these organisations are not eligible for membership of the Labour Party.

Many organisations which were, or are, subsidiaries of the Communist Party, were of short life, became merged into other organisations, or changed their title. This has caused some confusion, and many Constituency and Local Labour Parties, and their members, have been induced to give support to these organisations which have attractive titles, without a full appreciation of their origin.

The following is a list of Proscribed Organisations which are at present known to be in existence:

British Soviet Friendship Houses Ltd

Communist Party of Great Britain
Marx House
Scottish–USSR Society for Friendship and Cooperation
The World Federation of Democratic Youth
Women's International Democratic Federation
League for Democracy in Greece
British Peace Committee
Welsh Peace Council
Union Movement
British Youth Festival Committee
West Yorkshire Federation of Peace Organisations
World Federation of Trade Unions
The International Union of Students
The International Organisation of Journalists
The International Association of Democratic Lawyers
The World Federation of Scientific Workers
World Peace Council
British–Soviet Friendship Society
British–China Friendship Association
British–Czechoslovak Friendship League
British–Rumanian Friendship Association
The Society for Friendship with Bulgaria
British Hungarian Friendship Society
Musicians' Organisation for Peace
Teachers for Peace
National Assembly of Women
The Newsletter (Workers Press)
Socialist Labour League
Keep Left
Independent Nuclear Disarmament Election Committee

Attention is also drawn to Clause II paragraph (3) of the Labour Party Constitution which governs the position of other political organisations which have not been formally declared as proscribed organisations. Clause II paragraph (3) reads:

Political organisations not affiliated to or associated under a National Agreement with the Party on January 1, 1946, having their own Programme, Principles and Policy for distinctive and separate propaganda, or possessing Branches in the Constituencies or engaged in the promotion of Parliamentary or Local Government Candidatures, or owing allegiance to any Political organisation situated abroad, shall be ineligible for affiliation to the Party.

Appendix D: Estimated Soviet Subsidies to International Front Organisations

There is no doubt that vast Soviet subsidies of various kinds are regularly paid to the Soviet-controlled organisations described in Section II. Admissions to this effect have been made, from time to time, by Communist officials (see paragraph on Finance in the profile of the WPC*). Funds are also provided from Soviet sources to finance particular events. Some of this money is channelled through the Soviet Peace Fund. Because none of these organisations publish their accounts, it is not possible to quote detailed or up-to-date figures. An attempt was made in the United States in 1979, after careful scrutiny of all available sources, to produce estimates for Soviet subsidies for that year to the principal organisations. The results, which are given below, were published in the report of the Subcommittee on Oversight of the US House of Representatives dated 6 February 1980. It should be understood that these are 1979 figures; their equivalents today would be considerably higher.

	US$
Afro-Asian People's Solidarity Organisation	1 260 000
Christian Peace Conference	210 000
International Association of Democratic Lawyers	100 000
International Federation of Resistance Fighters	125 000
International Organisation of Journalists	515 000
International Institute for Peace	260 000
International Radio and Television Organisation	50 000
International Union of Students	905 000
Women's International Democratic Federation	390 000
World Federation of Democratic Youth	1 575 000
World Federation of Scientific Workers	100 000
World Federation of Trade Unions	8 575 000
World Peace Council	49 380 000

Appendix E: Comparison of Selected Passages From The WPC Programmes For 1985 and 1988

Introduction

1985 (Extracts)

The year that has ended [1984] saw tens of millions of women and men in all continents expressing, through the most varied forms of actions, their refusal to participate in the war preparations of the United States Administration, the other most aggressive member States of NATO and their allies and partners.

The Reagan Administration and its partners seek desperately to divide and weaken the peace and anti-war forces. The peoples must foil these efforts by building an even wider united mass movement for the prevention of nuclear war, which threatens all life on this planet.

1985 must see a vast expansion of the demonstrations and other actions in Europe, North America and in all continents against the deployment of Pershing II and cruise missiles in Europe and in other parts of the world, for a freeze on the production, development and testing of nuclear weapons, for reduction of military budgets, for a pledge by all nuclear-weapon powers not to be first to use nuclear weapons, for the establishment of nuclear-weapon free zones, for a total ban on nuclear and chemical weapons and other weapons of mass destruction.

A vital issue at this hour is that of preventing the sinister plans for the militarization of outer space, which have resulted in the danger of a nuclear war reaching unprecedented proportions. The Reagan Administration has publicly announced its determination to go ahead with these plans, despite worldwide opposition. This calls for the most effective actions throughout the world.

1985 must see an intensification also of the mass actions against the open and covert agression and intervention by the US Government and by those states with which it colludes, against the sovereignty and independence of countries in Central America and the Caribbean, the Middle East, southern Africa, the Indian Ocean, South-East Asia and the Far East.

The struggle for peace and for the prevention of nuclear war is one struggle. To fight in defence of the sovereignty and independence of countries is to fight for the ending of the armaments build-up. And equally, the fight against hunger and poverty is at the same time a fight against the armaments build-up. Each struggle for the defence of peace, for the building of a new world and for detente is part and parcel of the common struggle of all the peoples for the prevention of a nuclear war.

1988 (Full text)

In the nuclear age humanity stands at the crossroad: either survival, peace and cooperation or confrontation, nuclear war and annihilation.[a]

That is why disarmament, total elimination of nuclear weapons, peace and common security remain vital issues for the entire peace movement of which the World Peace Council is an integral part.

The possibilities for enhancing the process of peace and real disarmament are steadily growing. This is clearly manifested in the Soviet-American INF agreement, which is also the result of the vast mass movement for peace. But, to ensure that this process continues on a firm footing bringing new decisive successes, it is necessary to mobilise the vast potential of public opinion. This requires *cooperation and common actions* by all peace forces—at grassroots, local, national and international levels.

The peace committees, organisations and groups in 144 countries represented in the WPC constitute the strength and vitality of the World Peace Council as a whole.

This Programme has been prepared on the basis of proposals made by national peace movements and after discussions by the WPC Bureau at its session in Auckland, New Zealand, in October 1987. The important objective of this Programme, is *to further the contribution to the development of peace activities of national organizations*, and to render maximum practical support

---

[a] Declaration of the World Peace Council Session (Sofia, 1986).

to their actions, to national and regional campaigns and initiatives.

It is essential that all events in this Programme are implemented in cooperation with national peace committees, along with other movements. It is also intended to provide more possibilities for the exchange of opinions, experiences and ideas on strategies and concrete campaigns during WPC 'constitutional' and other relevant international events, and also in WPC publications.

It is important to put the main emphasis in all international actions and events on *campaigning and networking* in order to achieve the maximum publicity and effect on public opinion both within and outside the WPC framework (as with the Global Peace Wave 1987). This should be the task of both national committees and the elected international bodies of the WPC, the Presidential Committee and the Bureau—otherwise it cannot be effective.

The WPC is fully aware that in the realities of today's international situation it has become a vital necessity for peace movements holding varying viewpoints on the key issues of our time to work together.

As part of this process the *WPC will promote and strengthen contacts, dialogue and cooperation* with all peace organizations, movements and groups, with parliamentarians and other elected officials, trade unions, veterans' and solidarity groups, women, youth and students, scientists, physicians, ecologists and lawyers, physicists and engineers, teachers and educationalists, artists, writers and other workers of culture, religious circles, etc. The WPC will continue and increase its cooperation with the UN, UNESCO and other specialized agencies, the Non-Aligned Movement, the OAU and other intergovernmental bodies.

It will support and contribute to the Six Nations initiative and any step by any government, parliament or party for the prevention of nuclear war and the promotion of disarmament, development, national independence, a peaceful solution to regional conflicts, the respect of human rights and building a secure and non-violent world.

Such a broad, open and friendly dialogue must serve as basis for overcoming the enemy images of the 'cold war', developing mutual understanding, joint actions and promoting of people to people diplomacy.

In presenting this Programme of Action the WPC welcomes

all new proposals and initiatives from all peace committees and other national and international organizations and movements.

Arms Control and Disarmament

1985
PREVENTING NUCLEAR WAR, HALTING THE GLOBAL ARMS BUILD-UP, REDUCING AND ELIMINATING NUCLEAR WEAPONS AND ACHIEVING GENERAL AND COMPLETE DISARMAMENT
A. *An urgent Campaign of Mass Activities for the Prevention of War: Full Support to the UN World Disarmament Campaign on the following priorities issues*:
As the highest priority to conclude a treaty banning space weapons and the militarization of outer space to achieve a commitment by the US in reciprocation to that undertaken by the Soviet Union to observe a moratorium on testing anti-satellite (ASAT) or any other space weapons.

- To achieve an immediate withdrawal of US intermediate-range strategic missiles, the Pershing II and cruise missiles from Europe, as the deployment of these first-strike weapons has qualitatively increased the peril of nuclear war.

- To achieve a freeze on the development, testing, production and deployment of all nuclear weapons and weapons of mass destruction.

- To rapidly achieve negotiated simultaneous reductions, the elimination and the banning of all nuclear weapons (under international control and based on the principle of undiminished security for all nations) for a nuclear weapon-free Europe and a nuclear-free world.

- To secure a pledge by the United States to renounce the first use of nuclear weapons, as has been done by the USSR.

- To achieve an immediate moratorium on the testing of all nuclear weapons and to conclude urgently a Comprehensive Test Ban Treaty.

- To exert pressure to overcome the obstruction by the United States in the Conference on Disarmament so that negotiations may proceed on the prevention of nuclear war, on nuclear disarmament and security guarantees to non-nuclear states, and for a CTBT, and on banning space weapons.

- To create nuclear weapon-free and peace zones, such as in the Nordic countries, the Balkan countries, the Mediterranean region, the Indian Ocean and the South Pacific, etc.

- To support the initiative of the Swedish government to create a nuclear weapon-free corridor in Central Europe.

- To halt the qualitative escalation of the arms build-up which has accompanied the advent of first-strike nuclear weapons such as cruise missiles (which are being deployed on sea vessels and aircraft throughout the world, and which would present nearly impossible verification problems, thus threatening to make the arms race irreversible) and other first-strike missiles.

- To expose the myth of 'limited' nuclear war and US plans for waging a 'protracted' nuclear war, contained in strategies such as SIOP (Single Integrated Operational Plan) as well as to expose US global military strategy as a whole.

- To halt the increasing US military and nuclear presence in Asia and the Pacific and the planned deployment in those regions of new first-strike nuclear weapons, including the Pershing II and cruise missiles. To achieve a withdrawal of US nuclear weapons already deployed in various parts of the region.

- To disseminate widely scientists' findings that a 'nuclear winter' would engulf the entire world if nuclear weapons are ever used as well as other information on the horrors of nuclear weapons.

- To give all-out support and devote all activities to the World Disarmament Campaign of the United Nations.

- To achieve the implementation of the decisions of the First Special Session of the United Nations General Assembly on Disarmament (SSD I) which were reaffirmed by SSD II as being the most comprehensive and best programme for averting nuclear war, reversing the nuclear arms build-up and achieving general and complete disarmament simultaneously and under international control, as also reiterated time and again in UN General Assembly resolutions supported by the overwhelming majority of countries.

- To halt the imperialist military build-up, stockpiling of nuclear weapons, direct and indirect intervention, aggression and war around the world as in the Middle East, Southern Africa, Central America and the Caribbean, especially Nicaragua, El Salvador and Grenada, and the Mediterranean, the Indian Ocean, Asia and elsewhere.

- To seek the fullest possible adherence to and implementation of the Nuclear Non-Proliferation Treaty.

- To achieve a full implementation of the United Nations Charter which calls for the non-use of force or the threat of force in international relations.

- To conclude a treaty renouncing the use of force between NATO and the Warsaw Treaty nations, as proposed by the latter.

- To at all times seek to build the widest unity and common action based on these issues while at the same time consistently clarifying who supports and who opposes disarmament and the responsibility of the US Reagan administration for the arms build-up.

- To show the inseparable interconnection of the nuclear war danger, the arms build-up and the struggle for peace, independence, human rights and democracy, economic justice and development, against racism and apartheid, imperialist intervention and aggression, colonialism and neo-colonialism, the US Central Command and Rapid Strike Force— in the Middle East, Africa, Asia, the Pacific region, Latin America and the Caribbean and the Mediterranean.

[Here follow proposals for 36 specific activities to promote the above]

B. *Further Campaigns to Stop and Reverse the Global Arms Build-up, Against Nuclear and Other Weapons of Mass Destruction, for International Security, Cooperation and Détente on the following issues*:

- To prevent the further production and deployment of chemical and nerve gas weapons and to achieve a ban on chemical weapons—by overcoming the US obstruction of the negotiations in the conference on Disarmamant.

- To achieve a ban on laser, radiological and space weaponry—also achievable by unblocking negotiations in the Disarmament Conference and beginning negotiations on space weapons.

- To achieve a reduction in armed forces and armaments and the dismantling of military alliances.

- To accomplish a reduction in military budgets and the channeling of resources to economic development and human needs.

- To campaign for negotiations on every possible level through existing bilateral and multilateral fora but also in the UN Security Council and through the holding of the World Disarmament Conference called for by the United Nations.

- To encourage the widest exchange of contacts, trade, scientific and cultural exchanges between East and West.

1988 (Full text)
DISARMAMENT

- Support *actions and campaigns* at national and international levels aimed at: prohibiting and eliminating nuclear and other weapons of mass destruction; reducing conventional weapons; implementing a comprehensive nuclear test ban; ratifying and implementing the global INF treaty; reducing the strategic nuclear weapons potential by at least 50 per cent; maintaining and strengthening the ABM treaty; preventing the militarization of outer space; establishing nuclear weapon-free zones and corridors; demilitarizing the seas; withdrawing foreign military bases; achieving equal and comprehensive security for all peoples and nations.

- Promote dialogue, *cooperation*, joint actions and regular exchange of information and experience among peace movements and various other organizations and groups on peace and disarmament work; focus particularly on this issue at regional *meetings* of national committees.

- Contribute to the *preparations* of and participate in the Third Special Session of the United Nations Assembly on Disarmament (SSD III); contribute to the NGO preparatory conference on SSD III (Geneva, April) and other similar events; participate in the mass peace demonstration at the time of the SSD III (New York); promote broad cooperation among peace movements and other NGOs at national and international levels.

- Launch a *campaign* to defend the US-Soviet Anti-Ballistic Missile Treaty so as to ensure long-term adherence to it by the US and USSR; ensure full publicity coverage for this campaign and hold one major event in support of it.

- Hold an international *forum* on 'The Nuclear Strategic Situation—New Tasks for the Peace Movement' (Geneva, spring), followed by visits by *delegations* to the missions of the nuclear powers at the UN

- Convene a *seminar* on 'A Vision of a World Without Nuclear Weapons' (European country).

- Participate in *discussions* and activities in the aftermath of the INF accord.

- Sponsor *seminars* on the possibilities for cuts in the arsenals of conventional, chemical and biological weapons.

- Contribute to an international *meeting* on nuclear weapon-free zones (Sofia, spring).

- Hold a *symposium* on 'The verification process of the INF treaty: an example for future nuclear disarmament steps' (possibly Sweden).

- Support the *initiatives* of the Six Heads of State and the Non-Aligned Movement in the field of nuclear disarmament; promote national and international events to this end.

- Support the World *Conference* Against Nuclear Weapons (Tokyo, August); popularize the *signature campaign* on the Hiroshima and Nagasaki Appeal.

- Further develop *cooperation with the UN* Department for Disarmament Affairs, the Disarmament Campaign and other UN bodies on issues of disarmament.

- Contribute to the *UN/NGO cooperation* framework, particularly the Special NGO Committee on Disarmament and other existing machinery for regular INGO dialogue and cooperation.

Human Rights

1985 (Full text)
ACTIONS IN SUPPORT OF AND IN COLLABORATION WITH OTHER ORGANISATIONS:

■ Campaigns of solidarity with the victims of crimes perpetrated by fascist, neo-fascist and reactionary regimes, in violation of human rights.

■ Inquiries into the events related to the denunciation presented before the United Nations Environment Programme by the President of the Movement for the Preservation of Life in Brazil, on the crime committed by the transnationals resulting in the death of indigenous people and danger to the flora and fauna through use of defoliants chemically similar to dioxine employed by the US armed forces in Vietnam.

■ Continuation of the investigations into the violations of human rights in the Arab territories occupied by Israel since 1967 and into the crimes and genocide committed by Israel against the Palestinian and Lebanese peoples.

■ Categorical condemnation of South African colonialism and its crimes and the holding of inquiries and public hearings to denounce the gross violations of human rights by the apartheid regime in South Africa and Namibia.

■ Conduct inquiries and public hearings to denounce the violation of human rights in Malawi and Northern Ireland.

■ Hold a public hearing on the violation of human rights in Pakistan and South Korea.

■ Hold inquiries and public hearings to denounce the violations of human rights in El Salvador, Guatemala, Chile, Haiti, Uruguay, Paraguay, Honduras and Grenada.

■ Denunciation and exposure of the violations of human rights in the United States against the Black, Hispanic and indigenous peoples and other oppressed minorities.

■ Support the activities of the organisations working to end the 'professional ban' (Berufsverbot) in the FRG.

■ Support the activities of the International Commission of Inquiry into the Crimes of the Military Junta in Chile.

- Support the activities of the Anti-Imperialist Tribunal of Our America, Central and South American Organisation.

- Hold a public hearing to investigate the violations in Turkey of human rights as part of the governing junta's imperialist policy exemplified externally in the occupation of part of Cyprus and its development as a NATO base.

- Denounce and condemn the genocidal policy of imperialism against the countries of the Third World.

- Participation in national, regional and international conferences and other events related to human rights.

- Support the campaigns to declare torture and political kidnapping as international crimes against humanity.

- Consider as a human rights violation the plunder by transnational corporations of natural resources, especially energy resources, taking into consideration the effect this has on employment, food and social progress, and emphasizing especially the plunder of human beings as cheap, disposable labour.

- Cooperation with the United Nations Centre on Human Rights and the ECOSOC.

- Cooperation with other governmental and non-governmental institutions to exchange materials on human rights. Meetings and visits to exchange experiences.

- Look into the possibility of organising an activity jointly with the Peace University operating in San Jose, Costa Rica. In any case WPC should broaden relations with them.

- Denounce the US-inspired doctrines of 'national security' as developed in several Central and South American undemocratic states, which constitute the application of political violence originating in military build-up and which is a threat not only to internal human rights but to peace.

- Host an international Conference to denounce the violations of human rights of the Peace Movement and peace fighters.

- Sponsor an International Conference on Human Rights, the Threat of a Nuclear War and the Right to Live, in collaboration with Human Rights organisations and on the basis of the documents approved in the Conferences previously held in 1981 in Panama, 1982 in New Delhi, 1983 in Mexico and 1984 in Quito, Ecuador.

■ Participation in the Second World Congress on Human Rights to be held in Dakar.

1988 (Full text)

■ Support *actions* promoting the respect of human rights—the right to life and peace and other political, economic, social, cultural rights; develop *cooperation* with human rights organizations.

■ Contribute to the *celebration* of the Fortieth Anniversary of the Universal Declaration of Human Rights; promote the holding of an international *event* on human rights and peace.

■ Organize an international *meeting* of parliamentarians on cooperation of humanitarian issues (Moscow, June–July).

■ Contribute to *public hearings* on cases of human rights violations.

■ Send a *delegation* to the UN Human Rights Commission; cooperate with the UN Centre and Special Sub-Committee on Human Rights, and with other UN bodies.

■ Participate in the *work* of the NGOs' Special Committee on Human Rights and the Special Group on Development and Human Rights; develop *dialogue* with other NGOs on various humanitarian issues (right to peace, conscientious objection, rights embodied in the Universal Declaration and the covenants on social, economic and other rights, etc.).

Appendix F: Explanation of Consultative Status in the United Nations

Article 7 of the United Nations Charter established the Economic and Social Council (ECOSOC) as one of its 'principal organs'. ECOSOC consists of 54 Members of the United Nations, elected by the General Assembly under Article 61. Article 71 of the Charter provides that

> The Economic and Social Council may make suitable arrangements for consultation with non-governmental organisations (NGOs) which are concerned with matters within its competence. Such arrangements may be made with international organisations after consultation with the Member of the United Nations concerned.

In granting consultative status to NGOs, ECOSOC distinguishes between three types of relationship, namely

Category I: those organisations with a basic interest in most of the Council's activities, of which there are currently about 34, three of them—WIDF, WFDY and WFTU—being Soviet-controlled international organisations;

Category II: organisations with a special competence but concerned with only a few of the Council's activities, of which there are currently about 269, six of them—AAPSO, CPC, IADL, FIR, IOJ and IUS—being Soviet-controlled international organisations.

A Roster of organisations placed thereon for *ad hoc* consultations, arranged in three Types;

Type A: organisations listed by virtue of action taken by

the Council, of which there are currently about 185;

Type B: organisations listed by action of the Secretary-General, of which there are currently about 32;

Type C: organisations listed by virtue of their consultative status with other United Nations bodies or the specialised agencies, of which there are currently about 239, including the WPC, IIP, WFSW, FISE and certain other international organisations subject to Soviet control.

In addition, the UN specialised agencies also maintain lists of NGOs enlisted to consultative status limited to their area of interest. It is, however, the ECOSOC/NGO relationship which is central to an understanding of the political role and function of NGOs at the UN.

In 1987 the UN Secretary-General designated a number of NGOs with UN consultative status as 'peace messengers' and awards were duly made to, among a number of other international organisations:

WPC, CPC, IOJ, IUS, WIDF, WFTU, ABCP, BC, Generals for Peace and Disarmament.

APPENDIX G: SELECTED BIBLIOGRAPHY

BARRON, John. *KGB: The Secret Work of Soviet Secret Agents* (Hodder and Stoughton, 1974)

BITTMAN, Ladislav. *The KGB and Soviet Disinformation* (Pergamon and Brasseys, 1984)

CORSON, W. B. and CROWLEY, R. T. *The New KGB: Engine of Soviet Power* (Wheatsheaf Books, 1986)

CROZIER, Brian, MIDDLETON, Drew and MURRAY-BROWN, Jeremy. *This War Called Peace* (Sherwood Press, 1984)

GOLITSYN, Anatoliy. *New Lies for Old* (Wheatsheaf Books, 1986)

GORBACHEV, Mikhail. *Perestroika* (Collins, 1987)

GORBACHEV, Mikhail. *Towards a Better World* (speeches) (Richardson and Steirman, 1987)

GROSS, Babette. *Willi Muenzenburg* (Michigan State University Press, 1974)

KEEBLE, Curtis (Ed.). *The Soviet State: The Domestic Roots of Soviet Foreign Policy* (Gower, 1985)

KOESTLER, Arthur. *The Invisible Writing* (Collins and Hamish Hamilton, 1984)

LENIN, V. I. *Left Wing Communism, an Infantile Disorder* (Progress Publishers, Moscow Edition, 1950)

MERCER, Paul. *Peace of the Dead* (Policy Research Publications, 1986)

PINCHER, Chapman. *The Secret Offensive* (Sidgwick and Jackson, 1985)

REES, David. *Soviet Active Measures: the Propaganda War* (Institute for the Study of Conflict, 1984)

REVEL, Jean-Francois. *How Democracies Perish* (Wheatsheaf Books, 1986)

ROSE, Clive. *Campaigns against Western Defence: NATO's Adversaries and Critics* (2nd Edition) (Macmillan, 1986)

SCHAPIRO, Leonard. *The Communist Party of the Soviet Union* (Eyre and Spottiswoode, 1970)

SCHULTZ, Richard and GODSON, Roy. *Dezinformatsia: Active Measures in Soviet Strategy* (Pergamon/Brasseys, 1984)

SHEVCHENKO, Arkady. *Breaking with Moscow* (Cape, 1985)

STALIN, J. *Problems of Leninism* (Foreign Languages Publishing House, Moscow, 1947)

TUCKER, Robert C. *Political Culture and Leadership in Soviet Russia* (Wheatsheaf Books, 1987; now published by John Spiers Publishing)

The Communist Solar System, published by the British Labour Party, 1933

The Communist Solar System, an IRIS Survey, Hollis and Carter, 1957

The British Road to Stalinism, an IRIS Survey, Hollis and Carter, 1958

Contemporary Soviet Propaganda and Disinformation: A Conference Report, US Department of State, 1987

Soviet Influence Activities: Report on Active Measures and Propaganda, US Department of State, 1986

Soviet Propaganda Campaigns against NATO, US Arms Control and Disarmament Agency, 1983

How to Avert the Threat to Europe, Progress Publishers, Moscow, 1983

Statement by 81 Communist Parties, Moscow, December 1960

Report to 20th CPSU Congress, N. S. Kruschev, 14 February 1956

Report to 27th CPSU Congress, M. S. Gorbachev, 25 February 1986

Report on 70th Anniversary of the October Revolution, M. S. Gorbachev, 2 November 1987

The Meeting in the Kremlin, (Speeches from the International Forum in Moscow, February 1987) Novosti Press Agency Publishing House, Moscow 1987

Speeches by M. S. Gorbachev and others at the 19th All-Union CPSU Conference, June/July 1988.

'Soviet Active Measures in the Era of Glasnost', United States Information Agency, June 1988.

INDEX OF NAMES

GENERAL INDEX

ABOUT THE AUTHOR

SIR CLIVE ROSE, G.C.M.G., served in H.M. Diplomatic
Service from 1948–82, after serving in the Rifle Brigade in the
British Army for five years. From 1979–82 Sir Clive was British
Ambassador to NATO. In the period 1983–86 he was Chairman,
Royal United Services Institute for Defence Studies (R.U.S.I.)
and he has been Vice-President since 1986. Since 1987 he has
been President, The Association of Civil Defence and Emergency
Planning Officers, and since 1983 a Director of firms in the
Control Risks Group and a Consultant to the Group. He is the
author of *Campaigns Against Western Defence: NATO's Adversaries and Critics* (Macmillan, London; St. Martin's Press, New
York; 1985; 2nd edition 1987).